Finding the Fifties

by

Don J. Dampier

International Standard Book Number 0-9770558-0-9
Library of Congress Card Catalog Number 2005929188

Book layout by Asher Graphics
Cover illustration by James Asher

Manufactured in the United States of America

All book order correspondence should be addressed to:

DJ Discovery Press
124 Creekside Dr.
Georgetown, KY 40324

502-863-9378

~~djdiscoverypress@yahoo.com~~
dJPADAMPIER@GMAIL.COM

Dedication

To my classmates of the Class of 1955 of Carlisle (KY) High School – Each of whom inspired the writing of this book.

To our children, Debbie and David, and our grandchildren, Afton and Justin – may they better know who we are and, therefore, better know who they are.

To Pat, "my wife, my girlfriend, my best friend" … always by my side … always there for me … my life support!

Preface

What was so special about growing up in the '50s? More specifically, what are those enduring qualities that make small-town living so appealing? Over the past couple of decades, there has been much nostalgia and reminiscence, with a particular focus and fascination with the '50s. In addition to individuals who lived during those times offering their own remembrances, this lasting and unprecedented phenomenon is stimulated by numerous popular movies, television series, "oldies radio" featuring music of the '50s as well as other bygone eras, and books which focus on this time in history. Read on, and perhaps the features of the '50s that continue to fascinate generation after generation will be revealed to you!

Finding The Fifties is about growing up in the small town of Carlisle, nestled in Nicholas County of Central Kentucky, and attending the equally small, independent Carlisle City School System, culminating with the Carlisle High School Musketeers' senior year of 1955. This is a story of real and interesting people – all engaged in genuine events and activities in an actual place and time.

The reader is invited to join the members of the Carlisle Class of 1955 as they become the guides of a journey back in time for *Finding The Fifties.* Born of the Great Depression, they must first find their way through the darkness of the storm clouds of the World War II decade in the formative childhood and grade school days of the "Fearful '40s", then survive the wilds 'n' rapids through those high school teenage years of the "Fabulous '50s." Along the way, learn a bit of brief cultural history of the class members' hometown of Carlisle, along with something about some of the other small towns, with their small schools, that the class interacted with. You will be introduced to some brief early history of the carving out of the Commonwealth of Kentucky, how it fit in with the forming of our fledging nation, along with some of the national and international features of the decades of the '40s and '50s – all of which continue to influence our lives.

The classmates of the Class of 1955, along with their family and friends, should especially find Finding The Fifties most interesting, as well as current and former residents of Carlisle and Nicholas County. In addition, anyone who grew up in similar times, attending small schools in other small towns across the country, or those who are curious about the '50s phenomenon, will surely find this work a vehicle to transport them back to those good times! As you are introduced to the various personalities of the Class of 1955 and follow their many activities and antics, with the telling of their numerous good stories, you will very likely recognize several of your own classmates (probably with a different name) – some described as "characters" – who were involved in very similar situations in your own school and hometown.

Those of you who enjoyed *The GI Generation – A Memoir*, by Carlisle native Frank F. Mathias, a humorous and honest portrait of life in Carlisle and nearby Maysville from 1925 through 1943, should be pleased that *Finding The Fifties* takes up at approximately the period in history where Frank's fine book left off. This should provide the reader a complementary pair of works to describe life for countless individuals growing up in the element of small town/small school, rural America for over three decades.

It has been said, "A Kentuckian is a man who insists on telling you a funny story, usually about Kentucky!"

There is an old Irish saying, "A good story shortens the road by many a mile" The reader will discover many good stories contained within, and will view *Finding The Fifties* as "a good story". And perhaps, if life circumstances have burdened the reader with a long, rocky road ahead, that reading the stories of the Class of 1955 as featured in *Finding The Fifties* will shorten the road by many a mile!"

Table of Contents

I

Setting the Stage – Casting the Class

As The Carlisle School Bell Tolled, A New Beginning Was Signaled ...

In September of 1943, first-grade teacher Mary Ann Rogers warmly welcomed 44 youngsters to begin the 1943-44 school year at the Carlisle City School. These students would form the nucleus of the eventual graduating class of 1955. Except for church Sunday school or Vacation Bible School, this was the first experience at school for most of this first-grade class, since kindergarten was not available. Emotions surely ran high, ranging from eagerness and excitement, to anxiety for most, to outright fear for some! However, their first-grade jitters paled in comparison to the anxiousness, sadness, uncertainty, and fears experienced by their parents and adults of Carlisle and Nicholas County.

America was in the midst of World War II. The tragedy of Pearl Harbor had happened two years before on December 7, 1941. No one could foresee that D-Day was approaching in about a year on June 6, 1944. This event would pave the way toward the ending of the war in Europe. Under the policies of President Franklin D. Roosevelt, our parents were working toward recovery from the Great Depression of the previous decade. These were the times when the eventual class of 1955 began first grade. No doubt, the downtown Lyric Theater in Carlisle had a showing of Casablanca, the Academy Award winner of 1943. As first-graders, we did not recognize that it would later be named as one of the greatest movies of all time. The title of one of the most popular songs of that school year was very significant as the first-grade class of 1943-44 began its twelve-year "Sentimental Journey!"

This scenario was repeated in countless communities across

the Commonwealth of Kentucky and throughout our great nation – "from sea to shinning sea" – all closely interwoven and connected by "the strands" of a world at war.

There were approximately seventy-seven students, at one time or another, who boarded "the train of the Carlisle Class of '55" on its twelve-year journey toward graduation. Most disembarked along the way before the train's arrival at the final destination! Those who stayed the course became identified as "The Musketeers!"

Of the original forty-four who entered the first grade together in 1943, fifteen made it to the steps of Carlisle High School to begin senior year. However, after completing eleven years as part of the class, two of "the originals" sought an alternate route as marriage beckoned. They were Sonia Nell Shrout (now Arnold) and Mary Agnes Mann, who married Charles Carter (CHS Class of 1953). This left "The Thirteen Originals" to complete the journey as the Carlisle High School graduates of 1955. These students were Larry Paul Cameron, Donnie Joe Dampier, Gordon Lee Moreland, Jackie Wood Shepherd, Billy Elgin Vanlandingham, Anna Mary Clinkenbeard, Marjorie Anna Farris, Martha Sue Feeback, Norma Ann Harris, Barbara Allen King, Carole Woodson McLean, Wanda Reid, and Mary Phyllis Smith.

Two other students who were part of that first grade of 1943-44 spent eight or more years with the class and therefore were a significant part of history of the Class of 1955, even though they were not part of the CHS graduating class of that year:

Bobby Gene Anderson transferred to Nicholas County High School after completing the tenth grade at Carlisle High School and became part of the NCHS Class of 1955. The Blue Jackets, who did not play football at that time, had the better basketball program, which was part of the appeal to transfer for Bobby – to better pursue his dream of playing in the State Basketball Tournament.

So, did Bobby Gene realize his dream? Read on!

Billy Buntin spent the first eight years at Carlisle before transferring to Millersburg Military Institute, where he became part of the Blue and Gold Cadet MMI graduating class of 1955. So it was that the Class of 1955 for both Nicholas County High School and M.M.I. received a gain, while Carlisle High School experienced a loss.

With the exception of Jackie Shepherd, Billy Vanlandingham, and Donnie Dampier, each of whom left the class for a short while and then returned, ten of the thirteen completed all twelve grades together (all in the same building). Jackie completed eight years, then transferred to Maysville to spend one year with his Aunt Arlie Wells, a teacher in that independent school system. He then moved on to MMI for two years before returning his senior year to graduate from CHS. Billy Vanlandingham transferred to Nicholas County High for his junior year, then returned as a senior to graduate as a member of the Class of 1955. Donnie moved with his parents for several months to Southern Indiana, where he attended second grade during the time his Dad worked in a defense plant as part of the World War II effort. Donnie then returned for the third grade through the twelfth.

Meanwhile, over 100 miles to the southeast of Kentucky – in the small town of Barbourville – another wide-eyed little girl, experiencing very similar "first-grade jitters," began her twelve-year journey toward graduation in the small, independent Barbourville City School. She likewise would spend a one-year sojourn away from her hometown – this in Detroit, Michigan, also as part of the World War II effort. She would return to graduate as part of the Barbourville High School Class of 1955. Her name was Patricia Ann "Pat" Disney – and she would become the wife of Donnie Joe Dampier.

There were an additional six students who joined us en route to be part of the class that, on graduation night, marched down the aisle to gladly, and with gratitude, claim their diplomas. In the order of their arrivals they were ChaPatCha Lois May, Kenneth Jaynes Booth, Carole Jean Donovan, Jackie Gene Wells, Sylva Joy Owens, and Joseph Houston "Jock" Conley. This completed the main cast of characters of the production of the Class of 1955 of Carlisle High School, each of whom had significant parts to play in the multi-act performances presented in the following pages.

So it was, from this early beginning, that the "Original Thirteen" embarked on a lifetime journey, picking up new classmates along the way while saying goodbye to others. They lived experiences and adventures as they went, building upon their firm foundations and strong value systems, all the while earning an excellent education. And, with the gaining of lifelong friendships, it can be said that for the Class of 1955, the story of a "Sentimental Journey" continues. ...

II

The Fearsome '40s
Growing Up During the War Years of the '40s

"To every thing there is a season, a time to every purpose under Heaven: a time to be born, a time to plant, a time to harvest, a time to cry, a time to laugh, a time to grieve, a time to dance ... a time to hug ... a time to find, a time to lose ... a time for keeping ...a time to repair, a time to be quiet, a time to speak up ...a time for loving. ...a time for war, a time for peace."

Ecclesiastes 3: 1-8, the Holy Bible

Grade School in the Decade of 1940-1949

The Carlisle High School Class of 1955 entered and spent our formative grade school years in the decade of the 1940s. The '40s were a period that was pretty well defined and dominated by World War II. War production pulled America out of the Great Depression, and unemployment had almost disappeared as most able-bodied men had been drafted and sent off to war. In the cities, single women were actively recruited into the workforce to fill the gap. By 1943, as we entered first grade, most single women were employed, with married women now also allowed to work.

The famed "Rosie the Riveter," made famous by the Norman Rockwell painting that appeared on the cover of the May 29, 1943 issue of the Saturday Evening Post and who depicted the "You can do it!" spirit, was the symbol of the working woman, as women were needed to work in the urban factories on the home front. However, the GIs preferred another symbol of womanhood – the "pin-up girl," such as Rita Hayworth, Betty Grable (with her "gams" insured for a million), Lana Turner, Dorothy "Dottie" Lamour, and others!

The real-life World War II-era "Rosie" was Rose Will Monroe, a native of Science Hill in Pulaski County, Kentucky, who worked during the early 1940s as a riveter in an aircraft plant that made B-24's and B-29's in Ypsilanti, Michigan. As it turns out, the real-life Rose, who died in 1997 at the age of 77, has a kinship connection to Pat Dampier, Donnie's wife. Rose's daughter, Vickie, of Clarksville, Indiana, was married to Rick Jarvis, Pat's second cousin. Rick is the son of Louise Jarvis, who is the niece of Pat's mother, Jeree. Rose Monroe, with a lifelong love of flying and her "can-do" attitude, finally earned her pilot's license in the early 1970s when she was well past age 50. Her desire to fly was passed on to Vickie, who, along with her husband, Rick, became a licensed pilot, skydiver, and, skydiving instructor!

At the end of World War II, with the return of our servicemen – badly needing jobs as civilians – women in the late 1940s would be reverted to their previous full-time status as housewife, a move back into the kitchen, and the bedroom – the beginning of begetting the "baby boom." This sired those who became the last class of Carlisle High School. This would be only a temporary reversion, for in the decade to follow, women would re-emerge to find careers outside the home, working side-by-side in the workplace with their men-folks to assume their needed roles as part of the "two-income family." It was during this late '40s era that America began its transition from the rural-agrarian climate (with fewer and fewer of our servicemen returning to the farm) to an urban-industrial culture... a population that would quickly become a mobile society.

The "Rosie the Riveter" image, together with the very valuable contributions of the many real-life "Rosies" demonstrating that women were very capable of performing the so-called "non-traditional jobs" – built a strong foundation and began laying the brickwork that would pave the way for meaningful careers for women in the workforce in the decades to follow, including the girls of the Class of 1955.

Previous national policies leading toward USA isolation were forgotten as the United States emerged from the war as a world superpower. We of the Class of 1955 were very young during the WWII era, and by living in Carlisle we were somewhat isolated with limited understanding of the major consequences of the war effort. However, most of us will remember participating in scrap drives for steel, tin, paper, rubber, etc., and that rationing of food supplies began in 1943, the year we entered first grade. Even the seemingly minute activity was considered important, as we separated chewing gum wrappers in order to collect the aluminum foil. We helped our parents grow "victory gardens," and some of us continued gardening later in school as 4-H projects. With the seeds firmly planted, many of us have continued the self-sustaining pursuit and satisfying pleasures of gardening for most of our adult lives.

Wartime Drills – Many of our generation, who were school children during these tumultuous times of the WWII years, will remember school civil defense drills that required us to get under our desks until the teacher gave an "all clear!" There are some of us who may recall the occasional drone of scores of planes flying overhead in the dark night, presumed to be military aircraft flying from an origin and destination we knew not where. There were the air raid drills (thankfully, never the real thing in Carlisle), which required total blackouts with all lights diminished. Some of our fathers, and other men of Carlisle not selected for active military duty, proudly served as Civil Air Patrol and, with their official arm bands, walked the streets of Carlisle to make sure no light of any kind was visible (not even a flickering candle) until the signal ending the drill was sounded. For those of us in those early elementary years, they were scary times!

The drills were not looked upon as a game, but were considered very serious business. With the knowledge that we were contending with the massive military might of two formidable foes, Japan on our Pacific shores side and Germany from the Atlantic side, both of whom were bent upon world conquest and control, there were legitimate concerns and fears throughout our nation that our own considerable military resources could be overextended, which could open us up and possibly lead to air strikes and invasion onto our shores, so those on the home front remained very diligent and alert.

The war years of WWII, forging the four fear-filled years of 1941-1945, were desperate days for all our citizens, with the fears of our parents also felt by the Class of 1955, still in their early childhood days. The December 7, 1941 attack on Pearl Harbor, the first military act involving the United States, propelled our nation full-force into the war effort, which dictated the U. S. Congress, the following day, to declare war on Japan and then, three days later, on December 11, 1941 (the fifth birthday of Donnie Joe Dampier), to also issue a declaration of war on Germany and Italy.

World War II — A devastating chapter in our nation's history. We lost over 400,000 of our fighting men and women, falling on foreign fields in their service of fighting for our freedoms – with our small community of Carlisle/Nicholas County losing some three dozen as part of that nationwide number. The anxious folks back home dreaded the delivery of the telegram officially informing the household of their fallen family member, as across our Commonwealth of Kentucky over 9,000 souls were lost in the cause. Among those was the Barbourville, Kentucky household of Patricia Ann Disney (of the Barbourville High School Class of 1955, who would grow up to become the wife of Donnie Dampier), feeling the intense pain as a 6- or 7-year-old, along with her mother, Jeree, of the loss of their father/husband, Edison John Disney, at around the prime age of 33 … "Killed In Action" on the foreign fields of Italy.

Thankfully, most of our gallant men and women of the service did return home – who, standing side-by-side with their fallen comrades, were all members in good standing of the "Greatest Generation." Several of our local returning servicemen, back in their chosen civilian occupations, provided positive values contributions – along with our parents – in the lives of the Class of 1955, as we grew into adulthood … men such as Ben Pumphrey, Tebay Rose, Charlie Wilson, Frank Mathias, Jess Back, and Charlie Blake, to name only a few.

Charlie Blake, a name which most of us in our class would not readily recognize except for our classmate Jackie Shepherd, was one of those individuals possessing "a good story to tell." With his WWII wartime adventures, Charlie, a Nicholas County native and neighbor of the Shepherds of Scrubgrass Road, achieved hero status to the wide-eyed Jackie during the youngster's childhood years of around the ages of 5-9. Charlie, at some dozen years his senior and living close by, had taken Jackie under his wing as the twosome had become good fishin' buddies.

Jackie, always the inquisitive one, would continuously ask Charlie, while the soldier was home on furlough, to recount some of his wartime experiences, but Charlie, sensitive to Jackie's young ears as were most of his WWII comrades-in-arms, would usually remain mostly mum on his missions. Indeed, Jackie remembers that at times during their fishing trips, hardly a word was uttered from the lips of Charlie except, "The fish sure ain't bitin' today," or, "Boy, the fish sure are bitin' today," or, "See that shagpoke flying overhead" (a name the locals gave to North America's largest of the species, the pileated woodpecker).

Charlie Blake had apparently, on three occasions, been reported as "missing in action," generating fears among the folks back home that Charlie had either been captured or killed – and with Charlie's tough-as-nails reputation and his attitude of "never going down without a good fight," the latter was usually feared. It was no doubt these traits that influenced the "Old Coach," Ben Pumphrey, to name Charlie, usually an outweighed lineman, as one of Carlisle High School's best in the pre-WWII era of Musketeer football.

Charlie finally relented to his young friend's probing by describing how he and two of his company companions, had escaped from behind enemy lines in Germany – with German patrols, led by their sniffing search dogs, in hot pursuit. After Jackie's alert question, "But, Charlie, how in the world did you escape being caught by the sniffing dogs?" then Charlie recounted his escape escapade.

"Well, Jackie, we traveled at night under cover of darkness from farm to farm – then we hid out during the daylight. We used the 'manure method' to escape detection by the dogs by covering ourselves in each farm's manure pile (the 'fresher' the better!), leaving only a small hole for breathing. There was no sniffin' dog that could smell our scent once we were covered with sh--! We lived off the land each night by very quietly slipping into the farmer's henhouse and stealing a few eggs, which we naturally ate raw. We were very careful to not disturb the chickens and start them clucking – that would have been a sure-fire giveaway to our location if a farmer thought a fox was in the henhouse, when he would come out shooting with his shotgun! (Charlie discreetly never mentioned any "help" they might have gotten from "the farmer's daughter!") Jackie, we hand-milked dairy cows in the fields, and with no milk bucket we shot the milk stream directly into our mouth – you might say 'from tit (teat) to tongue' – and that, Jackie, is how we survived and escaped the German dog patrols until we crossed the border of Switzerland to safety!"

So, Charlie Blake, relying on his Carlisle/Nicholas County farm-boy resourcefulness to live off the land, was probably responsible for saving not only his life, but also those of his unnamed companions. Charlie Blake, who died some years later after the war – back in his Nicholas County home – was, like so many of his compatriots, a largely unknown and unsung hero of World War II, but he has remained a larger-than-life hero to our classmate Jackie Shepherd, who, sixty years later, still frequently and fondly reminisces with good stories about his boyhood friend, Mr. Charlie Blake.

The Ending of World War II – As the Class of 1955 was concluding its second-grade year, several significant events on the national and international stage unfolded that finally led to the conclusion of World War II and changed our world – events that would affect our thinking and outlook for the rest of our lives. Our president at the time, Franklin Delano Roosevelt, who led our nation through most of these tumultuous times, died on April 12, 1945. Our fallen president was succeeded in office by the vice-president, Harry S. Truman (1945-1953), who, after completing Roosevelt's unexpired third term, was elected in his own right to the office of president. Within a month after the death of President Roosevelt, V-E Day (Victory in Europe) occurred on May 7, 1945, with the unconditional surrender of Germany, bringing the official end of the war in Europe.

Then, on August 6, 1945, the USA employed the "secret weapon" when the first atomic bomb was dropped on the Japanese city of Hiroshima, followed, on August 9, 1945, with a second atomic bomb on the city of Nagasaki. The innocent-sounding code names for these two weapons of mass destruction were "Little Boy" and "Fat Man." They had been developed by the Manhattan Project, the code name for the top-secret project administered by the U.S. Army Corps of Engineers at Oak Ridge, Tennessee – so secret that Vice President Harry Truman did not know of its existence until President Roosevelt's death. At high noon Japanese time on August 15, 1945, Japan agreed to surrender terms, ending WWII. It was after midnight in the U.S. when many Americans, who were listening to a remote broadcast of Cab Calloway and his band, first heard the excited and elated radio voice loudly proclaiming, over and over, the most welcome news: "Flash – Japanese surrender. The War ... Is ... Over! The War ... Is ... Over!"

What a glorious time it must have been for our war-weary parents in Carlisle, and Americans everywhere, with newspaper headlines the next day such as, "JAPAN SURRENDERS – WWII ENDS!" We of the Class of '55, at only eight or nine years old, joined in the revelry without a full understanding at the time of everything that it entailed, but nevertheless we felt and celebrated the joy through the laughter, the smiles, and the tears of our parents. The citizens of Carlisle, and all of America, surely rushed out of their homes and businesses into the streets with the greetings, "Have you heard the news? The war is over!" They were exchanging hugs and kisses, handshakes and back slaps, with the joyous feelings that a huge weight had been lifted from their shoulders – and it had! Of course, at the time, no one knew of the devastating destruction inflicted upon the ordinary citizens of the two cities of Japan, which no doubt would have somewhat tempered the celebrations with a more somber effect of feelings for our fellow human beings.

With the dropping of the two atomic bombs, we were unceremoniously ushered into the "Atomic Age," unleashing upon our world forever the "mushroom cloud" of the threat of nuclear destruction. Of course, the vast power of the atomic nucleus can be, and has been, harnessed for some good through its utilization for atomic energy, but we still have a monster in our universe that the best minds and efforts of science to this day have not learned how to completely control, a fact of life we all must live, or die, with.

The Bikini atoll, a coral island in the South Pacific that was used by American scientists as the test site for nuclear weapons, became paradoxical as the name shifted from one associated with the creation of objects of destruction, to the objects of desire. In 1946, the skimpy, two-pieced bathing suit called "the bikini" – unveiled by its inventor, French car designer Louis Reared – was first bared on the beaches of the Mediterranean Sea, and was so named "because it also caused explosions!" We of the Class of 1955 were not fully "exposed" to the bikini until a couple of decades later, but we enjoyed singing, "She wore an itsy-bitsy teeny-weeny yellow polka-dot bikini, that she wore for the first time today!" The two-piece bathing suits worn by our girls of the '50s were much more modest and much less revealing, but no less appreciated!

Kenneth Booth, who had joined the Class of 1955 in the seventh grade and after graduation began a career as a Navy man, was the first of the class to be "exposed" to the bikini. In 1958 he had the opportunity to experience Europe, which included visits to Paris, France ("How you gonna keep 'em down on the farm, after they've seen Paree?"); Monte Carlo, Monaco (Kenneth lost at cards in the casino and boldly knocked on the door of the home of Prince Rainier III and Princess Grace Kelly – but, no answer!); Madrid, Spain, etc. In a post card, dated 11/13/58, sent to our classmate Miss Barbara King, Kenneth's reaction to viewing the bikini was, "Wow! Went to the French Riviera. The clothes they 'don't' wear on the beach. The girls wear bikinis."

Yes, almost six decades later, the bikini still exists and dazzles us with its "wow!" visual and cultural effects, now having expanded its influence from the Mediterranean to the American beaches. Even some modern-day women's medical practitioners have coined a phrase, "bikini medicine," with its focus on breast and female reproductive health. Yet, it is likely that most of modern-day mankind, except those of around the generation of the Class of 1955, probably "have not a clue" as to the origin of the name "bikini."

Further Facts and Fancies of the '40s

A few facts of the '40s revealed that our class was a very small part of a national population of around 132,122,000, with a life expectancy for women at 68.2 and for men at 60.8. The census of 1940 listed Kentucky with a population of 2,845,627, of which 70% was considered "rural." The average salary was $1,299, with teacher's average salary higher at $1,441, although, the grade-school teachers at Carlisle were probably not paid at that level.

The 1940 discovery, by Australian Howard Florey and Ernest Chain of Great Britain, of a process to purify penicillin, a powerful germicide produced by molds, revolutionized medicine.

This made penicillin available in a form that could be used to treat infectious diseases in man, thereby ushering in the "antibiotic age."

Statistics of the '40s decade revealed that 55% of U.S. homes had indoor plumbing, although that revelation had eluded much of Nicholas County at the time and many of our class were still familiar with "the old-fashioned way!"

Television made its debut at the 1939 World's Fair, but because further development was delayed during the war, it did not begin to be available to the public until 1947, when 13 commercial stations began broadcasting on the air. At the end of the war, only 5,000 TV sets were in American homes, but by 1951 some 17 million had been sold and we were on the way to "the TV generation." For many of the Class of '55, the first viewing of TV, probably beginning around 1949, was at a local restaurant (located between The Little House and Harper's Garage) where townspeople would gather as a community affair to watch Milton Berle, Ed Sullivan and, it seemed everyone's favorite, professional wrestling, headlined by Don Eagle, Farmer Brown, Lou Theis, etc.

It was during the early '40s that computers were developed, with the digital computer named ENIAC completed in 1945, weighing some 30 tons and standing two stories high! Computers, of course, meant nothing to the Class of '55 during our school years at Carlisle. Indeed, for most of us it would be some 10 to 15 years after graduation from high school before we were introduced to computers in the workplace, and not until the late 1990s when some of us began to utilize them at home.

Baseball, the "Great American Pastime," was threatened after World War II with player raids by the Mexican League, but U.S. Sen. A.B. "Happy" Chandler of Kentucky, who had become baseball commissioner in 1945, possibly saved the day by banning the return of players who left Major League teams to play in Mexico. He also fought for various player benefits and then paved the way for James Roosevelt "Jackie" Robinson, who joined the Brooklyn Dodgers in 1947, to become the first Negro (black) to play in modern organized baseball. Stan "The Man" Musial of the St. Louis

Cardinals in the National League and Ted "The Splendid Splinter" Williams of the Boston Red Sox in the American League were two of the leading hitters of the '40s and into the '50s, setting numerous records, with Musial winning seven NL batting titles, and Williams winning six AL batting titles. Ted Williams was, and still is, the last man to hit over .400 when he batted .406 in 1941, but his great feat was not enough to be named Most Valuable Player in the American League of that year, as "Jolting" Joe DiMaggio of the New York Yankees set the consecutive game hitting streak of 56 games in that great baseball year of 1941 – still the record, and considered one of the greatest individual sports accomplishments of all time!

Several Major League stars of that era, such as Ted Williams, Bob Feller of the Cleveland Indians, and Warren Spahn of the Boston and Milwaukee Braves, just to name three of many, had their baseball careers interrupted by serving their country in the armed forces during World War II, losing three to four years of statistical career records during their peak physical periods; however, several others lost much more by giving their lives in the cause of duty!

In the area of music and entertainment, radio was the life-line for Americans, including the folks of Carlisle and Nicholas County, with programming that included news, music, soap operas, mysteries, comedy, variety, etc., much like TV of today.

American-born composers produced some time-honored classics such as Aaron Copland's *Appalachian Spring* (1944) and *Rodeo* (1947), and William Schuman wrote his symphonies *No. 3* (1941) through *No. 7* (1949).

At the beginning of the decade, "Big Bands" dominated popular music, with Glenn Miller, Tommy Dorsey, Harry James, Artie Shaw, Duke Ellington, and Benny Goodman, "The King of Swing," leading some of the most famous bands.

It was on December 15, 1944 that Major Alton "Glenn" Miller, the founder of the Army Air Force Band, was listed as "missing in action" when his plane disappeared on a flight between Twinwood Airfield, Bedfordshire, England, and France. The remains have not been found to this day.

Be-bop and rhythm-and-blues (distinctly black sounds) grew out of the Big Band era toward the end of the decade, led by black artists such as Charlie Parker, Dizzy Gillespie, Billie Holliday, Ella Fitzgerald, etc.

The jitterbug made its appearance at the beginning of the decade, described as "the first dance in two centuries that allowed individual expression!"

The fad phrase "Kilroy Was Here" (with a cartoon drawing of eyes and a nose) was seen everywhere on walls, rocks, etc., in public places, probably with an origin to inject a little humor in otherwise anxious times. To add to the fun, it was a fairly common occurrence for a pregnant woman to come into the delivery room with "Kilroy Was Here" painted on her bulging belly! Local Carlisle physician Dr. Wendell Kingsolver has exclaimed, "Ah, yes, I remember it well," as he was occasionally surprised during examination of some of his "ladies in waiting" with "Kilroy Was Here!"

Magical Movie Moments – In addition to *Casablanca*, other 1940s motion pictures of note included *Mrs. Miniver, Lifeboat, Notorious, The Best Years of Our Lives*, and *Citizen Kane*. With movie stars galore, such as Gary Cooper, Gregory Peck, Humphrey "Bogey" Bogart, Alan Ladd, Katharine Hepburn, Spencer Tracy, Orson Welles, Cary Grant, Judy Garland, Lana Turner, Ava Gardner, Ginger Rogers, Fred Astaire, Errol Flynn, and many more, the 1940s were the "heyday" for movies.

Real Hollywood Heroes – With the advent of World War II, many of our actors, some in the midst of mega-movie-star status, went off to fight in the armed services (British, Canadian, as well as U.S.). Many were decorated, as they served with distinction – a fact that much of our modern-day population has forgotten. Some of these well-known actors – many of whom came back to portray "tough guy" movie roles – included Alec Guinness, David Niven, Charlton Heston, Ernest Borgnine, Charles Durning, Charles Bronson, George C. Scott, Eddie Albert, Brian Keith, Lee Marvin, Robert Ryan, Tyrone Power, and others, such as James "Jimmy" Stewart, who served as a bomber pilot with over 20 missions over

Germany, earning, among numerous metals, the Distinguished Flying Cross. Clark Gable, even though he was well beyond draft age when the U.S. entered WWII, enlisted as a private to serve on the European Front.

Even though released in 1939, the classic *Gone With the Wind* was very much in evidence in our local theaters during this time, and for many it was their first feature film to see. Recently listed as number four on the American Film Institute's "100 Best American Films of All Time," the movie starred the vivacious Vivien Leigh in the role of Scarlett O'Hara, and the dashing Clark Gable as Rhett Butler, who spoke the shocking line (for its day), "Frankly, my dear, I don't give a damn!"

Another of our all-time favorite movies, *The Wizard of Oz*, was also released in 1939. It is hard to say when or where the members of the Class of 1955 first viewed this film, but it possibly was not in the movie theater but at the first showing on primetime network TV the evening of November 3, 1956, or at the second showing in December of 1959. Sometime after those first two showings on TV, we have surely been part of the TV audience that has seen the movie probably more times than any other motion picture over a multidecade period, and still running every year during the Thanksgiving and/or Christmas season. The famous tornado segment still reigns as one of the most exciting and dramatic movie shots of all times, since it is likely that none of the Class of 1955 living in the hill country of Nicholas County had ever before witnessed the drama of an approaching tornado, which inadvertently, figuratively, connected it to that other famous movie release of 1939 when Dorothy, and her little dog, Toto, were swept up by the tornado and were *Gone With the Wind!*

The Wizard of Oz was rather unique in that the opening scenes were filmed in black and white, but when Dorothy and Toto were dropped into Oz, we were startled as the film suddenly switched to be in color!

Technicolor, the patented process for making color motion pictures that was developed by Herbert T. Kalmus in 1917, was not new to us, but was the exception for movies produced in the '40s, probably due to cost. Ironically, the first Technicolor full-length all-color film, *Toll of the Sea*, appeared in theaters in 1923, even before the first talking picture, *The Jazz Singer*, starring Al Jolson, was shown in 1927. We did get to usher in the wide-screen processes in the movie theaters, developed in the '50s, with *The Robe* establishing the success of Cinemascope and one of our all-time favorites, *Around the World in 80 Days*, scoring a triumph for Todd-AO.

Small-Town Movie Theaters – Growing up through grade school during the "Fearful '40s," a favorite pastime was going to the Saturday matinee movies at the downtown Carlisle Lyric Theater. We could attend for the large sum of a quarter – 15 cents for admission and another 10 cents for popcorn! On Saturday afternoons and evenings, large lines, sometimes three to four people wide, extended from the ticket booth of the Lyric up Locust Street to the Deposit Bank on the corner of Main.

This was the time of our lives for the Class of '55, when the buds of young love began to bloom, but ofttimes they were "nipped in the bud" and rarely continued into full flowering, as was the case with Donnie Dampier and Anita Ring Clark, who Donnie considered as one of his first Carlisle girlfriends of those grade-school years and thought of as his "dark-eyed senorita," no doubt inspired by the beautiful Spanish and Mexican actresses in movies such as *Zorro*, as well as others. Some of the girls of the class, such as Martha Sue, Mary Phyllis, and Barbara, remember an exception to the normal short-lived young-love romances even that far back, as Wanda Reid and Jewell Vice began eyeing each other at the Saturday afternoon movies. The twosome have not changed the focus of their gaze toward one another after all these years!

Those who grew up during those times will remember that our movie date usually consisted of meeting each other in the line going into the theater, or telling our chosen favorite, "I'll save a seat for you," and then, somewhat nervously, sitting together, occasionally being brave enough to gently hold hands and, after the movie, we would sometimes walk to one of the three downtown establishments with a soda fountain (the Carlisle Drug, Tureman's Drug, and Williams Restaurant) to share a Coke. It was amazing how much nonverbal communication was exchanged between us as we gazed at each other – from the end of a straw!

Since we were away from the loving disciplines at home for a couple of hours, this was our time to be mischievous in the theater by throwing wadded-up popcorn sacks, putting chewing gum under the seats, moving from seat to seat, and "whooping and hollering!" We kept the theater manager, Mr. Walter Wyrick (who passed away in December of 2003 at age 81), busy patrolling the aisles. However, when the lights dimmed and the movies started, our eyes were "glued to the screen!" We were entertained with cartoons, such as *Bugs Bunny* and Walt Disney characters, and with the occasional short funny of *The Three Stooges, The Little Rascals*, etc. Since few, if any, of us read newspapers then, and with no TV, our window to the world was the frequent news reels of events around the globe. Then, there were the serials, such as *Batman and Robin* and *The Lone Ranger and Tonto*, which were sure to bring us back for the next episode!

Our feature film heroes were usually singing cowboy stars such as Gene Autry and his horse, Champion; Roy Rogers, "the King of the Cowboys," with his horse, Trigger, together with co-star/wife Dale Evans, *Queen of the West*, and her horse, Buttermilk; and non-singing "Hopalong" Cassidy (played by William Boyd) with his white horse, Topper. There was Audie Murphy, at only 5-feet-5-inches tall and 110 pounds, portraying the tough cowboy roles, but who was a real life hero of WWII fame – "the most decorated serviceman of WWII." We laughed a lot at their comical side-kicks, such as George "Gabby" Hayes, Smiley Burnett, Pat Brady, Pat Buttram and Andy Devine. And, we would sing the songs of the Old West, such as *Don't Fence Me In* and *Water, Water* with the Sons of the Pioneers, or *Back in the Saddle Again* with Gene Autry and *Happy Trails* with Roy and Dale. Some of our other favorite cowboy stars were Randolph Scott, Sunset Carson, and Lash Larue, who with his trademark bull-whip may well have been the inspiration and preview to the *Indiana Jones* series of the 1980s. Many of us thought that our classmate Larry Cameron resembled Jimmy Wakely, who had a brief career in the movies as a singing cowboy.

The Saturday matinee movies, or, as we used to say, "going to the show," was part of our value system training since the "good guys," wearing the white hats, always won out over the "bad guys," wearing the black hats – except for Hopalong, a white-haired hero who wore all black, including his hat! We never could figure out, even when we tried to imitate the action, how our cowboy heroes never seemed to lose their hat in a fist fight with the bad guys!

III

The Contribution of the Comics

The comics, which were originally meant to be funny and thus were called the "funnies" whether they were in the form of the comic book, which first appeared in the 1930s, or newspaper strips, provided us with access and fueled our imaginations with vivid adventure, escape, heroes, humor, and entertainment, and was a source in helping us learn to read and develop a lifelong passion for reading. Comic books, which could be purchased for 5 to 10 cents and then traded between classmates for free, were an affordable diversion at a time when there was little extra money.

The contents of the "funnies" were certainly not up to the level of the classics, novels, fiction and non-fiction that we would later learn to love, but for many of us they served as an introduction to reading. Except for the Bible, which many did read on a regular basis, most of our households were not filled with books or magazines, and many saw only the occasional newspaper, so, for us, the comic books and the "funnies" filled a void.

Historically, the first widely known comic strip was *Hogan's Alley*, created by Richard F. Outcault in the 1890s, with its main character and hero known as "the Yellow Kid." While it is very unlikely that any of the Class of 1955 were familiar with "Hogan's Alley," there were many different cartoon characters that we grew up with in the '40s and '50s who were inspired from a variety of sources by their creators.

The war years spawned several, such as G.I. Joe; Steve Canyon; and Smiling Jack (a nickname we gave to Jackie Shepherd). Joe Palooka, created by Ham Fisher in 1930 as the good-natured heavyweight boxer, with his emphasis on fair play and sportsmanship – the first comic character to put on a soldier's uniform in World War II – inspired many of our boys to try their hand in the pugilistic art.

In 1931 Chester Gould created Dick Tracy, the police detective – who provided us with a symbol of law and order. With his two-way wrist radio and other technological gadgets to fight crime, he was way ahead of his time, sort of the comics version of the futuristic science-fiction writer H.G. Wells. And, we should not forget the likeable Ally Oop, a caveman possessed with strength of body and character, with the setting in the opposite time travel, backwards to prehistoric times.

The hard times of the Depression years inspired *The Katzenjammer Kids* (the title word actually means distress, depression); *Gasoline Alley*; *Bringing Up Father*, created by George McManus (with the henpecked Jiggs and his society wife, Maggie – which may remind modern-day TV viewers of the British comedy *Keeping Up Appearances*, featuring the characters of Richard and Hyacinth); and *Mutt & Jeff*, the long-running favorite created by Bud Fisher which, after his death in 1954, was continued by Al Smith.

We had our action heroes, who included Jerry Siegan's 1938 creation, Superman, a hero born on a planet in another galaxy and possessed of superhuman powers, described as a combination of Sherlock Holmes, Hercules, Robin Hood, and Sir Galahad. Our minds were so ingrained with Superman's alternate identity, Clark Kent, in which he posed as a meek newspaper reporter to hide his true identity, that even today, when Donnie Dampier makes reference to his good friend Kent Clark, a Barbourville classmate of Donnie's wife, he has to concentrate that he does not reverse the order of Kent's name.

Then there were Batman and Robin (we never wondered about this strange pairing); the Phantom; Captain America; and Captain Marvel, who, when invoking his magical transformation from the weak Billy to hero status, shouted "Shazam," adding a new word to our vocabulary. Among our favorites were Edgar Rice Burroughs' Tarzan, Jane, and Boy, whose roles we tried to act out by swinging from ropes we had fastened to tree limbs. Even more tenuously, we would occasionally find in nature the large grape vines, dangling from the upper tree limbs, which we used to play-act Tarzan by swinging precariously across a hollow nestled between Nicholas County hills!

At the time, we were not aware that some of our cartoons were filled with messages of political and social satire, with the likes of "Albert Alligator" with his pal, Pogo Possum; and, of course, Al Capp's 1934 creation of *Li'l Abner* and his mountaineer parents, Pappy and Mammy Yokum, with Daisy Mae, the hero's faithful but unappreciated girlfriend (that is, until 1952, when Li'l Abner finally married her). The gang of Dog Patch, USA, drinking their Kickapoo Joy Juice and running in their Sadie Hawkins Day Race (the one day of the year when it was permissible for the girl to chase the man, looking for her mate!), but the fun and laughter of the strip, paradoxically, also added to the unfair stereotype of the Appalachians "hillbilly."

It appears that most of the main cartoon characters were male, such as Donald Duck and his three nephews, Huey, Dewey, and Louie, along with Goofy, Mickey Mouse, Andy Panda, Bugs Bunny, his antagonists Elmer Fudd and Yosemite Sam, and Sylvester the Cat with Tweety Bird.

Of course, our girls had some cartoon characters they could relate to with Daisy Duck and Minnie Mouse, Little Orphan Annie, Olive with her Popeye, the Sailor Man, and Nancy, who was always getting the best of Sluggo, her boyfriend.

Then, there was the unsinkable Blondie, who continually stayed a step ahead of her husband, the bumbling, Dagwood Bumstead. By the time the Class of '55 began to read the *Blondie and Dagwood* comic strip in the '40s and '50s, its creator, Chic Young, had changed courses from the original format, created in 1930. Blondie began as a gold-digging flapper of the Roaring '20s, and Dagwood was the millionaire playboy, but as the influences of the Great Depression hit, the storyline changed: Dagwood was disinherited for marrying the calculating Blondie, and the twosome settled into the life of a middle class all-American couple with two kids and a dog, Daisy. Dagwood, without his millions, daily went to a regular job at the J.C. Dithers Company, working under his boss, the disagreeable and dislikable Mr. Dithers, and Blondie became the socially acceptable, long-suffering, happy homemaker. The *Blondie and Dagwood* strip was such a favorite of Donnie Dampier and his parents that he named his first dog, a brown and white mongrel who was lovable but frequently in trouble, as Dagwood!

It would be a stretch to say that we learned much about romance from the comics! Perhaps the greatest "sister for super-heroes" that our girls tried to identify with was Wonder Woman – "beautiful as Aphrodite, wise as Athena, strong as Hercules, and swifter than Mercury." As her creator, William Moulton Marston, wrote in 1941 when she first appeared in the comic book story "Introducing Wonder Woman," "She is known only as Wonder Woman, but who she is, or whence she came, nobody knows!" Well, she just added to the blossoming mystique of our girls, as the boys liked her also!

Legacy of a Library – At about the time that we of the Class of '55 were fifth-graders at around 10 or 11 years old, a public library was first established in Carlisle. A formal dedication of the Nicholas County Memorial Library was held on September 20, 1947, honoring the men and women who had served in the Armed Forces. The "little lending library that could" began its operation early in 1948, housed in one room on the second floor of the

Nicholas County Court House. According to The History of Nicholas County, it initially was open two days per week with an average of nine books checked out to the 271 borrowers in the first nine months. Donnie's mother, Ann Dampier, must have been a key contributor to those statistics, for she was an avid reader who frequented the limited library often. Donnie remembers accompanying her numerous times to watch as she checked out probably every edition of a murder mystery the library had available. Her favorites were the *Adventures of Sherlock Holmes*, the *Crime Club* series, *Ellery Queen*, and especially the English mysteries, led by the great writers Agatha Christie and Dame Ngaio Marsh, among others. This love of a good mystery has been passed on to Donnie, who enjoys the pursuit of subtle clues in a well-written story to try to solve the "who-done-it!" The little library contributed to this by providing access to these books that probably would not have been otherwise available or read during this particular time in Carlisle.

In 1966, the Nicholas County Library was moved into a new building of its own, with a dedication ceremony at its current location on Broadway, across from the Court House, and two doors down from the Conley and Conley law office.

IV

"It's All Elementary" – The First Six Grades

These were our formative years, in which we individually and as a class conscientiously developed much of our value systems and sense of right and wrong.

For most of the Class of 1955, memories are vague as to the experiences of that first day of school in September of 1943, or the rest of their first-grade year of 1943-44. Mary Phyllis Smith, although her mother and three aunts were all elementary school teachers, remembers, "I was so scared that I sat outside on the front steps and had to be carried into the school building on my first day at school!" Martha Sue Feeback and Wanda Reid remembered they were so petrified it was as if they were glued to their desks. Barbara King said she "was in such a 'fog' that she recalled nothing of that day!" But several of our boys – Larry Cameron, Billy Buntin, Bobby Anderson, Jackie Shepherd, and Donnie Dampier – all remember and admit to having a huge first-time "crush" on our very attractive first-grade teacher, Mary Ann Rogers!

Probably none of us, neither boys nor girls, had any previous experience with playground equipment, so with several of the boys scrambling for space at the top of the slide, Donnie was shoved off the top, landing on his back – with the breath knocked out of him! Another time, in clamoring to get a turn on one of the schoolyard swings, Donnie was clobbered in the back of the head – sending him to the doctor for treatment and stitches! When it was learned years later that Donnie's Kentucky founding ancestor, Henry Dampier – at the same first-grade age – had been kicked in the head by a runaway horse, the realization set in that if either blow to the head had resulted in disaster, this book of *Finding the Fifties* would never have been written!

Hoosier Hiatus – For Donnie Dampier, in his first venture/adventure outside of Kentucky, feeling he was so far from home, he could just as well have been "On the Far Side of the World." In his temporary home in Indiana he possibly learned that the unusual but famous nickname of "Hoosiers" may have come from the traditional Indiana pioneers' greeting to visitors: "Who's here?" While in Indiana during his second-grade year of 1944-45, Donnie and his parents, Elmer and Ann, resided in a motor court, which consisted of four to six one-room cabins, each with a bath, that sat behind a two-story farmhouse that served as the owner's office and home. The motor courts of the '40s and early '50s were the popular precursor of modern-day motels, which, at that time, often served as temporary residences for transients as well as overnight lodging for travelers.

During his sojourn in "Hoosier Land," Donnie gained many experiences in learning and lifelong lessons for living. One of his closest playmates was Peggy, the motor court owner's daughter, who, at a couple years older, frequently pestered Donnie, like the time she deliberately chased him into the swampy, smelly drainage fields of the septic system (much to the dismay of Donnie's mother, who had to clean him up). Despite all, she was a good buddy most of the time, although Peggy occasionally made Donnie doubt the truth of the old nursery rhyme that little girls are made up of "sugar and spice and everything nice"!

Another good friend that Donnie gained was Allen, also a year or so older, who lived upstairs over the hamlet's country store, located a short distance down the highway from the motor court. This could be described as a "Tom Sawyer-Huckleberry Finn" friendship, with Allen, the older, bigger, and more adventurous, in the roll of "Huck." They both had a love of reading and exchanging comic books, which was one of the few affordable "extras" of that time.

"The First Girl Friend" – It was in this picturesque, rural setting of southeastern Indiana that Donnie experienced the joys of his first girlfriend. Her name was Emma Brewster, a pretty little girl with reddish brown hair in long pigtails, freckles, and an impish, quizzical smile, who looked as if she had just stepped out of a Norman Rockwell painting depicting 1940s Americana! Down through the years, Donnie has always had trouble remembering people's surnames, but he remembers Emma, possibly because at the time he thought her last name was a funny name because it rhymed with "rooster"! Even at this early adolescent age, Donnie probably had the good common sense to not kid her about the rhyme and, therefore, had many good times with "his first true love" in the short time of only a few months that they knew each other! Even though Donnie has always considered Emma his first "official" girlfriend, classmate Mary Phyllis Smith could well have fit that distinction. Mary Phyllis, always a very pretty brunette, frequently visited her three aunts, the Botts sisters, who lived just a few houses down Upper Jackstown Road from the Dampier homestead. Mary Phyllis and Donnie ofttimes visited and played together during those early elementary age days.

The "Big Lie" – This was also the time that Donnie experienced an unforgettable lifelong lesson for living as a repercussion for telling a terrible tall tale! The "big lie" happened during the first few days of school in Indiana when the second-grade teacher asked her students to stand up before the class and tell something about themselves. Perhaps to impress Emma and his new friends with a shocking story, Donnie told the class that he had had a little brother who had been run over and killed by a train! The little country elementary school was located across the railroad tracks, parallel to a two-lane highway that was within walking distance of the motor court. Donnie had always been fascinated with trains, as he liked to watch from his front yard on Jackstown Road as the daily trains approached Carlisle. This no doubt influenced his tall tale, and he almost got away with it, except that the teacher saw his mother at the local general store a few days later and expressed her condolences to Donnie's very surprised mother! When Donnie's dad arrived home from work that evening and learned of the misdeed of deception, he ordered Donnie to go out and cut his own switch for punishment (it took about three trips before he brought in one that was acceptable to his dad) and, from that time on, Donnie had learned "the hard way" the value of truthfulness and the folly of lying – which he never forgot!

"Then you will know the Truth,
and the Truth will set you free."
Saint John 8:32

Home from Hoosier Land - So it was after the completion of that second grade school year in Indiana that Donnie and his parents followed the reverse route of Hoosier native and gifted songwriter Hoagy Carmichael's famous old refrain of *Back Home Again* *in Indiana*, when they left Indiana and returned to Carlisle later that summer of 1945 in time for Donnie to enter third grade and resume his journey as part of the Class of 1955. In recent year reunion remembrances, several classmates, such as Martha Sue, Mary Phyllis, Barbara, Wanda, and Larry expressed surprise and had forgotten that Donnie was not with them during second grade at Carlisle, and most exclaimed, "Donnie, you mean you missed out on being in Mary Frances Fisher's second-grade class!" Apparently, Ms. Mary Frances, an excellent but stern teacher, had left an indelible impression upon these students that caused them to remember her well, and all seemed to be disappointed that Donnie had missed out on the experience of her teachings!

It was in conjunction with the combination of the surrender of Germany on V-E Day and the official end of WWII in August of 1945, with the surrender of Japan, that Donnie's dad left his job at the Indiana defense plant and gladly gathered up his family for the return to Carlisle. During this anxious year of hiatus in Hoosier Land, Donnie's parents provided for the basic family needs but were frugal with Elmer's defense plant earnings, as they began saving in the hope of starting up their own business at that future time, which was then very uncertain, when conditions would allow them to be re-established back in their own home town.

Sadly, Donnie never again saw Emma, his first girlfriend, but she was not forgotten!

In that year of 1945, to begin the third grade, Donnie Dampier returned to rejoin his first-grade friends and resumed his place as one of the original thirteen of the Class of 1955. Even though missing out on the classroom of Miss Mary Frances Fisher, he no doubt felt her out-of-class instructions to "do your best" throughout the elementary years. As a result of his temporary hiatus as a Hoosier, he gained in wisdom from the many experiences he encountered and was now ready to be a part of the team, along with his classmates, in their ultimate quest to achieve in future studies, activities, adventures, and numerous class productions.

Productions of *The Tom Thumb Wedding* were popular, with

elementary students making up the cast, in small schools across the country in the 1940s. Tom Thumb, whose real name was Charles Sherwood Stratton, was a dwarf born January 4, 1838, to "normal-sized" parents. In 1842, P.T. Barnum discovered Charles, who measured 25 inches tall and weighed 15 pounds, and taught him to sing, dance, mime, and act. Barnum touted him with the stage name of "Tom Thumb," and together they traveled and entertained around the world, along the way meeting various leaders and royalty, including President Abraham Lincoln and Britain's Queen Victoria and Prince Albert.

The "wedding" was quite an event with its lavishness, which no doubt inspired the numerous grade schools play productions some 80 years later. Tom Thumb and Lavinia Warren, who was 32 inches tall, were married February 10, 1863, in New York City's Grace Episcopal Church. The newlyweds stood atop a grand piano to receive more than 2,000 guests. Tom Thumb died of a stroke on July 15, 1883, with more than 10,000 people attending his funeral. The fourth-grade class of Carlisle City School, under the direction of Mrs. R.T. "Nell" Brayfield, presented its version of *The Tom Thumb Wedding* in March of 1947. Headlines of *The Carlisle Mercury* of February 25, 1947, proclaimed, "Children To Give Tom Thumb Wedding," to be presented at 7:30 p.m. Tuesday in the school chapel, with special music under the direction of Mrs. James Williams and Mrs. Cleary Fightmaster.

Many of our class have little recollection this event, other than remembering that we were in the play; however, Jackie Shepherd remembers that he and Bobbie Anderson portrayed ushers. With the finding of an old photo, saved by his mother, of Donnie Dampier in a "tux," he knew that he was in the performance, but did not recall the role he portrayed until the old newspaper account, found by Mary Phyllis Smith, showed that he and Martha Sue Feeback were the father and mother of the bride. Larry Cameron adamantly remembers that he was "Tom Thumb," and that Carol McClain was the bride. Larry probably remembers his part so well because he was so excited to have the chance to be paired

Those Little Rascals
Third Grade 1945-46, Carlisle (KY) City School.

Front row, left to right: Mary Mann, Carole McLean, Nell Shrout, Maurita, Anna Mary Clinkinbeard, Margie Farris, and Bonnie Brammer. Second row: Lou Blake, Wanda Reid, Barbara King, Sue Feeback, Donnie Dampier, Larry Cameron, Jackie Shepherd, Faye Yates, Bobby Anderson, and Ben Henry. Third row: Billie Buntin, Mary P. Smith, J. C. Bussell, Billy Vanlandingham, Dora B. Morris, Eleanor Smart, Norma Ann Harris, and Eddie Frederick.

up with a pretty girl like Carol! David Odor, who joined the class in the fourth grade and stayed with us through the fifth, was the preacher. Those of us who knew of the robust and mischievous nature of David probably got a good laugh at him playing that ministerial part.

Completing the members of the cast of our "Tom Thumb" production, all appearing in evening costumes, were: Announcer, Billy Buntin; reader, Lou Blake; maid-of-honor, Wanda Reid; bridesmaids, Barbara King (now a Warren, but not believed to be a relation to the real Tom Thumb's bride, Lavinia) along with Nell Shrout; and the groomsman, Gordon Moreland. The flower girls were Nancye Fightmaster, Marjorie Farris, Brenda Thomas, and Anna Mary Clinkenbeard; the ring bearer, Larry Crawford. Tom Thumb's mother and father were Norma Harris and Billy Vanlandingham; grandfather and grandmother, Carol George and Eddie Frederick; wealthy aunt and uncle, Mary Phyllis Smith and Billy Buntin; cousins, Mary Mann, Bonnie Shannon, and Dora Morris.

Benjamin Bailey "Ben" Henry, who was one of our good buddies with the class through the first three grades before leaving for other parts, missed out on being in the "Tom Thumb" production; however, Ben was later reunited as a classmate to Jackie Shepherd in dental school at the University of Louisville in the early 1960s. Except for Larry, most of our memories are vague as to the details of our "Tom Thumb" experience; however, Mary Phyllis remembers that the high school auditorium was filled to capacity, with the support of family and townfolk, at each performance. From an entry in the 1947 diary of Ms. Ethel Botts, supplied by her niece Mary Phyllis, Ms. Botts recorded on March 4, "The Tom Thumb Wedding came off fine. They took in $61.00." Note that in the March 3 entry, Ms. Ethel entered, "Mary P. is spending the night. Ben Henry sent her a pen, spelling "Mary. It is right pretty!" Could it be that Ben Henry had a "crush" on Mary Phyllis?

Sylva Joy Owens, who joined us for one year in fourth grade, sang at the "wedding," an early introduction to her beautiful singing voice and an indication of many more renditions to come when she would return and rejoin the class for her sophomore year and remain as part of the graduating Class of 1955.

It seems that just about every year, as we made our way throughout our school days, our class produced a play, usually one for the public, and numerous in-class skits, acting out events of history or literature. We did miss one year, possibly the second grade, when most of the class missed much school with the chickenpox. These plays were very important in our social, mental, psychological, and educational development as they taught us to work together with teamwork toward a common goal, to stimulate and activate our brains by learning lines and memorizing parts, and, the teachers made sure that each classmate was involved and had a part in the production – from set creation and construction to prompting and "speaking lines." When we successfully completed the performance, and saw and heard the audience accolades and applause, there was a real sense of accomplishment, and probably also, from just about all of us, huge sighs of relief were heard!

Another "wedding" production that was popular during this era and into the '50s (before television) was "The Womanless Wedding." The all-male cast was composed of local adult men, and some of our class as school-age boys, dressed in women's clothes (borrowed from their wives, girlfriends, sisters, or other willing women), wigs, lipstick, and makeup, to "act" as women. These plays (or skits) were usually produced by the churches and organizations in the community, and were especially popular with the women, who enjoyed many a laugh from watching their men parade around in their role as women!

Molly Jane Flora was one of those students who joined us along the way and spent six years as part of the class from fifth grade through the tenth grade before transferring to Lexington Lafayette High School to become part of their Class of '55. The old English meaning attributed to the surname of Flora is said to be, "one who was born in spring," so leave it to Molly Jane to be different, since she waited until June 28, 1937, to be born, one week after the June

Solstice, which is the official beginning of summer.

It was during the fifth grade that Molly Jane suffered through one of those "most embarrassing moments" for her part in *The View*. It seems that Jane was sitting sideways at her desk in class, absorbed in a study assignment, with both feet in the aisle, when David "Scarcey" Craycraft came walking down the aisle toward the back of the room. Now Scarcey, another "Huckleberry Finn," was always looking for some mischief so he reached down, grabbed one of Jane's feet, and whirled her around while lifting her leg, which completely exposed her underpants – to the unobstructed "view" of those sitting down that aisle! David, never one to be known for his subtlety, added insult to injury by laughing and pointing at Jane's predicament! It was at this point that Ms. Earl Botts, our fifth-grade teacher, while probably not aware of the cause of the classroom disruption, turned around from making entries on the blackboard and ordered Scarcey back to his front-row seat. It is not recalled that any of us had to sit in the corner wearing a dunce cap, but our teachers made those of us who were bad in the classroom sit in a front-row seat where they could keep an eye on the culprit, and Scarcey got to sit in the front row often! Well, Molly Jane soon overcame her moment of embarrassment and indignity, but she "could have killed" Scarcey if Ms. Botts had not stepped in when she did to quickly bring order back to the classroom. For Donnie Dampier and any of the other fifth-grade boys sitting in that row, *The View* was a brand new experience, but as for Molly Jane – always a very pretty girl who naturally drew the attention of the boys – she did not need this type of additional attention!

Molly Jane Flora Abbott, while at CHS, followed her attractive older sister, Kay, as a cheerleader for the Musketeers and later, at her new school, was elected as Lafayette Band Sponsor during her senior year. Mollie Jane went on to graduate in 1959 with a degree in elementary education from the University of Kentucky, where she was a member of the Alpha Gamma Delta Sorority.

The "ChaPatCha" Challenge – ChaPatCha "Pat" May was on the verge of becoming a Cynthiana City High School Bull Dog until she moved to Carlisle in the early summer before the beginning of sixth grade so her mother could go to work for Lonnie Griffin Manufacturing Co. (Lonnie Griffin was Pat's uncle by marriage). Pat and her mother lived on a corner of Locust Street, one block from Molly Jane on Broadway, which provided an avenue for the two of them to become fast friends.

Most of us were not aware of "Pat" May's first name of ChaPatCha, a most unique and interesting name. Pat said it is of Native American origin that her mother had heard before she was born, and liked well enough to give her the name. She does not know the tribal origin or the Indian meaning, but has always been happy that "Pat" is in the middle, which has made it much easier in introductions or addressing herself.

This writer has been so intrigued by the name of ChaPatCha that, in traveling around the country with his wife (his "Pat"), it has become an interesting challenge to try to find plausible origins and possible meanings for the name. So, in areas where there is a sizable presence of Native American population and culture, Donnie has browsed through bookstores, and when possible, has talked with some of the native Indians to see if they might have heard of this or a similar-sounding name.

One such visited locality is comprised of the two villages of Moosenee and, right across the Moose River, its companion community of Moose Factory Island (the oldest English-speaking settlement in Ontario). Both are located in the northern part of the province of Ontario, Canada, situated at the base of the Arctic tidewaters of James Bay that, on its northern flow, blends into the Hudson Bay.

The unusual name of "Moose Factory" does not relate to a "factory" as we normally associate the word, and therefore it is not a place that "manufactures moose," as some on the tour jokingly said, but rather it refers to the extensive fur-trading operations of the renowned Hudson's Bay Company that began in the late 1600s. The "factor" was the title affixed to the man who was the operational head of the company in each trading post, and the administrative offices became known as the "factory." Hence, the name of Moose Factory Island became the administrative center for the entire James Bay area. Donnie and Pat Dampier traveled to this area in August of 2001, along with some 36 new friends, as part of the "Polar Bear Express" tour sponsored by the Kentucky Retired Teachers Association.

A Possible Meaning of ChaPatCha – This is found from the ancestral home of the Cree. In the short time allotted for strolling the streets of Moosenee and Moose Factory Island, Donnie made inquiry about "ChaPatCha" with some of the native Cree Indian women, who were marketing their native crafts. They indicated no knowledge of the name, but referred him to a small craft/gift/museum shop that contained a book section on the Indian cultures. It was there that a book of the Cree language was found, detailing their words and meanings, that could shed some light on the linguistic source for Pat's name of ChaPatCha. The Cree language reflects a culture that is full of respect for the land, the animals, birds, and creatures therein, and the natural spirits. For instance, from the Cree, "Cha" is a reference to the lark or the hawk; "Pae" is a reference to elements of nature, such as clouds, lightning, the rain, etc.; "Pa" – the sunrise; and "Pay" – the sunset. According to Pat, her mother heard the name Cha Pat Cha, which she found delightful enough to give the name to her daughter; however, she might have actually "heard" Cha "Pa" Cha, or Cha "Pay" Cha, or Cha "Pae" Cha, with the similar spelling and pronunciation, which possibly has a meaning such as "the lark sings at sunrise" or "the hawk soars above the clouds at dunset" or other such interpretations!

The traditional Indian people have grown up with a belief that they are caretakers of the land and that they must live in harmony with it. Therefore, in naming their children, the reference and meaning is frequently one of nature.

The Cree, a major Algonquian group (the largest group of linguistically related tribes of North America), are one of the great Indian peoples, numbering some 70,000 today, could well be the source of our classmate Pat's name, since they have expanded far from their original James Bay base and intermarried with people of European descent to create a large mixed-race culture known as the "Metis," with their culture, language, and influence possibly extending into Kentucky and the Southeast.

With over six hundred different Native American Indian tribes in the United States (some 381 officially recognized by the United States), as well as many more in Canada, there may be over a thousand different possibilities of Indian language combinations, with the Cree only one of them, to add to the "Challenge of ChaPatCha!"

Elementary school teachers for our first six years included: Grade One – Mary Ann Rogers, Grade Two – Mary Frances Fisher (CHS Class of 1906), Grade Three –Marie Flora (CHS Class of 1926), Grade Four – Nell Brayfield, Grade Five – Miss Earl Botts (CHS Class of 1914), Grade Six – Fanny Ruth Snelling. We were very blessed to have this group of teachers, for each one was dedicated to her craft, knew how to teach, cared for each one of us, and took pride in our progress and accomplishments. Once we advanced to the next higher class, the preceding teacher(s) kept up with us, even after we advanced beyond the elementary grades and throughout high school. If any of us were reported to be "slacking off" in our schoolwork in those upper grades, it would not be unusual for Miss Nell or Miss Fanny Ruth or any of our elementary teachers to chastise us in the hallways or lunch room or even downtown to "straighten up" and do the work we were capable of! Each of our teachers, from grade school through high school, adhered to and practiced the age-old wisdom, "Do not just give a hungry person a fish, but teach him how to fish!"

V

"It's A Wonderful Life" – Bred, Born, Belonging … The Joys of Small-Town Living

Small towns can be described in much the same manner as a famous winemaker revels in the flavors of a fine Pinot Noir red wine. … It is family and friends, warmth of heart, and generosity of spirit!"

Robert Mondavi,
California wine maker
and Phi Sigma Kappa,
Stanford University, 1936

Within the heart of Central Kentucky, as well as throughout the commonwealth and across the breadth of our nation, lie tens of thousands of small communities of various sizes, but considered small towns – each with a unique history, all with its story to tell.

Our small town was not unlike the setting and atmosphere of that portrayed in *Happy Days* or the mythical Mayberry of *The Andy Griffith Show* – except we enjoyed a time of winter or the occasional rainy day, and the character of Carlisle fit in with the recognizable theme of the popular TV series *Cheers* – a place "where everybody knows your name."

Our hometown of Carlisle, Kentucky was founded in 1816 when the county seat of Nicholas was moved from its original site at Ellisville to its current site on land donated by John Kincart, and was probably named by Mr. Kincart in honor of Carlisle, Pennsylvania (founded in 1751), the hometown of his father, Samuel, and where it is reported some of our early settlers came from.

Carlisle, Pennsylvania is historically known as the founding home of the Carlisle Indian Industrial School, from 1879-1918, as part of nationwide system of government-run American Indian boarding schools. It gained national fame as the home of legendary athlete Jim Thorpe and football coach Glenn S. "Pop" Warner. The story of the rise of Jim Thorpe, told in books and especially the 1951 movie *Jim Thorpe, All American*, starring Burt Lancaster, served as an inspiration for the boys of the Class of 1955 in the development of our athletic pursuits. We were all further intrigued by the name connections of the two "Carlisles."

The Carlisle Indian School probably was best known for its football teams coached by "Pop" Warner, who was not an American Indian. Coach Warner is credited with developing the "single-wing" and "double-wing" football offenses during his career, with the single-wing the offense of choice in its use by the Carlisle Musketeers during the 1953 and 1954 football seasons of the Class of '55.

There is also a small town of Carlisle, South Carolina, which, ironically, is located near the origination from which one Henry Dampier, as a young man of 19-20 years old, in the late 1790s left the safe haven of the home place of his father for an adventurous trek which led him into the wilderness of Kentucky to settle in the Blue Licks/Stony Creek area, near the land area which would later become our hometown of Carlisle and where Henry would establish himself as the "founding father" of the long line of Dampiers of Nicholas County. Was this possibly another "Carlisle to Carlisle" connection?

We could label the modern-day Carlisle of Kentucky as the City by the Creek (Brushy Fork). Actually, Carlisle has its own lake, and upper lake, which back in the days of the Class of 1955 we called the city lake, or the reservoir, which supplied Carlisle with its drinking water. During this time, the lake was a popular place for fish fries, church and club socials, picnics, family outings, a good place to fish, and, on moonlit evenings, it was secluded and quiet (except for the frogs chirping, or the screech and "hoot" owls, and, possibly, some "heavy breathing." It was a romantic place for young love, with occasionally some "older folks" who might slip in for an amorous adventure!

The origins of the naming of Carlisle, with its possible Middle Ages meaning traced back to the original Carlisle of northwestern England, is a fascinating story which shall be reserved for the telling in another book…

This appears to be a good time in the story of the Class of 1955 – as we are about to move from the "Fearful '40s" to those "Fabulous '50s" – to take a close look at our home town of Carlisle in the company of various members of the Class of 1955, who will guide us in a stroll downtown … and then on a cruise into the county.

Homespun "Homilies" of A Homogeneous Home Town … Carlisle, Kentucky – "The Little Town With the Big Heart," in the late '40s and the '50s, was a busy, bustling "burg" (as many residents called it). This was especially so on Saturdays and also on Tuesday afternoons, the time when "Downtown Came Alive," when many from the Nicholas County farming community came to town for socializing and supplies (possibly in conjunction with stock yard sales) – the "homilies" of conversation, discourse and humorous homespun stories carried on with the various Carlisle merchants, waiting their turns in the barber and beauty shops, as well as the pool halls, frequently on the street corners or while sitting on the courthouse wall. These were the frequent times in which the "townspeople" and the "country people," of a like kind or nature, came together singing a similar song in the harmonies of our hometown. Then, as if suddenly signaled by the 10 p.m. "gong, gong, gong' of the courthouse clock, the humming of the crowded Carlisle downtown became quiet – largely deserted – as the streets of downtown were "rolled up" for the night – until the next day of doing business.

Even as late as the early '50s some individuals came in riding horseback or with horse-drawn buggy or wagon. The original hitching (tethering) rings are still evident on the west side of the courthouse yard wall. There was still the occasional automobile and pickup truck of 1920s and 1930s vintage.

Many of our classmates remember when our family homes first received electricity or running "city" water with "indoor plumbing" or the telephone! These are items that many of us lived without during our early childhood days, but are now considered as necessities of life!

Privy "Councils" - Even those of us who lived in town with indoor plumbing were quite familiar and experienced with the outhouse, or outdoor privy (French for "private"), for most of us had grandparents, family, or friends we frequently visited in the country who were without the indoor facility made possible by running water. Contained within the "half-moon" decorative doors of these two-, three-, or four-seaters (assuring family closeness when all the members were seated "in council" together) was a very welcome companion – the mail-order catalog received from such as Sears Roebuck, Spiegel, J.C. Penney, or Montgomery Ward. The catalog provided many functions, such as reading material, and sometimes stimulation for the senses as the men and boys viewed the ladies' lingerie, while the women and girls gazed on the pictures of male models; or, more likely, the catalog served as a wish list of desirable items that were frequently not affordable; but mostly, the catalog's pages, strategically placed in the outhouse, supplied us all, after utilizing the facility, with a necessary utilitarian purpose!

Party Lines - When the folks out in the county did get a telephone installed in their home, it was most likely on a "party line," shared by possibly five to six other people in their neighborhood. In making a telephone call, there was ofttimes a handle on the side of the early phones, usually mounted on the wall, that was used to manually "ring up the operator," a "live person" located at the telephone exchange office who would then connect the caller to the desired party. When folks upgraded to the "cradled desk" phone and connected to the live operator merely by lifting the receiver, they were considered to "be uptown!" This was sort of like "Mayberry," when Andy or Barney made a telephone call with their recited line, "Sara, get me 'so-and-so'..." on the popular "Andy Griffith" TV series. The callers of these early-day times would often have company on the line from others on the party line. It did not take long for people to identify who on the party line was receiving the call by memorizing their individual rings, such as two longs (rings) and a short (ring), or three shorts and a long, etc. So, occasionally one or two people would eavesdrop on the calling parties (sometimes uninvited and unwelcome), but most often it was a welcome and good way for several of the neighbors to verbally visit and hear what was going on about – sort of the beginnings of the modern-day conference calls!

An Early 911 System – Occasionally the party line served as an "emergency help system," as was the time on a winter Sunday afternoon when the phones began to ring off the hook, with their distinctive rings, to report that a local neighbor was missing, an elderly and ill farmer, somewhere in the Persimmon Ridge, Stony Creek, or Goose Creek roads area. As the men-folk and the older boys went out looking for the lost man on a cold, windy, and snowy afternoon, the women-folk stayed inside on the party line to report progress. Donnie Dampier, who was probably about ten to twelve at the time, remembers hiking the hills with his dad, granddad, and uncles Raymond Hall and Bob and Hershel "Chee" Dampier to help in the search. Later that afternoon, at about dusk, the missing man was found by some neighbors near his home, very disoriented and nearly frozen, but before disaster took over. The news was quickly spread around the area that Sunday afternoon via the "party line," which had served as an aid in locating him, by the exchange of information between neighbors on reported times, sightings, and places of his last known whereabouts, and became the talk on the line for several weeks thereafter.

For the Class of '55 growing up in this era, we had the opportunity to experience history of mostly a bygone era of decades past on a firsthand basis that most of our big city counterparts missed out on!

We never thought much about "our excursions backwards into a history of past times" as we were growing up, but, in looking back, it was almost as if we, at times, were living experiences from decades before we were even born. Some of the features of "The Good Old Days" of these past times had not, as yet, changed much in Carlisle and Nicholas County. Indeed, on an occasion during the mid-'70s, while taking a work break, as Donnie Dampier was reminiscing some true stories of growing up in Carlisle, a female co-worker, knowing she was only some 5-6 years his junior – who had grown up in Owensboro – skeptically exclaimed, "Don, just how old are you anyway?"

Downtown Carlisle, along Main Street and a short distance north and south on the cross streets of Broadway and Locust, was usually crowded on Saturdays with shoppers and visitors in and out of the many thriving business establishments along this stretch. There were three drug stores, The Rexall Carlisle Drug, Hopkins Drugs, and George Gaffin's (Tureman's Drug); and, from time to time, two or three pool rooms, which served as adult male bastions of entertainment. The quaint Feeback Hotel, established in 1882 by the family of Martha Sue Feeback Taylor, was still in operation on Main Street until 1960.

There were barbering shops (which included Hunt's and Mathew Campbell's) and beautician shops, both of which also served as good places to catch up on local news and gossip. Jimmie Charles Hall, first cousin/stepbrother of Donnie Dampier, fulfilled his childhood dream of entering the barbering trade by owning and operating a barbershop in downtown Carlisle from the mid-'60s until his retirement in the year of 2001. The late Jimmy Charles did not have long to enjoy his deserved retirement from over forty years of barbering service to his community, as he died in January of 2003.

Three financial institutions, the Deposit Bank, First National, and The Building and Loan provided for the financial needs of the community. Nate Young and Nate Young, Jr., who operated The Nicholas County Building and Loan for decades in Carlisle, served the community in like manner as the role played by actor Jimmy Stewart in the movie *It's A Wonderful Life.* Donnie Dampier remembers his personal financial philosophy was developed in early life by watching the regular Saturday night ritual at "The B & L" of his mother and dad first making payment on their outstanding loan, then always setting aside some money for the future in a savings account.

For eating, there were always four or five restaurants and numerous grocery stores such as The A & P, Kroger, Coatney Brothers, Sextons (a "mom-and-pop" operated by Mr. & Mrs. Clyde Sexton), and Neal's Square Deal, "Where Ma Saves Paw's Dough," etc. Bobby Crockett, CHS Class of '49, and Wayne Gaunce, CHS Class of '51, were enterprising young men who established Crockett & Gaunce Grocery shortly after their graduation, and both continued in the food service business, with Bobby remaining in Carlisle. But Wayne, after marrying our classmate, Pat May and "throwing her over his shoulder," took her and his wares off to Glasgow, Kentucky.

In the clothing line there was the C.C. Cole Company (later to become Carter's), Lerman Brothers, Abrahams, and a shoe repair shop, operated by Herman McGinley and Rollie Cavanaugh, etc. On the second floor of the C.C. Cole building was located the Telephone Exchange. For variety, there was Western Auto, operated by Tommie Johnson, a jewelry shop, and at least two "five-and-dimes" (including Clinkenbeard's, Anna Mary's parents' shop).

Two business types which are not seen any more included: The Cream Station (for separating the cream from the milk), and The Freezer Locker where the local residents brought fresh meat from "hog killing," a beef, or game meat to be wrapped and stored in rented lockers. This was before most people had a home freezer and many still used the "ice box!" At one time, there was the ice (manufacturing) plant, located across Brushy Fork Creek, and, at the foot of the hill where Upper Jackstown Road begins, which later became the site of Griffin Manufacturing Company.

Home Deliveries – In the '40s and into the very early '50s, ice was delivered to those homes that were on the delivery list. Each homeowner tacked a large square card around the front door. Within the square was a circle divided into color-coded "pies," which designated if they wanted ice that day and, if so, how much. One color indicated "no ice today," and the other colors indicated how much, in poundage. The delivery person on the ice wagon, or truck, could see the card from the street, and, therefore, carry the correct size ice block to place in an insulated icebox that was kept outside the door.

"The Iceman Cometh" could well have been the calling card of Maurice King, who as a high school teenager in the late 1920s and into the '30s, delivered ice door-to-door for Raymond, his father, first while driving a horse-drawn wagon and then, when they upgraded to become mechanized, delivering from a 1929 Model A Ford truck. Of course, in the early '30s, Maurice would not have been familiar with that particular phrase of "The Iceman Cometh," the title of a masterpiece of the modern theater written by play-wright Eugene O'Neill in 1939 but not produced until 1946, and then revived on Broadway in 1956, the year after the Class of 1955 graduated. Maurice would later become the father of classmate Barbara Allen, but at the time he was delivering ice to the residents of Carlisle, as the "Iceman," Barbara was not yet even a glint in his eye!

In the issue of *The Carlisle Mercury* dated July 10, 1986, Emily A. Wolf began her weekly column, "Here Abouts," with the comment, "You might say Maurice King was easily the 'coolest' young man in Carlisle when he was growing up" (earning spending money by delivering ice). Her column stated, "The ice plant was owned by Kentucky Utilities … with Jack Goins (father of football star Jimmy Goins) as the first engineer." Jack Goins was a relative-by-marriage to the Dampiers, as he had married Ivy Campbell, the older sister of Ann Campbell Dampier, Donnie's mother. Jimmy Goins, who was Donnie's first cousin, possibly played football for the Musketeers in the early '40s, before the family was transferred to Bowling Green. He married Maxine McGinley, who resided about two doors from the Dampiers on out Upper Jackstown Road, and was a classmate of Frank Mathias of the CHS Class of 1943. By the early 1950s, when Barbara King's male classmates were looking for spending-money part-time jobs, the ice plant was near closure, so delivering ice door-to-door was not an option, but for Barbara's dad, the original "Iceman," it could also have been said of Maurice, working for his father, that he was "a chip off the old (ice) block!"

Many Carlisle residents of that day also had milk delivered to their doorstep by a local dairy. This was an era before throwaway plastic containers were used, so the milk was delivered in glass bottles, with the empties picked up, sterilized by the dairy, and then reused, over and over. There was little waste or filling up garbage dumps (we didn't have garbage land-fills back then), and the empty milk bottles also served a valuable function at youth parties for "spin the bottle" kissing games, giving us an acceptable excuse to "smooch" with our favorites of the opposite sex! This was also the time before the character of milk was changed by homogenization and which is now marketed with choices of "whole" or, fueled by our concerns with cholesterol, in the form of "1%," "2%," or "skim." The milk of the 1940s and 1950s came with a heavy layer of cream at the top, which was skimmed off and used in our coffee, cereals, baking, and in making that heavenly homemade ice cream. One of the local dairies of those times was located at the end of West Main Street, at the site currently occupied by the Nicholas County Board of Education offices.

"Car Talk" – It is hard to believe that in a small town of some 1,500 people, there were five thriving and successful automobile dealers: Harper's Ford-Mercury, Buntin's Dodge-Plymonth, H.C. Galbraith's Buick, for a short while Frey's Kaiser-Frazer, and Dampier Motors with Studebaker-Packard, with its companion business, created in the '50s – Dee Jay Auto Parts, in which, by the way, Elmer and Ann used the first and middle initials of their son, Donnie Joe.

In February of 1952, Studebaker, the fourth largest automobile manufacturer at the time, began its 100th year of operation. Studebaker, which started in South Bend, Indiana as a manufacturer of wagons in 1852, then, fifty years later started turning out "horseless" vehicles, was the only automobile company with a history of success that was older than the automobile itself! Elmer Dampier, Donnie's dad and owner of Dampier Motors, reported that since their appointment as dealer in Carlisle in September of 1950, they had sold almost 100 Studebakers and would soon celebrate the company's "century year" by selling their 100th Studebaker! Elmer Dampier always had a good business sense and a knack for timing, so that Dampier Motors, seeing the handwriting on the wall, had already dropped its dealership by the time the 1966 "Cruiser" became the last Studebaker to roll off the assembly line.

Before Elmer and Ann Dampier established the Studebaker dealership in Carlisle, they had served learning apprenticeships, first with Harper's Garage, then with Buntin's, where, even though the Dampier's would become competitors, they received the help, encouragement, and blessings of both Mr. Harper and W R. "Web" Buntin (Billy's dad) that enabled them to successfully venture out in business on their own by initially establishing a local dealership with the Willis Overland "Jeep."

The "Jeep" had earned near-legendary status with its mobile and dependable service as a primary transportation vehicle during World War II. As indicated by the large sales volume by Dampier Motors, the Jeep was readily recognized and accepted by the residents of Carlisle, especially by the farmers of Nicholas County, many of whom were just making the transition from the "work horse" to mechanism. The farming community frequently bought and utilized the "Universal Jeep" as a tractor. With its rugged construction, its power train, and the four-wheel stability, it was quite adaptable to the hilly farms of Nicholas and adjoining counties. This practical production popularity was probably coupled with the continued connotation of national patriotism – practiced by the folks of Carlisle/Nicholas County – which held the status of the Jeep in high regard!

It is said that "necessity is the mother of invention," and this was certainly true in the "invention" of the Jeep. Early on in the United States' entry into WWII in the European Theater to battle Hitler, it was learned that the Germans had developed a fast. rugged, and dependable vehicle for communication travel that would give them an overwhelming advantage, while the USA was still "relying on the horse" for this purpose. So, the nationwide call was sounded to bid on the development and manufacture of a vehicle of this type, under very rigid specifications, and under a very tight timeframe. Surprisingly, the very small company of American Bantam of Toledo, OH, with only 15 employees, not only won the bid, but designed and developed "a machine like no other ever built" in the remarkable period of only 49 days, which the proud employees named, the "Bantam Reconnaissance Car" (BRC). The American Bantam Company did not have large assembly line capability, so the actual production was awarded to Willis Overland Company, with the first "Jeep" rolling off the line in early November of 1941. This magnificent machine, described as "the embodiment of the war effort," was renamed the Jeep by Willis Overland after a cartoon character in the 1937 Popeye comic strip named "Eugene the Jeep."

It is interesting to note that the Jeep had replaced the horse on the battlefields and now, in peacetime, the Jeep was replacing the horse on the farm fields.

"Don't Put All Your Eggs In One Basket" – Even with the success of the new Jeep Products enterprise of the Dampiers, and recognizing the wisdom of this farming adage, they embraced the economic benefits of diversification by adding the dealership of Crosley Appliances to their budding business. The folks of Carlisle and Nicholas County readily received these time- and work-saving household products that manufacturers were now producing for peacetime home use across America shortly after the conclusion of the War. Some of the Crosley products included washing machines, dryers (even though many housewives still liked to hang their wash outside during nice weather, to gain the 'fresher smell'), refrigerators, deep freezers, radios and television sets.

Elmer Dampier even sold at least one Crosley Car in Carlisle; the identity of the purchaser is not remembered by this writer. The very small, white Crosley Car, with an engine that sounded more like it belonged in one of their washing machines rather than an automobile, was more a novelty than of practical use, and, therefore its production nationwide had a short life.

The Local Economy of the Times – The thriving community of Carlisle and Nicholas County that we knew in the late '40s and '50s was based on an agricultural economy, with much dependence on the sale of farm crops (such as milk, eggs, livestock, hay, corn, etc.) but primarily tobacco. A long-forgotten farming activity of the area was the production of "bluegrass seed." The foundation of this lifestyle was the strong work ethic and value system of the small family farm.

"Jot 'em Down Credit" – Farm families frequently had to delay payment for goods, supplies, and services that they did not produce until the sale of their farm crops. This resulted in a "local credit" system, devised by the Carlisle merchants, that usually consisted of the handwritten name, amount owed, and date on a piece of paper, a "jot 'em down" system which was stored in a cigar box next to the cash register until the person came in for payment; which was ofttimes extended and occasionally written off! This interest-free "honor system" was rarely ever abused, for honesty was an important value system of our community, a trait instilled in each of the Class of 1955.

Bartering was also an important part of our community economy during these times. This was an art in common practice throughout small-town rural Kentucky whereby an individual's produce, skills, crafts, or work was exchanged, in lieu of cash (not often in ready supply), for other goods, supplies, or services. This medium of "tender" was often viewed with greater value than cash, for it enabled an individual to demonstrate the fruits of his labor (for which he was proud) to another's fruits of his labor, for which he was equally proud. The practice of bartering was another value for life that we learned while growing up; that is, the need to work together and the dependency and importance we have for each other. The fine art of barter is rarely seen or practiced now days, primarily due to the modern credit card and the instant gratification mentality, which quickly provides "plastic" purchasing power without ready cash, but frequently leads to devastating debt with their heavy and unforgiving credit rates.

"Quiet Farming" – In this time of the late '40s and early '50s, tractors were beginning to make an impact on local farming practice and technique; however, most farm families still maintained and utilized teams of draft horses (referred to as "plow" or "work" horses) to do the heavy duty work of plowing, cultivating, and mowing. And, as an added benefit, the horses were willing and active participants in organically fertilizing the fields in a natural way! These very large animals, not as huge as the Clydesdales of Budweiser fame, were usually bestowed with names and were almost considered as part of the family. For instance, the team of horses owned by Raymond and Lorene Hall (Jimmy's parents and Donnie's aunt and uncle) were named "Sam" and "Joe." Once a team of horses completed their many years of "service in the traces," they were turned out to pasture to live a life of ease for their remaining 'retirement' years. This might be considered as the era of "quiet farming," since, in lieu of tractor noise, only the sounds of the farmer's horse commands of "get up" (giddy up) and "whoa," or "gee" (turn right or move ahead) and "haw" (turn to the left) filled the air, and not a discouraging word could be heard (well, maybe occasionally, when the horse, or mule was stubborn)!

"Horse-Pulling Contests," sponsored by the VFW, were a popular event of those times when proud farmers could show off the power and prowess of their teams of horses and could earn a little prize money to boot! These well-attended events were frequently held in a "sometimes-farmed" bottomland on Upper Jackstown Road in front of the Dampier home, until moved to the Nicholas County High School athletic field in the '50s.

The Carlisle/Nicholas County VFW Horse Show," touted and publicized as "Kentucky's Finest One-Night Horse Show," was very likely that, for it attracted both participants and patrons from far and wide (of all ages), including some from out of state, to show and marvel at the variety of gait and paces of these magnificent animals. Locals instrumental in the origination and success of this production were Mr. and Mrs. Frank Hardesty and the Frank Henrys, neighbors to each other, and next door to the Dampiers on Upper

Jackstown Road. Mrs. Hardesty always had horses ready to show, and she and Frank, with their widespread reputation for horsemanship, were influential in bringing in other show persons, including kinsmen Stewart Berryman and family from Nicholasville, as regular and successful competitors. During the era of the Class of 1955, the horse show originally was held at the CHS football/athletic field on the east end of Carlisle, but in the '50s it had been moved to the new Nicholas County High School athletic field. The annual horse show, which was held the first week of June each year, celebrated its sixth year with the 1954 event.

"Donkey Basketball" was a big hit with everyone in Carlisle during the late '40s and early '50s. This fun-filled entertainment event was played on the Nicholas County High School gym floor (Superintendent Davis of Carlisle High School would have never allowed donkeys on "his" gym floor!). The donkey's feet were surely wrapped with a material to protect the floor and keep the donkeys from slipping. Wrapping the feet of donkeys must have been an event in itself" It is not recalled how barnyard accident" of the donkeys on the gym floor were taken care of, but they were sure to happen occasionally. The object of the game was to dribble, pass, shoot, and score, all from the back of the donkey. If someone fell off, and some did, the other team was awarded a foul shot (from the donkey's back, of course)! Only the Harlem Globetrotters were as much fun to watch!

VI

The Decade of the "Fabulous '50s" – The Times

This was an uplifting period, a time spanning a decade in which our national mood was arising from the depths of previous decades of despair consumed by three world wars of major proportion, sandwiched around the desperations of a Great Depression into a time of relative peace and freedoms … a time of renewed hope.

The Times and Triumphs of the 1950s –
"Moving On … Fast Forward!"

We were teenagers growing into adulthood in a decade and era that would later be called "the Fabulous '50s" – an interesting and good time to grow up – an era that was filled with major accomplishments and change. The Class of 1955 are members of what demographers have labeled the "Silent Generation" (that fought the Cold War, launched rock 'n' roll, and put a man on the moon), sandwiched between the group containing our parents and elders – "The Greatest Generation" (revered for their grit and heroism during the Great Depression and World War II) – and the Baby Boomer Generation" (those born between 1946 and 1964, which includes most of Carlisle's last class, the Class of 1963).

Our country had grown by some 19 million over the preceding decade with the 1950 Census counting a population of over 151 million in the USA. In 1950, Kentucky experienced a 3.5% increase over the preceding Census to a population of 2,944,806, but with a decrease in the ratio in the rural category to now show 63 percent.

In 1951, aspirin tablets were first produced in mass quantities for direct public purchase and distribution by the Bayer Company of Germany.

On October 2, 1950, the new comic strip *Peanuts* (originally called *L'il Folks*), created by cartoonist Charles Schulz, made its first appearance with Charlie Brown, Lucy, Linus, Schroeder, and Snoopy, along with the rest of the gang.

Also in 1950, the comic strip character *Beetle Bailey* made his debut as a "college cut-up," but with America's entry into the Korean Conflict, cartoonist Mort Walker's star character "accidentally" enlisted in the Army, and, as they say, "the rest is comic-strip history!"

In 1950, Americans Frank MacNamara and Ralph Schneider, embarrassed in a fine restaurant when they discovered they were short of cash to pay the bill, launched their credit card, called "Diner's Club." Initially designed on cardboard, it allowed for payment to be made at the end of each month and initially was good to use in 28 restaurants listed on the back of the card.

The Korean Conflict – The '50s began with the dark, brooding storm clouds of yet another war with the terrible unofficially declared Korean War, which began June 25, 1950, when Communist troops from North Korea crossed the 38th Parallel to invade South Korea. Thankfully this "conflict" had officially ended by an armistice on July 27, 1953, with the final peace terms orchestrated by our newly elected president, Dwight D. "Ike" Eisenhower, in the first of his two terms. This was the first war in history in which troops of a world organization, the United Nations, acted as a police force to fight an aggressor nation (Communists controlled North Korea), as some 15 member-nations joined with the United States. This was one of the bloodiest wars in history as the USA suffered 157,554 casualties of dead and wounded, with 54,246 dead. It was certainly a major relief to both the boys and girls of the Class of 1955, as well as our parents, when the "war" was officially declared as over, just after the conclusion of our sophomore year at Carlisle High School. During our freshman and sophomore years our young men were anxiously mentally readying themselves for possible armed conflict on the Korean front upon graduation, and our girls (who were not permitted in combat service) had begun thinking about serving in the much-needed nursing profession.

Polio Is Conquered! – Dr. Jonas Salk, in 1952, developed a polio vaccine which became licensed during the year of 1955 to basically end that dreaded disease of poliomyelitis ("infantile paralysis"). To the youth of our day, polio was a consuming fear – an acute infectious virus characterized by paralysis and atrophy, ofttimes leaving the victim with permanent crippling disability and deformity, sometimes death – and for many of us, the thought of being confined and constricted within an "iron lung" was a fear almost greater than death itself! Thankfully, none of the Class of 1955 contracted this dreaded disease.

The Salk vaccine and the newly found freedom from war were perhaps the two most significant events of the decade, which uplifted us with the ability "to spread our wings and soar," making the '50s so fabulous!

Harry S. "Give-'em-Hell" Truman was our president (1945-1953), noted for his philosophical phrase, "If you can't stand the heat, get out of the kitchen!"

At the January 20, 1949 inauguration of the vice-president and president of the United States, Kentucky went all out for her "favorite son," Alben William Barkley, and her Missouri neighbor, Harry S. Truman. And truly it was Kentucky's day, as Supreme Court Justice Stanley F. Reed of Maysville administered the oath of office to Paducah native Barkley as the nation's thirty-fifth vice-president, and, at approximately age 72, Barkley became the oldest man to hold that office. Chief Justice Fred Vinson of Ashland, Kentucky, swore in Missourian Truman, whose grandparents once lived in Shelby County, Kentucky, as the thirty-third individual to hold the highest office in the land. It was President Truman who remarked at the inaugural ball later that evening that, "there seemed to be more Kentuckians present than Missourians."

It was on August 4, 1952, that Colonel Harland Sanders, the white-haired, goateed icon of Corbin, Kentucky – at the mature age of 62 – franchised Kentucky Fried Chicken, with his secret and original recipe of 11 herbs and spices. In that year, Pete Harman, an acquaintance of "The Colonel," became the first franchisee when he added to his burger business by selling the first piece of Kentucky Fried Chicken (under that name) in his Salt Lake City, Utah restaurant – and thus began a highly recognized and famous fast-food delicacy worldwide in over 80 countries.

On May 6, 1954, Oxford University medical student Roger Bannister of the United Kingdom set the "four-minute mile milestone" with a time of 3:59.4, a barrier previously thought to be unbreakable (there was never an expectation that our classmate, Jock Conley, would break that barrier!). Interestingly, on May 28, 1955, two days after our graduation, three runners broke the four-minute mile again, all in the same meet in London!

On May 29, 1953, New Zealand mountaineer Sir Edmund Hillary, with his Sherpa guide, Tenzing Norgay, reached the 29,028-foot summit of Mount Everest, on the border of Nepal and Tibet, and referred to locally as "Chomolungma," meaning "Goddess Mother of the World." We had all thought that Kenneth Booth, our most adventurous classmate, would be the first to accomplish that feat!

The girls of the Class of 1955 surely took note when the news arrived that in 1954, the "first shopping mall," which was designed by the Victor Gruen Firm, opened at the Northland Center near Detroit, Michigan, and they no doubt gleefully anticipated the future time when a similar mall (enclosed in an air-conditioned environment, containing 200-300 shops on several levels) would arrive in a closer city, such as Lexington. The stated purpose of the "mall" development – "The hope is that shopping centers will give new life to rundown American cities" – appears to have had an opposite effect by hastening the further decline and demise of our inner cities, as the malls were generally located on the outer fringes of our metro areas and, in the process, permanently consumed our farm lands along with large tracts of our natural landscapes.

It was during the year of 1950 that IBM (International Business Machines, Inc.) came to town … Lexington town, that is; which created a major positive economic impact not only to

Lexington, which began to see its population soar from around 50,000 (in 1950) to six times that number 50 years later, but also provided economic, and cultural opportunities for multitudes of smaller communities across central Kentucky. The culture of Carlisle changed to that of a commuting community, as many graduates of Carlisle and Nicholas County High Schools, such as Kimbal Booth, Bobbie McFarland, Jimmy McGinley, and many others, traversed the sixty-some round-trip miles "by car pool" daily to work at IBM.

In 1953, the first *Playboy Magazine* was launched with Marilyn Monroe on the cover, which had no date because publisher Hugh Hefner was not sure there would be a second issue! Naturally, we were all "too young and naïve" to be interested in such things at the time; however, it is thought that Larry Cameron was the first of our class to acquire a copy!

The *Today Show* began on NBC in 1952 hosted by Dave Garroway, and in 1954 Steve Allen pioneered, in late night network TV talk shows, the start of something big when he created *The Tonight Show.* In 1955, Disneyland Park opened its doors in Anaheim, California, a creation of the one and only Walt Disney, who happens to be a distant kin of Pat Disney Dampier, Donnie's wife.

While at the movies, the ten "Best Picture" Academy Award Oscar winners from the '50s were: 1950, *All About Eve*, 1951, *An American in Paris*, 1952, *The Greatest Show on Earth*, 1953, *From Here to Eternity*, 1954, *On the Waterfront*, 1955, *Marty*, 1956, *Around the World in 80 Days*, 1957, *The Bridge on the River Kwai,* 1958, *Gigi*, and 1959, *Ben-Hur*. Most of the Class of '55 viewed every one of the '50s Academy Award winners!

The "Best Song" Oscars awarded during these years, along with their movie, were: 1950, *Mona Lisa (Captain Carey)*, 1951, *In the Cool, Cool, Cool of the Evening (Here Comes the Groom)*, 1953, *Secret Love* (Calamity Jane), 1956, *Whatever Will Be, Will Be (Que Sera, Sera)* from *The Man Who Knew Too Much*, 1957, *All the Way (The Joker is Wild)*, 1959, *High Hopes (A Hole in the Head)*, and the following titles from movies of the same name: 1952, *High Noon,* 1954, *Three Coins in the Fountain,* 1955, *Love is a Many-Splendored Thing,* and 1958, *Gigi.* And, we have sang or hummed each song!

The popular "Big Band" dance music era of the 1930s and 1940s was on the wane, but thankfully it was to return in popularity in the 1990s. Teenagers across the country, during the '50s, were embracing a new musical beat called rock-'n'-roll, which was rolling in at a rush led by its "granddaddy," Mr. Chuck Berry of *Maybellene* fame. We were probably not aware in Carlisle at the time, but the term rock-'n'-roll had its origin as code words, which became slang for "having sex"! These were the words that occurred so frequently in R&B songs, for example, You got to rock with me, "Henry, all night long; roll with me, Henry, I don't mean maybe."

It was in the early 1950s that two classic automobiles were developed that would now be considered as collectables. In 1953, General Motors presented the public with the Chevrolet Corvette, a hugely successful sports car which used innovative materials such as fiberglass and Plexiglas, which had been key to the war effort, to achieve a molded, organic shape. The Ford Motor Co., not to be outdone, followed up with the introduction of the T-Bird Roadster at the Detroit Auto Show in 1954. The first Ford Thunderbird came off the Dearborn, Michigan assembly line October 22, 1954 (the 1955 Model), selling for a base price of $2,695, with the convertible selling for $2,765.

In the latter part of the '50s decade, the Space Age began with the first satellite, Sputnik I, launched into outer space by the USSR on October 4, 1957. A year later, the USA entered the "race to space" with the launching of Explorer I on February 1, 1958.

On the evening of the same date that Sputnik I was launched, the popular, long-running TV sitcom *Leave It To Beaver* was also launched; and, we had TV dinners, which were introduced in 1953, to accompany us while we watched "The Beaver!"

While most of the CHS Class of 1955, by the mid-'50s, had begun hearing of Fidel Castro and his rebellious activities in his homeland of Cuba, probably none of us paid more attention than classmate Kenneth Booth, who, being on active service in the U.S. Navy and stationed at the Naval Base in Pensacola, Florida, was likely quite aware and on alert because of the actions occurring on the island nation just 90 miles from the southernmost point of the United States. Fidel Castro Ruz was born August 13, 1926 on a sugar plantation and was well-educated with a Ph.D (law) from the University of Havana in 1950. Divorced in 1955, with seven children, and excommunicated from the Roman Catholic Church, he had spent time in exile in Mexico and the United States in 1955-56, and, upon his return to Cuba, led armed attacks against the government of Fulgencio Batista from 1956-59. The rest of us all began to pay attention to Castro and Cuba when, on New Year's Day of 1959, Castro's forces overwhelmed and forced the deposed dictator, Batista, into exile, and then, only seven days later on January 7, 1959, the United States recognized the new Castro government of Cuba.

Don Sullivan, a good friend of Donnie and Pat Dampier from their meetings on the dance floors of the Lexington Cotillion Club, and who played Triple-A minor league baseball for Montreal, a Brooklyn Dodger farm club in the International Baseball League during the 1950s, relates that in 1954, when Havana was admitted into the league, "One and the same Fidel Castro was a star performer in the outfield for the Havana, Cuba entry!"

Major League baseball in the '50s included eight teams in each league, which was roughly geographically situated in cities from the Eastern Seaboard through the Midwest, bounded in an area north of the Ohio River to the western extent of the Mississippi. The league decided to follow Horace Greeley's advice to "Go west, young man," with five Major League teams moving to other cities, extending their boundaries beyond the Mississippi to a national coast-to-coast alignment. The Boston Braves (NL) moved to Milwaukee in 1953, and the St. Louis Browns (AL) became the Baltimore Orioles in 1954. The Philadelphia Athletics (AL) became the first team beyond the banks of the Mississippi with their move to Kansas City in 1955. Perhaps the loudest and most traumatic cries of protest were heard from the loyal fans of the Brooklyn Dodgers and New York Giants when these two National League teams were moved, respectively, to Los Angeles and San Francisco in 1958. This ended the famed "Subway Series" of the World Series usually between "those Bums" of the Brooklyn Dodgers and the New York Yankees. Expansion, the process of adding new teams, did not start until 1961, when the American League expanded to ten teams. This was an era of baseball in which the fans needed a scorecard not only for player rosters, but also to know "which city was in and which city was out," and to keep up with the location of their favorite teams as well.

A seemingly new breed of baseball stars emerged in the '50s, combining speed, power, hitting-for-average, fielding, and base running, of which the most notable all occupied center field – Willie "Say Hey" Mays (Giants), Duke Snider (Dodgers), and Mickey Mantle (New York Yankees), each to be later enshrined into the Baseball Hall Of Fame.

Pat Disney, while on her Barbourville High School senior trip to Washington, D.C. in 1955, and who didn't even like baseball, nevertheless got to see Mickey Mantle (Donnie Dampier's all-time favorite player) play in person in a game with the New York Yankees vs. the home-standing Washington Senators (led by home-run-hitting Harmon Killibrew). Pat's high school group had seats in the center field stands right above "The Mick!" It was said that during the game Mickey occasionally "tipped his cap" to the cheering group from the Kentucky small town of Barbourville, and some of the classmates, with kidding, posed the question, "Did Mickey actually see and pick Pat out in the crowd and wave specially to her?"

Our governor during the first half of the '50s was Lawrence Winchester Wetherby, who served from 1950-55. As lieutenant governor, he served one year of the unexpired term of Governor Earl C. Clements, who had resigned to run successfully for the U.S. Senate (1950-1957); then, Governor Wetherby was elected on his own in 1951. A feature of his administration was bringing state and local government employees under the Social Security System.

In May of 1953, Miss Nell Wilson (Mrs. Robert Poline), CHS Class of 1949, was chosen as the Mountain Laurel Festival Queen, representing Eastern Kentucky State College (now EKU). In the beautiful setting of Laurel Cove Amphitheater in Pine Mountain State Resort Park, just outside the city of Pineville, Kentucky, Nell, our equally beautiful queen, was awarded her coronation by Governor Lawrence Wetherby.

Pizza – The pursuit of the pleasures of pizza, that delicious delicacy that just about everyone loves enough to eat tons of it and now takes for granted, was not introduced to most of the Class of 1955 until a year or two after we graduated from high school. Since this famous food is so commonplace nowadays in our eating habits, it may be hard for modern-day kids to believe that the kids of Carlisle through the mid-'50s did not have pizza parties.

During the era of the Class of '55, pizza was primarily a dish of the Eastern Seaboard and the upper Midwestern states and had rarely made it below the Mason-Dixon Line.

That First Taste of Pizza – Jackie Shepherd relates that his first experience with pizza occurred on a visit, in the late 1950s, to Columbus, Ohio, when some friends said, "Hey, Jackie, let's go have a pizza pie." Jackie remembers thinking that was a strange pronunciation for any "pie" he was used to, and when he walked into the eatery, he thought, "What is that terrible smell?" expecting the same sweet aromas of the pies he was accustomed to that emitted from his mother's kitchen when she was baking fruit pies such as cherry, rhubarb, or apple. Donnie's wife, Pat Disney Dampier, says her first memory of eating pizza was around 1956-57 when she and her hometown friend Gloria Knuckles Compton were visiting with friends in Hamilton, Ohio, and Donnie's first taste of pizza was in the year of 1956, in the small town of Carthage, Illinois, when he and his parents had driven across country to visit with his mother's family of the Campbell Clan. Jock Conley, who said his first memory of eating pizza was at UK but hailed from the St. Louis area, was possibly the first of the Class of '55 to have had pizza, which would have been before his high school junior year, when he moved to

Carlisle.

VII

High School Years of the '50s
... The Second Six Years

Junior High –
Grades Seven, Eight, and Nine – 1949-52

It was during the mid-point of our seventh grade year (1949-50) that the Class of 1955 left the previous decade of the "Fearsome '40s" to begin the new decade of the "Fabulous '50s," and, perhaps even more significant to each of us, most of us were also making the marvelous move from the innocence of childhood to the trials of being a teenager.

Carlisle City School had its own version of the BBC production of *Upstairs, Downstairs,* for when we entered seventh grade our classrooms were physically located on the upstairs floors, and we thought we were "growing up," as we were no longer considered the "children" of the lower six grades located downstairs.

Also, those of us in the class were entering the age when our hormones were rumbling. We began to notice the physically developing opposite sex, but now we knew why! As we were making the transition to the teenage years, dealing with the changes in our bodies and experiencing the sometimes wonderment, sometimes bewilderment, but always the curiosity of the opposite sex, our plight could well be illustrated by a cute joke which was circulating around that time:

"A little boy, trying to 'act big,' walks up to a little girl, grabbing at her blouse, and says, "I want, what I want, when I want it!" – to which the little girl responds, after pushing him back, "You will get, what I got, when I get it!"

Upstairs Now
Seventh Grade 1949-50, Carlisle City School.

Forward to "Radiators", Left to Right: Billy Buntin, Donnie Dampier, and Mary Mann. Second Row: Jackie Shepherd, Barbara King, Wanda Reid, Pat May, and Nell Shrout. Third row: Bonnie Brammer, Kenneth Booth, Norma Harris, Dora B. Morris, Marjorie Farris. Third row: Anna Mary Clinkenbeard, Kenneth Cartmill, Molly Jane Flora, Gordon Moreland, Marie Bussell, Billy Vanlandingham. "Radiator row": Larry Cameron, Martha Sue Feeback, Carol McLean, Mary Phyllis Smith, and Bobby Gene Anderson. Standing, Home Room Teacher, Mrs. Mary L. Cavanaugh (Social Science, Civics, English).

This was a time when, for most of us, our libidos were advancing at a faster speed than our corresponding physical bodies were developing, so we paid more attention to the older, more developed students ahead of us than to our own classmates. Upper-classman girls such as Marietta Hardin, Rose Ballard, Kay Flora, Joy Shrout, Helen Roundtree, Carol Shrout, Betty Caywood, Betty Sexton, Jewell Farris, and Jane Ellen Gillespie, were just a few in whom our boys expressed some interest, and, for our girls, who were a bit more coy about their interest, there were upperclassmen such as Billy Blake, Wayne Gaunce, Jimmy Hardin, Brooks Pitman, Gary Flora, Jim Shepherd, and Jim Hughes. Ms. Frances Metz, a very attractive "older woman" (in her early twenties!) who was our junior high English teacher, would frequently sit on the front corner of her desk and discreetly cross her legs, helping to stir those early biological awakenings in most of us boys!

It was during this period that we gained two new classmates who would become graduates of 1955. In the seventh grade, Kenneth Booth, first cousin to classmate Wanda Reed and a transfer from Moorefield Elementary, came boldly bounding in from the hamlet of Frogtown to add a rugged and robust spirit of adventure to the class personality. Then, in the eighth grade, Carole Donovan came to us from Parks Elementary. It could be said that Carole, with her rather quiet, perhaps somewhat naive, demeanor, added some additional sweetness to the mix, whereas Kenneth added some vim and vinegar to the class stew! Coincidentally, as seniors, Kenneth ("old Blue Eyes") and Carol were crowned as king and queen of the Class of 1955 during Commencement Week!

Kenneth Booth seemed to be one of those kids whose body developed physically at an earlier age, enabling him to be bigger and stronger than most of the other boys of his age. Donnie Dampier's first memory of Kenneth, whom he did not know at the time, was at the Saturday afternoon movies, probably when Kenneth was around ten to twelve. Kenneth loved to sit in the front row, and in the "rowdy" period before the movie started, some of the smaller kids were always trying to climb onto his back. Donnie recalls watching Kenneth tossing these smaller kids around as if they were rag dolls and thinking, "Who is that guy?" Little did Donnie know at the time that, in a couple of years, Kenneth would be his classmate at Carlisle and become one of his best friends.

In grade nine (1951-52) the class gained three new students who would be part of the class through high school into our senior year: Jackie Wells, Wanda Mattox, and Billy Hollar entered in January, 1952. Prior to the beginning of our freshman year, the family of Frank Albert Mattox, a plumber, had moved into the community of Carlisle, bringing three very attractive daughters: Janet, the oldest, who would be a part of the Class of 1953, Wanda of the Class of 1955, and younger sister Bonnie, who is not listed as a Carlisle graduate.

The Class of 1955 had twenty-six students enrolled in grade seven, twenty-seven in grade eight, and twenty-five in grade nine. Miss Mary Lou Cavanaugh, taught social science (civics) and mathematics and served as home-room teacher in the seventh and eighth grades. Freshman-year home economics teachers included Ms. Marie Lowe and Ms. Betty Locke, who split the year.

From Near-Tragedy to Triumph – During our freshman year in November of 1951, we tragically almost lost one of our classmates. Norma Ann Harris, as a teenager of about age fourteen at the time, was a passenger in a near-fatal automobile accident; however, a Carlisle resident who came upon the scene some fifteen minutes after it happened possibly saved her life by applying emergency procedures. Norma Ann, who was one of the class's "original thirteen," gave us all a scare as she was listed in critical condition for several days, but thankfully, she fully recovered from this near-tragedy to graduate with the Class of 1955.

On a more pleasant note, through the triumph of theater, the freshman class, in the spring of 1952, produced a 1938 play written by Ned Albert titled, *Comin' 'Round the Mountain, A Hillbilly Comedy in One Act.* With the tremendous popularity scored by hillbilly entertainment on the radio, there had been a noticeable demand among amateur groups for a play with hillbilly characters

Sassy Smiling Sophomores
Tenth Grade 1952-53, Carlisle High School.

Kneeling, Left to Right: Jackie Wells, Bobby Anderson, Billie Hollar, Larry Cameron, Kenneth Booth, Donnie Dampier, David Hardin. Second Row: Billy Vanlandingham, Nell Shrout, Molly Jane Flora, Marjorie Farris, Wanda Mattox, Carole Donovan, Martha Sue Feeback, Carol McLean, Anna Mary Clinkenbeard, Gordon Moreland. Third Row: Mary Phyllis Smith, Mary Mann, Norma Ann Harris, Pat May, Marie Bussell, and Wanda Reid.

and comedy. The cast of characters, as played by the freshman class in a spirited and enthusiastic manner, was:

Maw Judkins (Elviry), a typical mountain woman in her middle 50s (Martha Sue Feeback);

Pap Judkins, her husband, a tall, powerfully built mountaineer in his middle 50s, rough in his speech and manner (Kenneth Booth);

Daisy Judkins, their daughter, a pretty girl of seventeen (Mary Phyllis Smith);

Zeke Bemis (Gordon Moreland), a tall, gangling boy of nineteen who tries to propose to Daisy;

Dynamite Ann, a mountain woman in her 50s and the sheriff of Fishhook County (Wanda Reed);

Mrs. Hortense Belmont-Cliff, a society matron who is a large woman in her late 40s with a haughty and domineering manner (Wanda Mattox);

Millicent Lovell, her niece, age twenty, sweet and charming (Carole Donovan);

Carey Newbold, a young Northerner, who is a tall, fine-looking youth in his early 20s, well-poised, clean-shaven and attractive (Donnie Joe Dampier).

In the following spring of 1953, the Class of 1955, as sophomores, produced yet another play – a comedy in one act – titled, *Life O' The Party*. The production of 12 characters (six boys, six girls), all with choice parts, was about a disappointed 13-year-old boy not invited to his own sister's first party – yet enlisted to help out – who absent-mindedly pours sleeping medicine (intended for his "sleepless" father) into the party punch – leading to much confusion.

Musketeers, "One For All, And All For One" – Upon entering high school, school/team spirit began to take hold. We now identified ourselves as the Green-and-White "Musketeers!" It was during one of the Class of'55's numerous reunions of recent years, probably the 2000 gathering, while the class alumni, after much storytelling, had sat back in one of those quiet and rare reminiscent reposes, that Kenneth Booth, himself a former Musketeer footballer, suddenly broke the temporary silence, as he posed the question, "Donnie, what in the world is a Musketeer?"

This was not an unusual question, nor one with an obvious answer, for even though most people have heard of Musketeers, their understanding of the real meaning of "Musketeer" has been skewed by the way they have been depicted in the movies. French novelist Alexandre Dumas (1802-1870) had popularized and romanticized them in his 1844 book *The Three Musketeers* as "swashbuckling swordsmen," who were also later portrayed in like manner in numerous movies. However, the term "Musketeer" derives from "musket," a heavy, large-caliber shoulder firearm carried by infantry. It was a unique and fitting mascot, since we at Carlisle High School were also part of an "elite group" that embraced the Musketeer motto, "One For All, and All For One!"

Kenneth's innocent and open-ended question had an expanded and long-term effect by stimulating the historical curiosity of this writer as to when, why, and how the mascot name of "Musketeers" was chosen to be the identity of Carlisle High School.

The "Musketeer Mystery" was solved as revealed in the Thursday, November 12, 1925 edition of *The Carlisle Mercury*, with the front-page headline, " 'The Musketeers' Chosen For Name": "In a "Name the CHS Mascot" contest, which was sponsored by *The Carlisle Mercury*, the winning name was submitted by Miss Shella R. Shannon, of 122 East Main Street, Lexington (her address at the time), who was a former student of the Carlisle High School, in which she also claimed the $3 cash prize offered for the winning entry. After reviewing, and considering, over 200 suggested name entries, the selection committee, comprised of: Joe T. Embry, athletic director and coach at Carlisle High School, John Parker Ross (CHS Class of 1920), and Allen Hopkins, board member, made the final selection, in a meeting held on Monday evening of November 9, 1925 – the official date in which Carlisle High School, Kentucky became, for evermore, 'The Musketeers!' "

The Lexington Herald followed up in its Friday, November

13, 1925 edition with the headline: "Carlisle Plays Admirals – Musketeers Is New Name for Former Eleven – (Special to The Herald), dateline, Carlisle, Ky., Nov. 12 – The Carlisle High School 'Musketeers' will play the Danville Blue Admirals. … 'The Musketeers' is the name selected by the Carlisle Athletic teams."

The school colors of green and white had previously been adopted by Carlisle High School sometime in the early '20s, with newspaper football accounts occasionally referring to "the White and Green," the "Big Green," and "the Green and White."

The first time Carlisle High School took the athletic field as the Musketeers was on the November afternoon of "Friday the Thirteenth" of 1925, but there was no jinx, as the football Musketeers rose to the occasion and defeated the strong Danville Blue Admirals by the score of 3-0. The appealing reference to the new identifying mascot name, presented with pride, was in full evidence in the game account in *The Carlisle Mercury* on November 19, 1925, as written by John Parker Ross:

"'One for all and all for one' – Dumas, 'Three Musketeers'" Friday, the Thirteenth, held no fears for Carlisle High School's Musketeers. The Carlisle High School Musketeers defeated the Blue Admirals of Danville High School on Jackson's Park last Friday afternoon with a score of 3-0. … D'Artagnan, Porthos, Athos, nor Aramis of the far famed 'Three Musketeers' never fought more valiantly than did the little band of Carlisle Musketeers on last Friday. … The locals outplayed the Blue Admirals in every department of the game."

The Carlisle players making history by playing in this first game as Musketeers were seven seniors (CHS Class of 1926), Martin, McClanahan, Moore, Hutchings, Poe, Gaffin and Blake. They were joined in the starting lineup by Barton, Huddleston, Cook, and Clark. The subs who participated were Parker and Allison, so there were thirteen who played on that Friday the Thirteenth in that eventful first game as Musketeers!

In the preceding week, before officially becoming Musketeers, Carlisle High School began a longstanding tradition when, on November 6, 1925, Carlisle High School hosted and played in its first homecoming game. Many of the local merchants had closed their businesses to enter into the festivities and joined in to become part of a huge homecoming crowd, along with a large visiting delegation from Maysville. In the Friday afternoon game, played out on Jackson's Field, with the kickoff at 2:30 p.m., Carlisle High School lost to Maysville High School for the first time in four years, by the score of 27-0.

And so it was, in the 100th year (1825-1925) after Lafayette, the famous French hero of the American War for Independence – a real-life "original Musketeer" – in his visit through central Kentucky, had traveled perhaps only 4-5 miles from the home of the newly formed "regiment" of the elite guard – the "original" Kentucky Musketeers of Carlisle High School!

Administrators and teachers during senior high included: Mr. Robert E. Davis, superintendent (history, vocations); Ms. Nancy E. Talbert (CHS Class of 1915), principal (English, Spanish); Ms. Jimmie B. Barton, secretary (commerce); Mr. G. B. Leonard, agriculture; Mrs. Glennie F. Gilley, mathematics; Ms. Mary L. Cavanaugh, social science (civics) and English; Mr. Charles E. Wilson, industrial arts; Ms. Marie S. Lowe, home economics; Ms. Jamie Griggs, home economics during our girls' sophomore year; and Ms. Julia Ann Johnson, home economics and FHA chapter advisor for the junior and senior years. Ms. Margaret Pitman and Mrs. Cleary (Martha) Fightmaster were directors of choral music, with Mr. Carroll G. Hall leading the band.

The creation of the Industrial Arts Department at Carlisle High School, under the direction of Mr. Charles E. Wilson, occurred in August of 1951. Mr. Wilson, a decorated member of a tank division in the European Theater of WWII, related many stories to us of the war effort. The new Industrial Arts Department was housed in a building next to the gymnasium that had previously served as a "community cannery" during the '40s.

Some of the Class of 1955, as grade-school kids, may remember accompanying their mothers to assist in canning vegetables and fruits in Mason jars, in a setting with its steam and heat that would be akin to a modern-day spa.

The woodworking shop, expertly directed by Mr. Wilson, was well equipped with the tools to prepare us for future do-it-yourself projects, as Mr. Wilson elevated our experiences with hand tools such as the hammer, saw, level, or screwdriver, with, for most, an expanded first-time introduction to the shop power tools such as table saws, scroll saws, the drill press, lathes, etc., all with detailed safety and utilization instructions. We had a better understanding of the varieties of nails, screws, glues, and other fasteners, and we learned to apply a series of steps of fine finishing techniques with the variety of sandpaper levels, pumice and rosin, shellacs, varnishes, or linseed oils, etc.

The skills and techniques of working with wood that we were taught were all a very valuable hands-on experience to last a lifetime. It is remembered that Billy Berry (CHS Class of '56) found his niche, being especially adept in our newfound art of woodworking. We all followed the refrains of the popular song, sung by Johnny Cash to his wife, June Carter Cash: "If I was a carpenter, would you … If I used my hands … and worked with wood …"

The girls had "home ec" and the boys had "shop." For most of the boys, this was their first exposure to working with fine woods such as cherry, walnut, oak, maple, mahogany, tulip (yellow poplar), etc., and many of us still have lamps, bookshelves, and other items created in shop. In the start-up school year of 1951-52, the Industrial Arts Club was formed by members of the Industrial Arts Training Course. Sponsored by Mr. Wilson, it included both boys and girls, with the purpose to better understand industry and its problems and to help students choose a vocation or a worthwhile hobby.

During the last week of the 1955 school year, Mr. Wilson organized an Industrial Arts "open house," with our parents and the public invited, to allow the class to "show off" through a demonstration and display of many of their projects completed during the year.

Building a Band of Note

In August of 1951, there was an expansion of the Music Department, which included reorganizing a CHS Band with Carroll G. Hall, a graduate of Morehead State College, as the initial director. The CHS Band was first organized in 1935 under the direction of Mr. Cleary Fightmaster, a post he directed for some 12 years until he was succeeded by Captain Blake of MMI in 1947. Since there was no mention of a band program in the Musketeer Memories yearbooks after 1947, and until 1952, it is assumed the band program was suspended for some three to four years until it was reinstituted by Mr. Hall.

This newly established Carlisle High School Band (1951-1952) had approximately 29 members, of which at least seven (Mary Phyllis Smith, Anna Mary Clinkenbeard, Jane Flora, Carole McLean, Pat May, Wanda Mattox, and Gordon Moreland) were a part of the Class of 1955. The following year at the football home opener, the CHS Band made its debut as a marching band, calling themselves "The Marching 32."

During the Carlisle High School tenure of Carroll Hall, *The Music Man*, the Green and White Musketeer band expanded and developed into a fine musical unit of some forty-two members, culminating with a "superior rating" at the annual State Music Festival in Lexington in May of 1954. This was the first time a local unit had received the top rating, having received "excellent" ratings the preceding two years.

Led by junior Gordon "Gorky" Moreland, who received numerous solo awards with his trusty trombone, other junior members of the Class of '55 who participated in the band program during high school were Martha Sue Feeback (base horn) and Mary Phyllis Smith (baritone horn), with Carol McLean and Pat May on snare drum. Mary Catherine Allison (now, Mrs. Kenny Knapke), a sophomore, was also awarded a Superior rating for her French horn solos. A brass sextet, composed of seniors Betty Sexton and Bobby Curtis, sophomore Mary C. Allison, and Class of '55 members Gordon Moreland, Mary P. Smith, and Martha Sue Feeback, received a rating of Excellent. The CHS Band had also performed very well, with an overall rating of Excellent, at the Regional Music Festival, held in April of 1954 at Morehead State Teachers College.

Mary Catherine Allison and Gordon Moreland had earlier been selected with the honor to represent CHS at the annual All-State Orchestra in Lexington during February of 1954, so, the Class of 1955 did not have a first team "All State" performer in either football or basketball, but, with Gordon, they did have one in band.

Yes, Carroll Hall could be considered as Carlisle's version of *The Music Man*, but unlike the fictional Professor Harold Hill of the theatrical and movie musical production, Mr. Hall came in with a genuine "motivation to mold a band of note," and he had qualifying credentials, of course!

Mr. Carroll Gene Hall, the band director at CHS for the preceding three years (1951-1954), resigned at the end of our junior year (1953-1954) to take a position of directing the bands for the school year of 1954-1955 in the Jessamine County schools at Nicholasville and Wilmore, before returning to Carlisle for a short tenure to be the band director at Nicholas County High School to begin the 1955-56 school year.

It was in September of 1954 that our "sister school," Nicholas County High School, had organized its first band in school history, with Mr. William E. Steiden as director. After many years of struggles to gain proficiency, the NCHS Band, in the 1990s, has achieved recognition as one of the top bands in its class in Kentucky by earning numerous awards statewide.

Carroll Hall is still frequently seen playing in local bands in Central Kentucky, such as The Men Of Note, Jazzberry Jam, Jay Flippin, etc., for dances and concerts. Donnie and Pat Dampier, members of the Lexington Cotillion (Ballroom) Dance Club, danced at numerous cotillion dances in the 1990s in which Carroll Hall was a playing member of the dance band.

Jackie Shepherd never played in the CHS band, but later learned to play the mandolin, and with some other locals from Georgetown formed a bluegrass band in the 1990s in which Jackie was very instrumental in naming the performing group as The Bull Sheps! Those of us that know Jackie well will recognize and agree that this is a very fitting name, but one must be careful to not try to say the name too fast in certain mixed company.

Mr. Jack Vals replaced Mr. Hall as band master during our senior year, a position he held for that one school year (1954-1955). At the 1955 Regional Festival of Music, held on the campus of Morehead State College on the first two days of April, several members of the Class of 1955 highlighted their senior year by helping the Carlisle High School Band achieve numerous awards for their performances. The full band won "Superior" for its three numbers played; a brass sextet, which included class members, Mary Phyllis Smith (now Cameron), Martha Sue Feeback, and Gordon Moreland, also won "Superior"; and Mary Phyllis Smith Cameron received an "Excellent" rating for her baritone solo.

In the following school year of 1955-56, the successor to Mr. Vals was William E. Link, a native of Henderson, Kentucky, and graduate in music education from Western State College in Bowling Green. Mr. Link was greeted by many fine carryover CHS Band performers, which included some younger siblings of the now "Moving On" Class of 1955 ... William "Bill" Conley (Jock), Marita King (Barbara), and Loretta Farris (Marjorie).

Mr. Don Trivett was the next-to-last band director at Carlisle High School, serving from 1958 until May of 1962, when he resigned to become band director at Lafayette Junior High School. Like singer/entertainer Tennessee Ernie Ford (famed for his recording of "Sixteen Tons"), Mr. Trivett hailed from the "Tennessee" side of the town of Bristol where Main Street serves as the state line between Tennessee and Virginia.

Donnie and Pat Dampier were privileged to meet (for the first time) and fellowship with Don and his wife, Joyce, at a Year 2001 Lexington Cotillion Club dance, having been introduced to the couple by the Trivetts' good friends, Mark and Linda Snelling Brown. In later and numerous cotillion conversations with the Trivetts, Don and Joyce both indicated how much they enjoyed their time in Carlisle, especially the helpful and welcome hand received from the residents. Tebay Rose served as their school superintendent, having returned from his coaching stint at Harrodsburg High School during their tenure as Musketeers at Carlisle High. Ms. Nancy Talbert was still the school principal and even enlisted Don Trivett to serve an additional academic function as the French teacher for a school term, and, as he would later say, "This was not his specialty!" Sadly, with life's passages of time, Don Trivett died on February 1, 2005, at age 69, thus ending a friendship just beginning, all too quickly.

The Last CHS Band Director – In August of 1962, Maurice Hale, a native of Madisonville and graduate of the University of Kentucky, was employed as band director/music teacher and, as it turned out, had the distinction of serving as "the last band director." Mr. Hale performed in that capacity during 1962-63, the last year of existence of Carlisle High School, as the old school played its last music at the annual Spring Concert on May 16, 1962, and closed its doors in consolidation with Nicholas County High School.

In 1954, as the Class of 1955 was "marching" in senior year, conducted by the faculty of Carlisle High School, toward their crescendo of graduation, brass band lovers everywhere were celebrating the 100th birthday of John Phillip Sousa, who was born in 1854, and who, incidentally, shares the birth "day" of November 6 with Pat Disney Dampier.

Noteworthy and Influential Writers of Carlisle

Through the power of the written word flowing from the pen of each of these interesting writer personalities – both then and now – our lives continue to be influenced and enriched!

A member of the CHS English faculty during our freshman and sophomore years, Mr. Walter Tevis brought national and international fame to himself as a published writer, and indirectly to Carlisle and the Class Of '55. Mr. Tevis, with his "Ichabod Crane" appearance, was a truly brilliant man reputed to possess a photographic memory. In addition to introducing us to *The Works of Shakespeare* in an interesting way, he was able to mesmerize us in English literature class with near verbatim reciting of writings, such as *The Tales of Edgar Allan Poe, The Perfect Crime*, and his own short stories, which were usually about pool players.

Mr. Tevis was truly fascinated with the game of pool and gaming, and most afternoons after school was occupied in the local billiards (pool) halls. The pool rooms, as they were called, were considered off-limits to us non-adults; however, a few of us would occasionally sneak in for the fun and adventure of it and watch Mr. Tevis. This became the subject and setting for much of his published works, some of which became popular movies such as *The Hustler* (with Paul Newman and Jackie Gleason), and the sequel, *The Color of Money* (with an older Paul Newman and young Tom Cruise). These were based on Tevis' most famous novel, *The Hustler*, published in 1959, which is about Fast Eddie, a young pool player who climbs to the top by defeating Minnesota Fats. A real-life "Fast Eddie," Eddie Parker, a legendary pool player who some have said may have inspired the movie character, died while performing at a pool tournament on February 2, 2001! However, the colorful characters in Tevis's stories were his own fictional creations developed as early as 1950, and, who knows, perhaps some of the characters in his novels had been inspired by those he observed in the Carlisle pool halls!

His second novel, published in 1963, *The Man Who Fell To Earth* (also made into a movie, with David Bowie), was a science-fiction work about an alien who lands into the small-town setting of Irvine of Estill County, Kentucky.

After a couple of years at Carlisle, Walter married the sophomore home economics teacher, Ms. Jamie Griggs, and eventually moved on to the University of Kentucky as an English professor, where Donnie Dampier had him in the classroom again for college freshman English. Sometime after the successes of these two novels and movies, Mr. Tevis began drinking heavily and became an alcoholic, which led to a seventeen-year gap in his writing production. However, Mr. Tevis got help, quit drinking in 1975, and, fully recovered, got his life back to achieve even greater success. From 1979 to 1983, Mr. Tevis published four successful books including *Mockingbird* in 1980, *Far From Home* in 1981, *Steps of the Sun* in 1983, a story about a real estate tycoon living in New York during the 21st century, and *The Queen's Gambit* in 1983, the story about a girl chess champion from an orphanage in Mt. Sterling, Kentucky.

Donnie Dampier was privileged to again visit with Walter Tevis in April of 1983 at an event of The Frankfort Arts Foundation that featured Mr. Tevis with his reading titled *At the Edge of the Woods* at its Annual Poetry-Prose Reading. As Donnie approached Walter at the wine 'n' cheese social after the reading, Donnie held out his hand and said, "Mr. Tevis, you probably don't remember me ..." but Walter, looking at him, immediately replied, "I sure do, you're Donnie Joe Dampier!" After nearly twenty-eight years, Mr. Tevis's "photographic memory" was evident as he immediately recognized and remembered Donnie, followed by a good time of reminiscing those high school and college days, which was enjoyed by both. Sadly, one year later, on August 9, 1984, Walter Tevis died of lung cancer at the young age of 56, but not until he had prevailed to end up "at the top of his game."

Classmates Jock Conley and Jackie Shepherd both missed out on experiencing Walter Tevis in the classroom, as Jackie was attending his freshman and sophomore years at Maysville, while Jock had not yet arrived in Carlisle from Saint Louis; however, Jackie well remembers "The Hustler" in the local Carlisle pool rooms, as Jackie had often ventured into the adventure of the "off-limits" establishments.

In 2003, Jamie Griggs Tevis published a book titled *My Life With The Hustler*, in which she recounts her twenty-seven year marriage to Walter Tevis. Our two sophomore-year teachers married in Carlisle just prior to the Christmas break in 1952. While at the 22nd Annual Kentucky Book Fair, held in Frankfort, Kentucky on November 8, 2003, Donnie Dampier visited with Jamie, one of the

170 featured authors, as he reminisced with her about "The Hustler," but on that day, a special reunion was held, as Jamie was reintroduced, after a fifty-year lapse, to Mary Phyllis Smith Cameron, Martha Sue Feeback Taylor, and Wanda Reed Vice, all home economics students of Jamie during their sophomore year of 1952-53 at Carlisle High School.

It was during this reacquainting time that classmate Barbara King Warren, who had lost touch with Jamie over the years, renewed communications with her. It seems that Barbara, while also one of Jamie's sophomore home economics students, had taught the young and inexperienced Jamie the art of making good homemade chili, and to this day, Jamie says she thinks of Barbara's skill in this culinary art each time she creates a crock of chili.

Jamie also disclosed a revelation of which none of our class was previously aware, including Barbara, in that Walter Tevis had used Barbara King as his fictionalized "heroine" in one of his early short stories, which was sold to a Toronto publisher and distributed in a magazine throughout much of Canada in the early '50s! Apparently, the "character" of Barbara had attracted the literary attention of Mr. Tevis, as he taught us literature, as "a student who was restless and loud in class, but a young lady with the soft heart of a teddy bear!" Time has obscured the title of this short story and the magazine it was published in, but it would surely be great reading, if found, by the Class of 1955!

Carlisle/Nicholas County has been blessed with other published writers, most notably the following:

Joan Estelle Weissinger Conley, the late wife of Jock , produced a fine work as editor and compiler of *A History of Nicholas County*, published in 1976. In 1974, the people of Carlisle joined in with countless communities across America, organizing to celebrate the 200th birthday of the United States. The Nicholas County Bicentennial Committee was thus formed, which then led to the incorporation and founding in April 1974 of the Nicholas County Historical Society, Inc., with the goal that a history should be written, and published to coincide with the founding date of our nation on July 4, 1776, "as our county's lasting memorial to the bicentennial ... so that future generations ... would reap the benefits derived from a printed history of their heritage."

Frank F. Mathias graduated from CHS with the Class of 1944, the same year the Class of 1955 completed first grade. His most memorable published works include *G.I. Jive: An Army Bandsman in World War II* (1982) and *The G.I. Generation: A Memoir* (2000). Another of Frank Mathias's publications, *Confessions of a 1950s Old Gold Salesman: Kentucky History by the Carton,* appeared in *The Register of the Kentucky Historical Society* (Summer 2002). Frank, also an accomplished musician, occasionally returns to Central Kentucky from his home in Dayton, Ohio, to lend his talent on the saxophone, playing "big band" music with local bands, led by his long-time friend, Byron Romanowitz, a retired Lexington architect.

Joan Conley and Frank Mathias were both contributing authors and consulting editors of *The Kentucky Encyclopedia,* a comprehensive volume of work published in 1992 to commemorate the bicentennial of Kentucky statehood on June 1, 1792.

Barbara Kingsolver – acclaimed author and agrarian advocate – attended elementary school at Carlisle City School prior to graduating in 1972 from Nicholas County High. Many of us were patients of her father, Dr. Wendell Kingsolver, who served as our family doctor. Some of her widely acclaimed and "best-seller" novels and essays include *Animal Dreams, The Bean Trees, Pigs In Heaven, Homeland and Other Stories, High Tide In Tucson: Essays From Now or Never, The Poisonwood Bible, Prodigal Summer,* etc. Novelist Barbara, with many influences from her days of growing up in Carlisle and Nicholas County, has received numerous awards and honors for her work, including the National Humanities Medal presented by then-President of the United States Bill Clinton in December of 2000.

Dr. Eslie Asbury – a noted surgeon/physician practicing in Cincinnati, Ohio – had family ties to Nicholas County. Dr. Asbury, who was born in 1895 in rural Central Kentucky, had a kinship to

Jackie Shepherd by virtue of being a nephew of Ms. Adaline Asbury Shepherd, Jackie's mother, whom he always referred to as his "favorite aunt." There were also family ties to the Galbraiths of Carlisle. Eslie Asbury's published works include *Horse Sense and Humor in Kentucky, Both Sides of The River* (1984), and *Not Under Oath* (1987).

Community and Church Life In Carlisle and Nicholas County

"Just give me that old time religion ... that old time religion ... is good enough for me!"

The work week that we grew up with was generally longer and with less leisure time than today. Most folks worked nine- or ten-hour days from Monday through Saturday, with pay day occurring on Saturday, rather than Friday. Some of the businesses would take a midweek break by closing on Wednesday afternoons to catch up on home chores, or to just enjoy a brief respite from work akin to the "siestas" of our neighbors "south of the border." Farm families would work from sunup 'til sundown, and ofttimes longer. It was said they "went to bed with the chickens" and "got up with the rooster's crow!" Whereas nowadays we think nothing of driving to Lexington or Louisville or Cincinnati for an evening of entertainment, that was rarely done in the '40s or '50s, so the local community events were very important to provide a leisure activity. Most businesses were closed and little work was done on Sunday to accommodate attendance at church worship services and activities, and to practice our belief to keep the Sabbath holy.
Religion, worship, and church life were instrumental.

Elmer Dampier, "Keeper of the Sabbath," was a man who strived to keep the Sabbath (Sunday for the Gentiles) holy by not opening up his business on Sundays; however, he fairly frequently received calls, or sometimes visits, on that day, usually from local farmers wanting one or more parts for their tractor or pickup truck. When Elmer reminded them that he was not open for business on Sunday, but they could come in on Monday for the service, they usually respected him and his desire to remain closed on Sunday, and waited. However, Elmer was much aware that the demands of farming often dictated an immediate need, regardless of whether it was Sunday or not, and, at those times, he would relent and supply their needs.

Elmer, who was well-known for his Christian beliefs through his long-term service as a deacon, elder, and Sunday school superintendent of the adult department at the Carlisle Christian Church, as well as Sunday school teacher of the adult "Broadcasters" couples class, relied on his weekly studies of the Scriptures by saying, "I believe Jesus approved of necessary work on the Sabbath when He rebuked the Pharisees by answering, 'Thou hypocrite, doth not each one of you on the Sabbath loose his ox or his ass (Donnie's dad would never use this term for 'donkey' in mixed company) from the stall, and lead him away to watering?" (Luke 13:15).

Church life in Carlisle and Nicholas County was a very important element, then and now, in the well-being of the community, not only in terms of its primary purpose of worship, but also joining with our schools as focal points for community social events and fellowship. Most of the CHS Class of '55 were members of one of the denominational congregations and/or were involved and included in the various church youth programs and revivals, ofttimes with different denominations from our family church, all of which enhanced our moral and ethical value systems and added strength to our lives. The typical worship week began with Sunday school followed by the morning worship service, then late-afternoon Bible study or youth programs, with the concluding Sunday evening service. Wednesday evening was prayer meeting night, often held in conjunction with a pot luck fellowship supper. There were four churches located behind the courthouse within a block of each other; at the corner of Chestnut and Locust stood the Baptist, Christian, and Methodist, and around the corner on Broadway stood the Presbyterian; then, down East Main, at the entry to Dorsey Avenue, stood the Pentecostal, and at the corner of East Main and Eastern Avenue stood the Catholic Church.

On occasion, some of the church congregations would conduct joint ecumenical special services, which fostered better understanding of different dogma, theology, and approaches to worship. Those of us of the Protestant persuasion, although not fully understanding the order of the worship service, often attended Christmas Eve Midnight Mass at the local Catholic Church. So, even when various members of the Class of '55 thought they had reached that age as teens when church was not so important, we were surrounded by influences that kept us from straying too far, especially since much of our social life was provided by, and in, the churches.

A sideline event of church attendance that frequently happened could be called the "hat and overcoat exchange." Back in the '40s and into the mid-'50s, most of the men-folk wore dress hats on a regular basis to church services and other social events. These were felt fedoras that were usually purchased at the C.C. Cole Clothing Company, which was later owned by Jimmy Carter (CHS Class of 1952). In most of the churches, a hat-and-coat rack was located in the hallway leading into the sanctuary, and everyone hung up their hats and overcoats in inclement weather. Since most of the hats looked alike, with similar shades of gray, black, and brown, it was not uncommon for a man to inadvertently pick out the wrong hat and/or coat to wear home. This was sometimes discovered and corrected before leaving the premises, especially if a "38" size man was left with a "44" size coat, or a No. 7 hat was left for a No. 7-? size, etc. Often as not, the "exchange" was made back to the rightful owner during the week, or at the next church service, always with a good laugh at the mistake.

Small country churches were scattered throughout Nicholas County, as well as the adjoining counties. Rural families that lived close to a bordering county (sometimes their farm boundaries overlapped county lines) would frequently attend church services outside Nicholas – there is no boundary to the expression of worship!

It is interesting to recognize that the birthplace of the three major Christian Church denominational groups (with modern-day membership exceeding two million) occurred right in the back yard of the Carlisle Class of 1955.

"Lay Preachers" – Worship services in many of these small country churches were not always held on a regular Sunday morning basis because a full-time minister was frequently not available. During these times when an ordained minister was temporarily not available, and inspired by a devout need for communal worship, church services were sometimes conducted by non-ordained local men, devout and religious "self-styled" preachers, but who, nevertheless, proved to be very effective in leading the local congregation in a meaningful worship experience. The grandfather of Donnie Dampier, Mr. Daniel Thomas "Tommy" Dampier, whose regular occupation was full-time farming, was one of these "lay preachers" that occasionally led services at the Stony Creek Christian Church. Another of these 'lay preachers' was William "Bill" Davis, the grandfather of Donnie's wife, Patricia Disney Dampier. "Mr. Bill" owned and operated a barber shop six days a week in downtown Barbourville, but occasionally preached in a small Baptist church in the little rural community of Himlar (named for a horse), located in southern Knox County

Most of the small country churches in Nicholas and surrounding counties that we were familiar with in the '40s and '50s, as well as throughout Kentucky, could not afford an indoor baptistry, so folks in those small country congregations during those times received their sacrament of baptism into the Christian community through the ritual use of water in one of the local creeks and rivers. While it is improvable that any of the Class of 1955 received our baptism, signifying our spiritual rebirth, in the great outdoors, it is likely that many of our parents and grandparents did.

On occasion, "dinner on the grounds" was part of a Sunday country worship experience, which provided welcome socializing and fellowship as well as great country cooking. In the Class of 1955's "growing-up period" from the late '40s to the early '50s, it was not unusual to see some farm families arrive in a horse-drawn carriage, wagon, or on horseback, and some in what we would now categorize as "antique automobiles" of 1920s and 1930s vintage.

These mostly all-day country church gatherings always adjourned in mid-afternoon in time for the farm folks to get home to milk the cows and tend the livestock who were there patiently awaiting their return.

The country church Sunday morning gatherings fostered occasions for the farm families to all come together for overnight visits at the family home-place, then get up on Sunday morning, share a good country breakfast, and attend church services together. As a child, Donnie Dampier remembers his mother and dad, aunts, uncles, and first cousins getting together on late Saturday afternoon after work at the home of grandparents "Tommy" and Edna Dampier. Donnie and three or four of the boy cousins, which included William Thomas and younger brother Paul Dampier, Jimmy Hall, and Donald Merle Bowles, about the time when they were ages 5 to 8, all slept in the same feather bed in an upstairs bedroom under a tin roof. With boys of this age, "bed wetting" could sometimes add to the "warmth" of the occasion! This was a cozy time, with all that family, in a moderate sized farmhouse, especially so on a cold evening when listening to rain or sleet fall on that tin roof!

A "Water Witch" – While Daniel T. "Mister Tommy" Dampier was occasionally called upon to preach the Gospel, his services were also frequently sought out for "witching." These seemingly paradoxical pursuits were in reference to his "gift" as a "water witch" in locating underground sources of water where a well might be drilled. The official name for this art is "dousing," and a recognized practitioner is called a "douser." The reference to "witch" apparently had its origin from the Appalachians, where early settlers and Native American Indians observed that the witch-hazel (Hamamelis virginiana), a shrublike tree that grows along low-lying stream banks, was "always seeking water." So they determined that by cutting a forked branch of a couple of feet long and holding a fork in each hand with a single pointed branch forward, when walking along, the "divining rod" would pull and dive downward seeking water to locate underground water sources. This ability or gift, originally called "witching for water," was possessed by only a few individuals who then became known as water witches. Eventually it was determined that other types of tree branches, such as the peach or apple, etc. would work for those with the gift, but the "witch" name stuck. Apparently, Tommy was pretty successful at the art, because he was called upon often.

In the modern day, several of the old country churches that some of us attended in our youth are gone; however many are still standing, even though infrequently used for worship services, but continue to be structurally maintained, especially those with cemeteries.

Scouting Adventures

Boy Scout Camp McKee, located in Montgomery County, was a summer scouting outing and camporee that lasted a week that some of our boys in scouting participated in. Ironically, it was at Camp McKee that Donnie Dampier first met (in a camp football game) and befriended Billy McKee of Cynthiana High School. Billy went on to become a star of the CHS rival Bulldogs football team (and later football coach at Harrison County). Even though Donnie and Billy were fierce competitors on the football field, they maintained their friendship off the field to the extent that Billy introduced Donnie to his cousin, Nancy McKee, and other girls of Cynthiana. One of those girls was a preacher's daughter whom Donnie dated for a short while during the summer preceding senior year. Her father/preacher frequently referred to Donnie as "The Little Tiger" ("La Petit Tigre") due to his confident strut when walking up their sidewalk to pick up his date (he never sat in his car and blew the horn for his date to come out). Donnie continued to use this assigned nickname from high school well into the years of college, but then stopped when he and Pat, his future wife, were betrothed and increased maturity began to set in.

Carlisle's Boy Scout Troop 15 – The boys of the Class of 1955 and those of numerous other classes benefited greatly by having an excellent and active Boy Scout troop (#15), led during our era by Scoutmaster Mr. Everett M. "Smitty" Smith (CHS Class of 1924), with Assistant Scoutmaster Kenneth 'Scout' Campbell (CHS Class of 1949). Some of the previous scoutmasters included Paul Garrett, Ralph Shearer, and Joe Roundtree. The Carlisle Scouts, which were organized as Troop 15 on February 9, 1943, during the first-grade year of the Class of '55, were part of some 18,000 Scouts and Explorers registered in Kentucky during that time. The Carlisle boys had their own Boy Scout meeting cabin, located on East Main Street near the football field, as well as Camp Blackhawk, consisting of four to five buildings overlooking the Licking River in the Myers Station area. In May of 1947, the older boys and Explorer Scouts razed a donated clapboard-covered log barn located on the farm of W.N. Young, brought the logs to the Carlisle playground, and re-erected it as a log cabin (partially funded by the Carlisle Rotary Club), which served as the Scout meeting house for many years. There was also Smitty's (personal) cabin located near Camp Blackhawk that we had access to, subject to his frequent approval. Very few scouting groups had the facilities that the Carlisle boys had! In addition to Camp McKee there was Camp Offutt in Jessamine County, and some of the Scouts trekked off as far away as Philmont Scout Ranch in the mountains of New Mexico.

It was at Camp Offutt that the Carlisle boys of Troop #15 did very well in the overall camp competitions, including a 100-yard dash in which Donnie Dampier, Bobby Anderson, and Jackie Shepherd finished 1-2-3, respectively, with Donnie being unofficially timed at 10 seconds flat!

At a "Scouting Board of Review" in September of 1952, several future Class of '55 boys were promoted and awarded merit badges; Billy Vanlandingham and Kenneth Booth were promoted to Second Class, while those promoted to First Class were Bobbie Anderson, Jackie Shepherd, and Donnie Dampier. The review at that time awarded one merit badge to Bobbie Anderson, three merit badges to Donnie Dampier, with Jackie Shepherd the champion of that evening with the receipt of seven merit badges. It is not recalled that any of the Class of '55 ever reached the highest rank of Eagle; however, both Jackie and Donnie, and possibly Bobbie Anderson, achieved the second highest rank of Life Scout before the attention to scouting (of all the boys) was diverted by other interests such as girls, cars, sports, work, school, and (did we mention) girls.

The whole scouting adventure proved to be valuable to us throughout life in providing training in a variety of mental, physical, and social skills, including activities in teamwork and a value system of truth and honor as stated in the Boy Scout Oath Of Honor: "On my honor, I will… ." Most of us began as Cub Scouts at around age nine, before graduating to the level of Boy Scout at around the age of twelve.

Joe Blount was a Carlisle young man (we sometimes called "Little Joe") who probably benefited from the scouting experience as much, and perhaps more so, than most of the other boys. Joe, who was raised by his grandmother and without the blessing of a loving father at home, benefited from the "father figures" of the Scout leaders, as well as the male role models of the older Scouts. Jackie Shepherd and Donnie Dampier, who were two grades ahead of Joe in school, sort of took Joe under their wing on scouting activities and outings, sharing their tents, sleeping bags., etc, as well as their experience – to remain close to Joe throughout high school. As a grade-school youngster and before Joe benefited from scouting training, he had picked up quite a wide vocabulary of "salty" language, and he exercised his "right of free speech" quite liberally. The story is told …

"On one afternoon, as the youngster Joe was standing on a street corner in downtown Carlisle, an out-of-town minister approached Joe and asked if he could help the minister find the local post office. Joe reportedly retorted, "Well, 'bleep', the 'blankity blank blank' Post Office is only a 'bleeping' block down the street!" The minister, shocked and stunned at the profusion of profanity coming out of the youngster's mouth, said, 'Son, if you keep using bad language like that, you will never get to Heaven, but I can help you find your way to Heaven.' The story goes that Joe eyed him suspiciously and scornfully replied, "Well, mister (not knowing that he was speaking to a minister of God), if you can't even find the 'bleeping' post office in Carlisle, how in h--- do you think you can help me find my way to Heaven?"

Well, our "Little Joe," who should not be confused with the youngest of the three Cartwright brothers on TV's *Bonanza*, matured and grew up to be as big as the rest of us and, with the Scouting influences along with the teachers of the Carlisle City School, did desalt his salty language to a more savory flavor.

A "First Fling At Football" – We had no "little league" in Carlisle back then, to provide early participation in team sports; however, our Cub Scout troop did field a football team, which gave us the opportunity to compete against boys of our age range from other Cub Scout troops in the area. Jackie Shepherd and Donnie Dampier played together on that team, but once those days were over, it would not be until our senior year in the fall of 1954, upon Jackie's return to Carlisle High School, when the two would be reunited as football teammates. Jackie's and Donnie's only lasting memories of that time on the grade-school gridiron were running around, hardly knowing what they were doing or why, and playing in the pouring rain, mud, and sometimes snow, but it must have had a lasting impact, for Donnie later on developed a love for the game of football, as did Jackie! Years later, and on numerous occasions, when Donnie would go to visit the "Shepherds on Scrubgrass," Jackie's dad, Walter, would almost always reminisce about standing on the sidelines with Donnie's parents and "watching those little fellows playing hard, getting knocked down, getting up, and running around that football field – getting after somebody!"

"Scouts 'Surround' City Hall" – For many of the young men growing up in Carlisle, including those who would be part of the CHS Class of 1955, the Scouting adventure and all its related experiences and activities was an important part of our upbringing, which influenced much of our value systems we brought into adulthood. An example of this was found in the February 9, 1950 issue of *The Carlisle Mercury*, with the front-page headline, "Youths Take

Over City and County Offices As Oldsters Vacate." No, this was not a siege, nor hostage taking, with the local boys barricading themselves within the Court House, City Hall, and the other local government offices, but the article was reporting on Carlisle's way of observing "Boy Scouts of America Week," a common practice among small-town communities across America in the 1950s. Following is the verbatim recounting of the article as written:

"You'd better watch your 'P's' and 'Q's' because today (Thursday, February 9) is Boy Scout Day in Carlisle, being held in connection with the 40th annual observance of 'Boy Scouts of America.' City and county officials are vacating their offices for the day in favor of the scouts, who assure residents that 'law and order will be well in hand.' Running the affairs of the day in place of W. C. Talbert is "Mayor" Everett Earl Pfanstiel, ably supported by M.H. Ruddell, Chief of Police, and his three deputies, William Berry, Joe Blount, and Harold Wasson. The office of city attorney has a new face in the person of Billy Vanlandingham. Billy Gilly is capably handling the duties of the water works superintendent, assisted by James Woodard and Charles Shrout. In the courthouse Billy Joe Morrison is tackling the duties of county judge, giving Spencer Taylor a "breather." Sheriff Gary Flora and his deputies, Kimball Booth and Ronnie King, will turn any person obstructing justice today to jailers Bobby McFarland, Billy Buntin and Wayne Berry. John and Wilhelmina (Suggs) are enjoying a much-needed vacation as Brooks Pitman and Donnie Joe Dampier don the duties in the county clerk's office. Billy Blake and Fred Hammonds are learning the tricks of the tax commissioner's trade, while Jimmie Shepherd, following in the political footsteps of his daddy, and James ('Cookie') Becket are holding forth in the office of the circuit clerk. James Hardin and Jackie Shepherd are performing as county attorneys. Doubtlessly, weddings, mock trials and various arrests will take place today, as the younger generation really takes over the town."

The above Scouting article was reprinted in a recent February 21, 2003 issue of *The Nicholas Countian* & *The Carlisle*

Mercury in the "It's My Opinion" column, with a commentary by Bill Crawford, Publisher/Editor".

"I don't know about the rest of you who have just read this week's column, but writing – or copying it from the February 9, 1950 edition of *The Carlisle Mercury* – sure did give me a good feeling. It also made me wonder why we don't offer opportunities for our young people today like those that were offered the Boy Scouts back then. Maybe we ought to do such things again."

This writer wholeheartedly agrees with Billy Dale's commentary in that this hands-on experience in the early days of our youthful trek into manhood further assisted our acclimation with the adults in our community, which led us to a sense of public awareness and civic responsibility, and there is little doubt that each of the participants of Boy Scout Day In Carlisle was inspired to view the freedoms of our citizenship seriously – to become regular voters at the polls in each election after we reached the age of eighteen and gained our eligibility to do so.

Delivering Newspapers - There is no doubt that Scouting helped to prepare our young men for responsible citizenship. Another enterprising endeavor that helped to prepare many of us for adulthood and which many of our CHS boys participated in was delivering newspapers door-to-door, such as *The Lexington Herald, The Lexington Leader, The Louisville Courier Journal,* and *Grit,* as well as the local papers. Bobby Gene Anderson was one such "carrier," and in a letter addressed to him dated October 4, 1952, postmarked Philadelphia, PA, from the *Louisville Courier-Journal/The Louisville Times,* Bobby received the mailing in a special envelope and stamp, "Official First Day Cover – Honoring America's News-Paper Boys – (for their faithful service to the public and their country and for their devotion to the task of preparing themselves to be useful, responsible citizens)." Following are some excerpts from Bobby's letter:

"Today, as a signal honor to you and your fellow newspaperboys (note: this is the exact way this was written in the letter), the government has issued a special postage stamp in recognition of the valuable service you perform …we are sure you will want one of these commemorative stamps and are therefore sending this in a 'first day cover,' which is a collector's item.

"You should be proud that you are a newspaperboy for you are following in a great American tradition. Since the days of Ben Franklin, the first newspaperboy of record, ambitious American boys have rendered the important service of distributing newspapers to the people of their communities. You and your fellow carrier-salesmen are, in a large measure, responsible for making and keeping the American public the best informed public in the world today.

"… It is no coincidence that many leaders in every field of American life – General Eisenhower, Justice Douglas of the Supreme Court, Joe DiMaggio, Arthur Godfrey, Bob Hope, Ralph Kiner, Thomas Edison and many, many more – began their careers as newspaperboys. By doing the same job you are doing today they learned the importance of dependability, service and thrift in the attainment of success and they also learned to understand and appreciate the American free-enterprise system.

" … Today we join the nation in saluting you and all newspaperboys for the important service you now render and for the more important job you are doing to educate and prepare yourself to assume a responsible place in the adult world of tomorrow."

Most of the boys who delivered newspapers during the '50s never thought of ourselves, at the time, in quite the high esteem that the *Courier-Journal* letter to Bobby Anderson proclaimed, and our girls will surely notice the exclusive reference to boys only, for in this period of time, delivering newspapers was considered as a job not suitable for a woman, a way of thinking that has certainly changed, for the better, with succeeding generations.

Junior Year – 1953-54

During our junior year, Sylva Joy Owens rejoined the Class of '55, bringing her beautiful singing voice to enhance our class makeup. She had originally spent one year with us in fourth grade. Sylva Joy had frequently favored us with her singing, but she also made us proud when she received a rating of Excellent for her solo at the State Music Festival at the University of Kentucky during our senior year.

Sylva Joy, whose father was a minister of a nearby church, lived out in the county, possibly on Abners Road, on a hill overlooking beautiful Pleasant Valley of the Licking River. On Highway 32, a couple miles from Sylva Joy, Molly Jane Flora had moved from Carlisle with her family, a year or so before leaving the CHS Class of '55, to a small farm situated at the beginning of Pleasant Valley. The Floras' place, just across the Licking River Bridge located at Myers Station, was bordered by a country road that led to a remote area called "Mexico" or, as some of the locals referred to it, "Mysterious Mexico." Even in modern-day times, the area apparently still has retained some of that intrigue of the unknown associated with it.

The Ol' Swimmin' Hole – On down Highway 32 toward Fleming County, accessed by a dirt lane east of the highway, was the famous swimming hole called "the Blue Hole," situated in a section of Fleming Creek. During the growing-up days of the Class of '55, there were no public or private swimming pools in Carlisle and Nicholas County (Lake Carnico with its swimming pool had not been built as yet), so those of us who learned to swim likely did so at the Blue Hole, the Licking River, or farm ponds. Actually, some of our boys who were in the Cub Scouts troop did have the opportunity for swimming lessons at the old Paris YMCA. Apparently, this was another activity where our girls did not have equal opportunity. The Blue Hole was a quiet, isolated spot, with unpolluted, unspoiled water that was deep enough to safely allow us to drop from a rope swing into its waters!

This was a place where the kids could even unabashedly go "skinny dipping" if they liked. It was said that occasional "coed skinny dipping" occurred (possibly on moonlit evenings), but only those with specific memories of such events can recall … "If they should dare, since they were bare!"

The beginning of junior year, David Hardin became a member of our class for one year before rejoining his Class of 1954. Billy Vanlandingham had transferred to Nicholas County High School for his junior year.

The Coming of the Conleys

In the spring of 1953, a very thin student named Joseph Houston Conley sauntered in from Kirkwood, Missouri to join the Class of '55. Wearing tight, low-cut, hip-high jeans, this kid with "big city" ways from a suburb of St. Louis was a sight not seen previously in Carlisle! However, "Jock," as he is better known both then and now, quickly adapted to small-town Carlisle/rural Nicholas County. He was straightway received and accepted by his classmates; so much so that Jock was elected as junior class vice-president. This was no doubt a precursor to Jock's successful tenure in the legal profession of public office by first serving as Carlisle City Attorney followed by then serving twenty-five consecutive years as County Attorney of Nicholas County before retiring from that elective post in 1999.

Upon his arrival, Jock wasted no time in becoming acquainted with the young women in his new surroundings, as he laid claim to Bonnie Mattox, the younger sister of classmate Wanda, who had moved with her family to Carlisle two years prior, as his very first girlfriend of Carlisle – and what an attractive young couple they were, as photos of the time reveal!

Jock recalls the first day of attendance at his new school of Carlisle High – to begin his junior year – when, during the homeroom first period, the announcement ring out, "Any student interested in singing in the school chorus, please report to the school auditorium." Now, even though Jock had always sung in his Catholic School's choirs back in the St. Louis area and had always enjoyed singing (he still does), he remembers thinking on this occasion, "Man, I don't think I will volunteer to sing in this chorus.

These Carlisle 'country boys' will think I am a 'soft sissy.' " So Jock tried to ignore the call by looking intently at the pages of his text book, when, upon hearing shuffling all around him, he suddenly realized that he had been left "Home (room) Alone," as most of his class, including all the Carlisle High "country boys," had gleefully left the room to join the choir! So, Jock joined the chorus that morning and, along with the rest of the boys – his newly found friends – combined their voices with our girls in mixed-chorus harmony – to later earn "superior" awards in singing competitions.

As the "new boy in town," Jock had already proved himself physically, both willing and worthy, that fall of junior year as a first-year Musketeer on the Carlisle High School football team, yet he still felt the need to also show that he was party-proof – with some libations of "100 proof" – to be just "one of the guys" on the Carlisle Drinking Team, which led to…

The Story of the Sadly Soiled Suede – So it was on New Year's Eve of December 31, 1953, that Jock was included as one of the eight boys that climbed into Donnie's Studebaker Starlight Coupe and clamored toward Myers Station, headed to Smitty's Camp, for some pre-stroke-of-midnight celebration. This was probably Jock's first introduction to the adventurous culture of procuring the product of the bootlegger and/or moonshiner of a dry county, as was Nicholas. As most any young man trying to make an impression on new friends might do, Jock enthusiastically joined in the New Year's celebration, drinking too much, too quickly. After a short while at the cabin, the boys were ready to head back to Carlisle to attend the midnight movie at the Lyric, but as Jock unsteadily climbed into the back seat, feeling not-so-good with wooziness and nausea, he found himself squeezed into the middle of the back seat without much air, surrounded by five of the guys, with senior Bobbie Feeback leaning up on the front seat – directly in front of Jock – and wearing his brand new Christmas gift, a beautiful brown suede jacket.

The tightly packed band of Musketeer boys had traveled about one-third of the six-mile trek back toward Carlisle on State

Highway 32 when, from the deep depths of the middle of the back seat, a weak "distress call" emitted from Jock – those dreaded "seven little words" the boys in the back seat of a very crowded car hated to hear: "I think I'm going to be sick." This was quickly followed by panic cries from the "frantic five" in the back seat – "Donnie, stop the car quick" – but before Donnie could pull over to the side of the highway, the "rumblings" from within Jock erupted like a volcano, as Jock "upchucked" with the full force of the "lava" flow covering the back of Bobbie Feeback's beautiful brand new brown suede jacket!

Miraculously, at least from the standpoint of Donnie's Studebaker, the excrement was contained on the back of the suede jacket and on Jock's lap. The boys, who had quickly scampered out of the car, pitched in as best they could to help clean up the mess on the jacket and Jock by using snow from the side of the road. Another of those Musketeer moments of "One for All, All for One!" Then, almost as miraculously, Donnie was able to safely navigate back into town – but now with five guys squeezed in the front seat, making it difficult to drive! Meanwhile, Jock and the jacket were relegated to one corner of the back seat, with the other two guys practically sitting on top of each other in the other corner – as the "Merry Musketeers" (now beginning to laugh about the sad situation) drove back into town – both windows down – in the sub-freezing temperatures!

Upon arriving in downtown Carlisle and parking near the Lyric, all the boys went to the movie except Bobbie Feeback, who hurried home, hoping to find a way to clean and save his sadly soiled suede jacket, and Jock, now coiled up asleep, was banned by the boys to stay in the car, still surrounded by the scent of his "aromatic aura!"

After a short time in the theater, Donnie, becoming concerned that Jock might freeze in the sub-freezing weather, went back to the Studebaker to check on his new friend, and, finding him still sound asleep, rolled up the windows and started the car with the heater full blast long enough to warm up the inside. Then, Donnie covered up Jock with a large, thick blanket taken from the trunk, which Donnie always kept in his car to live up to his Boy Scout motto to "Always Be Prepared," after which Donnie turned off the motor and, leaving Jock asleep in the back seat, "snug as a bug in a rug," went back to the New Year's Eve midnight movie, rejoining the rest of the Musketeers.

Now Jock Conley, with his easygoing, laid-back personality and seemingly "innocent" demeanor, has frequently, down through the years, been "The Right Stuff" for a "good story," so, in the wee morning hours to bring in the New Year on January 1 of 1954, Jock, in his way, continued this story. …

As Donnie returned to his Studebaker at the conclusion of the movie, and finding Jock still asleep in the back seat, Donnie drove him home to the Conley residence at 315 Sycamore Street (the home place in which Billy Buntin grew up in during childhood years until his father, Webb, had sold it to Joe Frank shortly after the Conleys' move to Carlisle). Upon waking up Jock, he helped him into the house and was about to leave when he noted that Jock, still "reeking 'n' rockin'," had starting taking off all his clothes, and was now clumsily creating some household noise – at around 3:00 a.m. – as he was fumbling around trying to figure out how to start the washing machine and perhaps "hide the evidence" of his evening escapade. It was at that time that Donnie, hearing Jock's mother descending the stairs – to check out the commotion – decided it was time for him to leave the scene!

Jock was about to quickly discover, along with the rest of us teenagers of the '50s, that we would be much mistaken if we thought we could put much over on our parents of that day and time – especially our mothers, who had developed that special "scientific" technique of being able to "sleep with one eye open and one ear open," and certainly Ms. Kathryn was no exception! The mothers of teenage boys were especially adept at this special trait!

So it was that Jock Conley, on his first night out in his quest to be drinking buddies with the rest of the boys, did indeed make a lasting and unforgettable impression with the Carlisle boys from that night on. Shoot, the truth be told, most of us who were teenagers and young men of the era of the '50s – this writer being no exception – had, at one time or another, very similar experiences by consuming too much, too quickly, and even Bobbie Feeback, who, as it turned out, was able to salvage his cherished gift of the Christmas jacket, held no hard feelings toward Jock's mishap of that night, in the "Story of the Sadly Soiled Suede!"

The Treasure of a True Friendship – From the standpoint of the casual observer, it is ofttimes not easy to see on the surface those special properties of personality which will bond two individuals together in a close, lasting, and lifelong friendship. Such has certainly been true in the friendship of Jock Conley and Donnie Dampier, for when the two initially met, it would have been very difficult to find two individuals with more diverse backgrounds … one, a boy hailing from the big city, the other, a country boy … one with a background honed in a metropolitan urban atmosphere, the other, in the setting of a small town … both brought up with a strong religious foundation, but one well-grounded as an Irish Catholic, the other equally well-grounded as a Protestant "Campbellite" of the Christian Church. Indeed, the only apparent commonality as the two first met was that both were Caucasian, with even a slight difference there in that, while the two young men frequently ran around in the summertime shirtless and hatless, Jock rarely sunburned, whereas Donnie frequently suffered from sunburns. Yet, their very close friendship, very evident to all now, was immediate from their first meeting, as neither can ever recall when they were not close – the true treasure of a enduring friendship, the bonds of which grow ever tighter each year – a friendship that has now exceeded 50 years (a half-century) as this is written!

Conley Clan Connects To Carlisle – Jock Conley was born on December 29, 1937, only 18 days from the birthdate of Donnie Dampier, but in the year later, in the city of Washington D.C., spending his first five years there before the family moved to the heartland of America in the Gateway City of St. Louis, Missouri. The ancestry of the Conleys of Carlisle can be traced to County

Clare in the Province of Munster of the "mother" country of Ireland, located in the west-central part of the Emerald Isle with its borders on the western shores opening into the North Atlantic Ocean.

Just to the south of Clare County is County Limerick, with its main town also of the same name of Limerick, associated by name with the witty, nonsensical verse of five lines (lines 1, 2, and 5 rhyme, and lines 3 and 4 rhyme), referred to as "limericks," containing puns or wordplay and, in the case of Irish limericks, ofttimes a bit bawdy!

The Irish Conley ancestors of Hibernia (Ireland, as so dubbed by the Romans), no doubt passed on the talent and trait of the telling of a good limerick, as we soon learned that Jock was quite versed in the reciting of the light and humorous verse form ... and, perhaps, sometimes with a bit of the bawdy.

The circumstances that brought Jock to Carlisle began in February of 1953 when Jock's uncle, James Patrick "Pat" Conley, who had passed the bar exam in June of 1949, resigned his post as master commissioner of Nicholas County (he previously had served as Carlisle City attorney) to accept a position as supervisor and legal advisor for Claims and Adjusters of the Panama Canal Company in Balboa, Canal Zone. Ironically, William Conley, another uncle to Jock, at that same time was living in Panama City, Florida. That spring, Jock's dad, Joe Frank Conley, and mother, Kathryn Gibson Conley, moved the family to Carlisle to take over his brother Pat's law practice of several years' standing in the community. "Joe Frank," as he was widely known by his friends and acquaintances, was a native of Carlisle and graduate of the Carlisle High School Class of 1924. After graduating from the University of Kentucky and completing law school at George Washington University in Washington D. C., he entered federal government service in that city; then, in 1942, he was placed in charge of his agency's regional office, which had resulted in locating the family to St. Louis, whence came Jock.

In June of 1955, shortly after graduation of the Class of 1955, Jock got his first taste of political campaigning as "Joe Frank" entered the race for state representative in the 67th District, composed of Nicholas and Bourbon Counties. Jock's dad, always well thought of, was very affectionately know as "Mr. C" by Donnie and Pat Dampier.

Jock's grandfather, Mr. W.C. Conley, had also practiced law in Carlisle up until his death, with previous terms of serving as Carlisle City attorney and master commissioner as well. So, Jock's legacy is his lineage of a long line of lawyers! Although to date Jock has not received an appointment to either the state or national Supreme Court, he would make a fine choice as a justice!

In addition to Jock and his parents, the family that came to Carlisle that spring consisted of Jock's younger siblings, William Lester "Bill," and their younger sister, Kathryn. Another brother, Patrick "Pat" Carter, would not be born into the family until one year later, in 1954, the year Jock turned 16. The "Carter" is from the family name of their grandmother, so, that it is a cousin of Jock, and kinship of the Conley family, Charles Rankin Carter, that married our classmate of the Class of 1955, Mary Agnes Mann. Charles's father, George Rankin Carter (CHS Class of 1932), and his mother, Eula, who lived for several years on a 'hill top' farm on Goose Creek Road, were very active in the Carlisle Christian Church, and were close friends of Elmer and Ann, Donnie Dampier's parents.

Premature Passing – A Family Loss – In January of 1959, a tragedy beset this fine family when Jock's younger and only sister, in her early teens, began experiencing severe headaches, and suddenly died of a brain aneurysm. At the time, Jock and Donnie Dampier, accompanied by their "pinned" girlfriends and future wives Joanie Weissinger and Pat Disney, had driven down to Florida with Donnie in his 1953 Chevy and were enjoying their final spring break at Ft. Lauderdale Beach, Florida, prior to entering the final semester of their senior year at the University of Kentucky. Joe Frank, knowing that Jock had traveled with Donnie, called on the Dampiers to help locate Jock. Elmer Dampier immediately contacted the Ft. Lauderdale police with a detailed description of Donnie's '53 Chevy, along with the license plate numbers, as well as their place of accommodations. Donnie had left all of this information with his parents before leaving for Florida, just as a precaution in case of an emergency, which, unfortunately, did happen. The Ft. Lauderdale police, not finding them at the motel, quickly located Donnie's car at a beach parking lot. Donnie was quite surprised when he walked back from their beach setting to his car to get something and found a policeman standing there, but then Donnie's alarm turned to grief as he had the unpleasant task of going back to the beach where the group was sunbathing and telling Jock the sad news about his sister.

Arrangements had been made for Jock and Joanie to immediately fly back to the Greater Cincinnati Airport, while Donnie and Pat would drive back. It was a cold and snowy evening when Jock and Joanie landed, but there to warmly greet them at the airport and drive them back to Carlisle were Donnie's parents, Elmer and Ann Dampier.

The premature passing on of Kathryn Gibson Conley, named after her mother, with her bubbling personality and zest for living just as she was entering into young womanhood, is one of those passages of life we all struggle to explain. In honor of Jock's sister, Jock and Joanie named their first daughter Kathryn Gibson "Kay" Conley (Anderson), born on July 30, 1962. Then, Jock and Joanie's son, Michael, named his daughter the same, making four generations in this family with the name of Kathryn Gibson Conley.

As seniors, Jock and Pat May were named as "Best Dressed." To this day, Jock is considered by many to be a "dapper dresser," but the rumor that he wears a coat and tie to breakfast on his days off is not true!

From a group of twenty-two students, the class officers selected for junior year were: Kenneth Booth – president, Jock Conley – vice-president, Wanda Reed – secretary, and Donnie Dampier – treasurer.

Junior-year enrollment at the Carlisle City School in September of 1953 was reported at 382, with 90 of that number in high school (this probably included the upper four grades). The class ahead of us, the senior class of 1954, graduated 21 students in May of 1954. The officers of this class were: Bobby McFarland – president, Saranell Seamonds – vice-president, Jewell Farris – secretary, and Barbara Reid – treasurer. In some of the other years preceding the Class of 1955, the numbers of graduating seniors were: 1949 = 26; 1950 = 15; 1951 = 26; 1952 = 18; and 1953, 21. By comparison, enrollment for the 1953-54 school year in the Nicholas County System was approximately 930, with 264 in high school. There were thirty-two NCHS graduating seniors in 1954. Enrollment figures early in each school year were imprecise in both school systems due to a number of students who were allowed to start late in order to finish cutting tobacco, the family livelihood for many.

"**Honors**" – There were some extracurricular recognitions and honors received by some of our classmates during junior/senior years. Early in 1954, Mary Phyllis Smith, representing the 4-H "Busy Bee Club," was named "District Best in the Achievement Contest" sponsored by the Kentucky Utilities Company. In May of 1954, Martha Sue Feeback was honored with consecutive titles as Miss Nicholas County at the Style Review during 4-H Week, where she modeled the outfit she had made! Mary Phyllis Smith had previously received this same honor in May of 1952. In June of 1954, Wanda Reed was chosen by the faculty of CHS to attend Girls State at Georgetown College sponsored by the American Legion, while Donnie Dampier had been selected in 1953 to attend Boys State held at Millersburg Military Institute. It was during December of senior year that Jock Conley's essay, titled "How Water Conservation Benefits My Community," was judged second best among the 44 entries received in the annual Soil Essay contest.

It was in April of 1954 that one of our good friends, Donnie Lynam, a graduate of NCHS, was awarded an Excellent rating for his delivery of "The Values of Good Leadership" in the public speaking contest at the Northern Kentucky FFA Day held in Cynthiana. Donnie joined Jock Conley, Billy Buntin, and Donnie Dampier as Phi Sig fraternity brothers at the University of Kentucky, then later married Judith "Judy" Galbraith, a graduate of the CHS Class of 1958 as they enjoyed a long marriage of over forty years. Judy, who sadly passed away on December 11, 2003, was the sister of Gatewood Galbraith, a two-time candidate for the office of governor of Kentucky and the daughter of Dottie Galbraith, who has amazingly won each year in the "Age-80-and-Over" running event of the State Bluegrass Games.

Wanda Reed wrote a weekly column titled 'C.H.S. Highlights' for *The Nicholas County Star* in 1954 and throughout our senior year.

The *Nicholas County Star,* a second local newspaper along with *The Carlisle Mercury,* was started in 1947 and closed shop in 1963 (the same year Carlisle High School closed its doors). The headlines of the final issue, which ran on July 3, 1963, read " '63 Festival Promises More Music, Fun & Frolic than Ever," which was a reference to the Blackberry Festival. *The Star* apparently consolidated with *The Kentuckian-Citizen,* described at the time as "the oldest newspaper in the Commonwealth."

The 1954 Junior-Senior Trip – As juniors, we accompanied the Class of 1954 to make up the 39 students who participated in the annual Junior and Senior Trip of that year. On the five-day trip we visited Bardstown (My Old Kentucky Home), Hodgenville (Lincoln Memorial), and Mammoth Cave in Kentucky. Then, on to Tennessee to visit the State Capital at Nashville along with the Hermitage (home of Andrew Jackson), Chattanooga (Lookout Mountain), and Gatlinburg with a drive through the Smokies to Cherokee, N.C. The trip continued to Asheville, North Carolina, and a tour of the Biltmore House before returning home to Kentucky by way of Cumberland Gap and Renfro Valley.

Accounts from that time indicate that there was rain and/or fog for much of the trip; however, our spirits were not dampened! It was also thought that at Mammoth Cave, the boys, influenced by "hip" students from other areas, were first introduced to the new teenage style rage of pink shirts and black pants!

Martha Sue Feeback wrote an account of the school trip as guest columnist in "Along the Star Trail" for *The Nicholas County Star* in May of 1954.

There were several significant community events and happenings in the year 1954 that generated interest and activities on the part of members of the Class of 1955 as well as most of the local residents:

The Blackberry Festival, which is still in existence, was possibly in its heyday as it began its sixth year with the July Fourth activities of 1954. The festival, which was estimated to draw some 10,000 persons annually, was initiated in 1949 as a homecoming for former Carlisle/Nicholas Countians to return and join the local residents in celebrating Independence Day. Even though the title was taken from the abundance of blackberries that grew wild throughout the county, it has been a rare occasion for fresh blackberries to be available during the festival because they do not normally ripen until late July. During this period, we thought the festival was loads of fun with carnival rides (set up in the Court House yard), numerous food and crafts booths sponsored by the local merchants, churches, and civic clubs, contests such as "husband calling," "human wheelbarrow races," "wrestling the greased pig," etc. Each night Main Street between Broadway and Locust was roped off for street dancing, usually country square dancing, clogging, or individual improvisation! It seems that an annual highlight was an address and singing by A.B. "Happy" Chandler, the former (1935-39) and future (1955-59) governor of Kentucky. He had a strong voice and was noted for his renditions of *My Old Kentucky Home, Gold Mine In The Sky,* and, of course, his trademark *Happy Days Are Here Again.*

On July Fourth of the 1955 event, classmate Carol McLean, the vibrant former cheerleader of the CHS Class of 1955, was named Queen of The Blackberry Festival and crowned by A.B. "Happy" Chandler, the festival speaker of that year.

An act by the 2004 Kentucky State Legislature could bring additional acclaim and appeal to the 2005 Carlisle/Nicholas County "Blackberry Festival," with their official declaration that blackberries (Rubus), a member of the rose family, are now the state fruit of Kentucky. For those of us with vivid memories of picking wild blackberries in the countryside during the 1940s and 1950s, we could suggest that the Kentucky General Assembly also give consideration to naming the chigger as the "State Insect" and the black rat snake as the "Kentucky State Snake," as those two creatures always seemed to be in abundance to accompany the blackberry brambles at picking time!

Prior to the Blackberry Festival, "traveling carnivals" were a regular, welcome diversion to the drudgeries of work for the Carlisle/Nicholas County residents. At a time before they were set up downtown as part of the festival, they were usually held in the same bottomland location on Upper Jackstown Road as the horse-pulling contests and frequently ran for the duration of a week. Apparently, some of these carnivals that set up on the outskirts of town included adults-only "hootchy-kootchy" shows that featured a strip tease! These shows, positioned in a back tent off the main thoroughfare, were most likely attended by men only, although women were not restricted. Women would probably publicly express their dismay over this type of activity, but many were possibly pleasantly pleased later in the evening by the amorous attention received from their men!

It is rumored that some of the adolescent grade school boys would try to satisfy their curiosity by attempting to sneak in under the back flap of the show tent, but were almost always caught by the show people before they got in; however, it is likely the boys did not know what they were looking for that they were not supposed to see!

All in all these traveling carnivals provided good family fun entertainment that included thrill rides (tame in comparison to modern rides), games of chance or skill, cotton candy, snow cones, hot dogs, and other attractions that were enjoyed by our citizens, including many of the eventual CHS Class of 1955.

The discovery of prehistoric mastodon and mammoth tusks, jaw, and leg bones of gigantic mammals of the Pleistocene or Glacial Period in Kentucky was uncovered at Blue Licks in August of 1954. The discovery, at the time termed "one of finest of all times," was uncovered in the bottom land of property owned by Ed Hunter in an area that included the Old Blue Lick Springs, the old hotel, and a store building.

Excavations of this area of Blue Licks had been undertaken since the late 1800s in an unsuccessful attempt to relocate the original Blue Lick Springs, for which the place was named, which had disappeared decades before. The famous vein of water has never been relocated; however, in its place, the massive bones were found. For the Class of '55, this was indeed, an out-of-doors classroom to observe the studies of archeology and paleontology. Several of us went to the site and perhaps participated in the dig.

At one time this area was a popular resort which drew people from far and wide seeking the restorative powers of the spring water. Some enterprising folks from Carlisle formed the Blue Lick Water Co. and marketed water in a brown bottle labeled as "BLUE LICK ... From 'The Famous Blue Lick Springs of Nicholas County, Kentucky.' "

One-Room Schools – Nearby was the old one-room school in which Ms. Adeline Shepherd, Jackie's mother, inspired her students in one of the beginning locations of her long teaching career, which was continued well into her eighties. The Blue Licks School was the third and largest (with some 50-60 students) of the progression of one-room schools in Ms. Shepherd's early teaching resume, all possibly situated within a long day's walk of each other – "just a stretch of the legs" – having come to Blue Licks from the one-room school in the tiny Robertson County community of Alhambra (with approximated two dozen students), located some six miles from Blue Licks in the tip where Robertson, Fleming, and Mason counties joined together.

The circumstances that led to giving this remote Kentucky community the exotic place name of Alhambra has probably been lost to history. The name originated not from the Bible, as many believe, but from the Arabic word of Al-hamra (meaning "Red" or the "Red One") and is the name of the great 13th-century palace and citadel of the Moorish kings built between 1248 and 1354, situated high above and overlooking the Spanish city of Granada.

According to Jackie Shepherd, his mother's first one-room school was located in Nicholas County at the Brierly school (which she estimated had about one dozen students), believed to have been somewhere in the Ball Hill and Tanner Branch area between Barterville and Blue Licks. Some years ago, Jackie quizzed Ms. Adeline: "Mother, how in the world did you handle and teach all of these students at the same time, with their ages ranging from first grade to approximately the sixth-grade level, and even though high school?" Ms. Shepherd laughed and responded, "It was really rather simple. I developed lesson plans and objectives for each level, then I had older students at each grade help teach the younger students in grade ages below them, such as second-graders helped first-graders, third-graders helped teach second-graders, etc., etc."

So, by involving her students in the teaching process and thereby providing them with ownership in their own educational pursuits, she "practiced what she preached," which was, "The best way to learn a subject, is to teach the subject!"

Ms. Shepherd had broken the mold of most women of that day by earning college credits leading toward a degree. That was at Midway College for Women (a two-year school at the time, which was originally founded in 1847 as the Kentucky Female Orphan School), when Ms. Adeline Shepherd, herself an orphan, completed her studies in 1921 as a classmate of Fanny Ruth Snelling, who also broke the mold and would later become our sixth-grade teacher.

The Historic Blue Licks Church, built in 1864, which had burned to the ground in February of 1954, was rebuilt during the year with a dedication for the new church in October of 1954. The historic church had been truly ecumenical in its day by serving congregations that were Methodist, Baptist, Presbyterian, and, at the dedication, Christian. This was especially significant to Donnie Dampier, for he had taken part in rebuilding the church. Donnie worked during the summers for Mr. T.W. Bailey of the Moorefield community, a Master Mason who had performed the concrete and bricklaying work for the church. The church, located on U.S. 68 adjacent to the Blue Licks State Park entrance, is pointed to with pride by Donnie on each of his occasional visits to the park. In some three summers, Donnie helped build another church in Mt. Olivet, two houses in Carlisle, and Mr. Bailey's own house in Moorefield, all of which he can proudly say "are still standing strong and in use!"

Pride in performance and the final product was well in evidence in the small-town and rural atmosphere of communities like Carlisle and Nicholas County during the '50s. Mr. Bailey's pride in performance was dramatically demonstrated as he was eyeing their work-in-progress while Donnie was cleaning up tools to conclude a workday in which they had spent around 10 hours laying courses of brick of over waist high and extending down the entire side of the house they were building on the corner of North Street, across from the CHS school grounds. Donnie was startled with Mr. Bailey's quitting-time instructions, "Donnie, when you get here early in the morning, tear it all down. The wall is not plumb. We must start over!" Donnie's inexperienced eye did not initially detect this flaw, but when Mr. Bailey demonstrated with the plumb bob, Donnie could see the wall was ever so slightly leaning outward and, if continued, by the time they reached the top course, the side wall would have probably been some two or more inches out of plumb. Over time, this flaw would have weakened the overall structure, causing considerable problems – so, there is a pride in performance to drive by the house a half-century later and observe that the walls still stand straight, strong, and tall!

In this unofficial apprenticeship Mr. Bailey taught Donnie the fine art of masonry and bricklaying, combined with a pride of workmanship, that enabled Donnie to singlehandily design and build his own "crowning glory" work, a large brick and concrete barbeque grill (very popular in that mid-'50s day) in the backyard of Donnie's old home place on Upper Jackstown Road. It is still standing in working order some fifty-years-to-date later, as this is written!

Donnie, at around age 12-13, in 1949-50, had also participated in the tearing-down of the original small four-room house which, at the time, sat on the line just beyond the Carlisle City limits, and the building of their new home at this location. This was in conjunction with the arrival of "city water" lines installed out Upper Jackstown Road.

So, it could be said that the design-plans of the new house were designed to center around the Elmer Dampier family's first-ever bathroom featuring indoor plumbing. Specifics are not recalled in detail from that time so long ago; however, this significant cultural life-changing event was probably initiated by a private family christening of the commode ceremony!

Elmer and Ann Dampier lived here until around 1967, when they moved into another new home they had built on Upper Sycamore Street. Elmer and Ann apparently desired living at an address that began with "Upper."

In July of 1954, a gentleman by the name of Walter E. Devine came wheeling into Carlisle on the last legs of his quest to tour, on bicycle, the state capitals of each of the forty-eight states. Yes, when the Class of '55 was in high school, there were only forty-eight states! In our history and political science lessons at the time, we did not know there would soon be fifty states. Alaska, "The Last Frontier State," became the 49th state on January 3, 1959, the first new state added to the Union in 47 years and the only state separated from the other states by a foreign country (Canada). Close behind was Hawaii, "The Aloha State," on August 21, 1959, as the 50th state.

A water pipe line running between the Carlisle reservoir and the Licking River at Myers Station was completed in September of 1954. This was a significant event to assure an adequate water supply to Carlisle residents, who had experienced severe water shortages during summer months for several years at the time. Both the city and farm communities were also exploring "cloud seeding" as a possible solution for the droughts they were suffering in the early 1950s. The Carlisle High School Band, under the direction of Mr. Jack Vals, opened the ceremonies for the Waterline Celebration, a thanksgiving program for the completion of 'operation pipeline'!

Mixing In With Millersburg

The Town of Millersburg, with only some seven or eight miles separating the two towns, was and is the closest neighbor to Carlisle. With the proximity of the two small communities, there was much interaction among their residents, including the Class of 1955, in family relations, work, education … and romance.

Millersburg in the 1950s had settled in to be a quiet and pleasant small town and, with a population of approximately 800 (some 200 fewer than the probable peak of the late 1800s), it could be called by some "a sleepy little village." However, during this period of "back to the '50's," with a site on the back and side street(s), the local youth sometimes had some rather rowdy parties while the rest of the town slept! Some of the CHS Class of 1955, such as Jackie Shepherd and Billie Buntin, with their MMI connections, and possibly some of our girls, joined in.

Donnie 'n' Polly – Donnie Dampier, who had a summer romance with Polly Vice, a local Millersburg girl, was frequently included in these parties. It is not specifically remembered the circumstances in which Donnie and Polly met, perhaps as Donnie was running around with Millersburg buddy Jeff Layson or, more likely, as Donnie was "cruising" Millersburg, he spotted her sitting on one of the local boys' cars, adorned as a hood ornament, in front of the two popular Main Street restaurants, Bridgett's Kitchen and, only two doors apart, the Kadet Inn, both of which also served as local youth "hangouts." Those of us who grew up in the '40s and '50s will remember that hood ornaments were the standard that served as an identifying symbol and adornment on most automobiles of the day, such as the ram on the Dodge, the sailing ship on the Plymouth, a figurine of Mercury (the Roman god who serves as herald and messenger of the other gods) on the Ford product of the same name, etc.

During the summer or two in which Donnie and Polly dated, it was probably thought of as a rather unusual romance in that, since Polly had neither an automobile nor a telephone, she frequently enlisted and convinced some of the Millersburg boys to drive to Carlisle to fetch Donnie for one of their parties. It is rather remarkable the hold that an attractive young woman can have on the boys, since Donnie would probably have been considered as a competitor for Polly's charms by some of the local boys she enlisted. However, Polly's influencing hold would have been well understood by the young male mind of the day, in that Polly, with dark eyes that complemented a well-endowed and proportioned female figure, could have been accurately described as "five foot four and one to adore" more so than "five foot two with eyes of blue!" The local boys that she recruited to fetch Donnie thought that by doing her bidding, they would have a later chance to win her to them, so Donnie rarely had any problems of competition with the locals – except on one occasion ...

"A Tossing Through the Closed Screen Door" – This one-time confrontation happened in the kitchen at a summertime party located in a home on the outskirts of Millersburg. While Donnie was talking with some of the other party attendees, a local young man, with too much to drink, began to berate Polly for bringing the "outsider" to their party. His loud talk attracted Donnie, who turned in time to see the young man beset upon Polly, first shaking, then shoving her down to bounce her butt on the kitchen floor, then, adding insult to injury, proceeded to empty a crock of snack potato chips onto Polly's head. Donnie quickly came to the rescue, whirled Polly's antagonist around, grabbed the front of the young man's shirt with both hands, and, with a combination of lifting and pushing across the kitchen floor, shoved him through the closed kitchen screen door into the yard, at which time the young man thought, "Boy, I've had enough of this party," and went home! Donnie then turned to find Polly, a bit embarrassed but otherwise unhurt, with a beaming smile across her face at Donnie's quick action, then, after helping her up, he spent much of the remaining evening picking crumbled potato chips out of Polly's hair. The next day, Polly and Donnie returned to the house with an offer to the owners to repair the busted kitchen screen door. As for Polly's antagonist, who made his unexpected exit "through" the screen door, there was no more trouble between Donnie and him, and, who knows, with the way things were back then, when young men had confrontations over a girl (a fairly frequent flare-up), the two of them may have gotten together later and joked about the incident!

In the 1950s, Millersburg Military Institute (MMI), a small all-boys school of approximately 200 students in high school, including the "Junior School" which sat about three blocks down the street from the main campus and standing seven miles from the downtown of Carlisle, was considered as a miniature high school version of the United States Military Academy, "The Army," of West Point, New York. The school, founded by Colonel C.M. Best in 1893 with the operational motto "Right Training Is Better Than Riches," and which did not open its doors to females until the 1970s, was well-noted for its disciplined, well-rounded academic and athletic programs. MMI was, perhaps, approaching its zenith in 1953, the year in which Colonel W.R. Nelson retired as the long-time head of the school. In the 33-year period in which Colonel Nelson served as commandant, his leadership resulted in a rise of enrollment from 18 students in 1920 to over 200 cadets by 1953. Several Carlisle young men had added to these numbers.

Donnie at Boys State – In 1951 MMI hosted, for the first time, the annual Bluegrass Boys State (Citizenship Camp) for 300 outstanding academic and civic-minded young men selected from high schools from across all parts of the Commonwealth, a commitment to the highest ideas of education. In the 1953 session, Donnie Dampier, who had just completed his sophomore year at Carlisle High School, was selected by the American Legion of Kentucky, which was the program sponsor (as part of the nationwide project), to participate in the weeklong camp, which ran from Thursday noon of June 18, 1953 through the conclusion the following Wednesday of June 24, 1953. Donnie, through the foresight of his mother, has saved the 42-page Manual of Functional Citizenship, which cited the aims and objectives of Bluegrass Boys State as "a training school in citizenship ... as a model of self-governing American democracy ... presumes the freedom and independence of the individual ... to assume the responsibilities to assure their continued freedom of thought and action ... an intelligent citizenry is essential ... etc."

In the intense and regimented non-stop schedules, which ran each day from 6 a.m. *Reveille* through the 10 p.m. *Taps*, Donnie was privileged to gain many friendships of young men from the far extents of our state and was able to acquire some two dozen autographs (with comments) on the back pages of his keepsake manual.

One of those was Charles Berger of Harlan County, who went on to serve many terms in the Kentucky State Senate (district including Harlan, Bell, Letcher, and Perry Counties) during the 1980s and early '90s. During this legislative period of years, especially the 1990 regular session, Donnie testified numerous times on state employee issues before the Senate State Government Committee, of which Charles Berger was a member; however, after the lapse of some 35-40 years, the two probably did not remember each other and that they were good buddies during that once-in-a-lifetime week of the 1953 Bluegrass Boys State.

Donnie was also able to meet several delightful young female visitors to Bluegrass Boys State and acquired some of their autographs in the back page of the manual, with their descriptive notes of themselves. It is interesting to note that back in the early '50's, some of the young ladies more formally addressed themselves as "Miss"! Alas, each of the young ladies lived at too greater distance for the 16-year old Donnie to pursue at that time!

Just like so many people we meet along the way, it makes one wonder, "What ever happened to all these guys and gals?" with the hope that they have each had satisfying lives – all of which are certain to have gained from the influences and practiced the principles of Bluegrass Boys State.

Although Jackie Shepherd and his family had always planned for him to be a graduate of CHS, he transferred to Maysville and MMI to gain from their stronger programs in higher math and science. With limited resources, these disciplines were one of the few academic deficiencies at old CHS. Jackie, who would say he went to MMI not to become a soldier, but to be better educated in the sciences, benefited in these moves in that he was able to graduate from Georgetown College in only three years. However, down through the years, he has also said that he wished he had stayed for the normal four years to more fully enjoy and benefit from the college experience. Jackie has had a very successful practice of dentistry in Georgetown for nearly forty years, and, along the way, he has embraced modern computer technology in developing one of the most progressive dental offices in Kentucky!

In addition to his considerable intellect, academic and athletic contributions, Jackie Shepherd, who at the time was frequently thought to have a strong facial resemblance to Bob Hope, brought to the Class of 1955 a "gusto" enthusiasm for life along with a hearty, infectious laugh.

The Drive To Drive

If one were to select a single icon which best symbolized the 1950s, it would likely be the automobile. Hot cars! Hot rods (such as Kenneth Booth's "skeeter")! Tail fins, whitewall tires, chrome trim, hood ornaments – big cars with plenty of horsepower and speed.

Ever since the early fears of the "horseless carriage" were put aside and the initial skepticism and lack of acceptance were overcome with expressions of "That 'thing' would never replace the horse and carriage" as the chief mode of transportation, America has embraced and developed a continuous love affair with the automobile. Even though there were many fine and elegant "classic" cars built before by numerous entrepreneurs, the introduction of the "Model T" Ford, "the Tin Lizzy," in 1908 – mass-produced in numbers for the first time by Henry Ford – made available an affordable automobile for the average man in the street. Beginning, perhaps, with the 1920's and thereafter, the automobile provided an avenue for "the loosing of the reins" (pun intended!) for the young and young at heart by providing mobility, distance, and a private place away from the watchful eyes of parents or other chaperons during those critical courtship days!

"A Love Affair ... A Passage of Manhood" – At no previous time in history, and some would say not since the '50s, has the love affair with the automobile been more evident, and perhaps unparalleled. Some factors that were key to the unprecedented popularity of the automobile, as we entered the '50s, were the conclusion of both World War II and the Korean Conflict, which provided for peacetime availability of the materials required for the production and operation of the automobile, such as steel, rubber, plastic, glass, and gasoline and oil. We were entering a period of relative prosperity and, with the burden of war removed from our shoulders, there was a renewed sense of freedom, accompanied with the unencumbered feeling that we could now drive around, just for the pleasure of driving. Especially for the young man of the '50s approaching the legal driving age of 16, to acquire that driving license and to have access to a set of wheels was akin to a passage of manhood! What they drove was an expression of who they were.

For the young woman of that day, possibly due to the cruising culture that usually expected the boy to drive and the girl to ride, attaining the driving license at age 16 appeared to be less important; however, they possibly saw the redemptive opportunity if they "were 16 and never been kissed," since that omission could now be alleviated in the newfound freedom in either the front or back seat of their boyfriend's wheels! From the girls of the Class of 1955, it is remembered that only Wanda Reid and Anna Mary Clinkenbeard acquired their driver's licenses during high school, probably as they entered senior year, and were allowed to occasionally take out the family car for "a spin," which frequently involved gathering several of the girls and parking on Main Street in front of the Court House (in their "private" sanctuary) to engage in "girl talk" while watching for the boys! Martha Sue Feeback, who did not get her license until she graduated from college at Morehead State, remembers that Anna Mary, when not accompanied by adults, would drive "like a bat out of hell," especially on some of those rare straight stretches found on the roads of Nicholas!

There was no less urge in the "drive to drive" for the boys of the Class of '55 and the other boys of Carlisle and Nicholas County, as they felt it was their birthright to learn to drive, get that license, and then drive either a used old clunker or the family vehicle. There was no driver's education in high school or a local driving school, so we usually were taught by our parents, most often the father. Actually, most of the boys who lived on a farm setting, such as Jackie Shepherd, Jackie Wells, and Kenneth Booth, as well as the boys of Nicholas County, had been driving around the farm fields and on the nearby county roads since they were about 14 years of age, and some even younger.

It was apparently legal, back then, for farm boys, at age 14, in application with farming activities, to even drive tractors or farm pickups on the highways. From about the age of 14, Jackie Shepherd's dad had assigned him the job of driving their ton-and-a-half farm pickup to Flemingsburg, the site of the nearest mill, on a regular basis to pick up a special mixture of grains for their dairy cows, which Jackie described as their "dessert." The very day that Jackie celebrated his 16th birthday he went in to Carlisle for his "legal" driver's license test. After passing the written portion of the test with a perfect score, the actual driving portion of the test, administered by the state patrolman, consisted only of Jackie driving once around the Court House and parking straight in, not even parallel parking, which most new drivers dreaded. Thinking that the test was usually much more comprehensive than that, a concerned Jackie asked the patrolman if he had done something wrong that might have caused him to fail on his first try. Laughing, the patrolman's reply was, "Oh no, you did fine, but you see, I have watched you drive that big pickup around here for the past two years, so, I already knew you could drive!"

There was much less motivation and little precedent for the girls of that era to obtain their driver's licenses as soon as they were "age eligible," with many not getting their license to drive until late high school or after graduation. Indeed, many of the moms and womenfolk of Carlisle and other small towns of Kentucky, who served as role models and influences for our girls, did not drive, or did not drive until later in life, and, for some, never. Many of the adult women who had a husband or man to drive for them did not see the need, plus, the automobile apparently was viewed during those times as a man's prerogative and, with its mechanical makeup, it was considered as more a "man thing" that was looked upon as less ladylike by some women. With the changing times, this is certainly not true for the young women of today, who are just as anxious as the boys to get their licenses as soon as possible! And, it was not just the boys who were "hot rods," as several of the girls were prone to "put the pedal to the metal!"

In the small towns of Kentucky, like Carlisle, most of the kids who attended the city school walked most places they needed to go. However, several of the Class of 1955 lived outside the environs of Carlisle, which frequently necessitated a ride; for instance, Kenneth Booth, Larry Cameron, Jackie Wells, and Jackie Shepherd all lived in the country, and, some of the girls lived on the outer fringes of the city limits, such as Martha Sue Feeback, Nell Shrout, Anna Mary Clinkenbeard, Mary Phyllis Smith, Sylva Joy Owens, and Carole Donovan. Even when we got the official and legal driver's license, there were still numerous occasions when we walked, rather than drove. Remember that this was prior to the modern day when it is common to see two, three, or four automobiles in the driveway, for, back then in the '50s, most families had only one "family car," and it was not always available or permitted for use by us teenagers.

In the small town of Barbourville, where Pat Disney (Donnie Dampier's future wife) grew up, most of her girlfriends walked nearly everywhere, including school, church, the local stores, each other's homes, and Jack's Restaurant, located on the downtown courthouse square, which was their teenage hangout (the equivalent of the Carlisle Drug or William's Restaurant in Carlisle). And, occasionally, they would all load up in some lucky boy's car for a jaunt in the country, or to an out-of-town game.

Pat, who had been taught to drive by her uncle Fred Davis,

did not get her driver's license until the month before she began her freshman year of college, and her mother, Jeree, showing her "true grit," finally obtained her license three years later (at about age 43) in the summer before Pat began senior year at the University of Kentucky. Pat and her mother, along with Donnie, took some courses at UK that summer of 1958, which also gave Jeree the opportunity, while staying in Lexington, to take driving lessons for the first time, and a short while later, Pat and her mother bought their first-ever family automobile, a used 1957 Chevy two-door hard-top Belair, an automobile that nowadays would be considered a classic. Jeree apparently was an inspiration to other ladies of her similar age range back in Barbourville, stimulating them to also learn to drive after they heard of her determination and observed her newfound freedom.

The First "Legal Solo" – Sometimes that first time out driving solo after obtaining that legal driving license can set the tone and have a lasting effect on a person's driving attitude and habits from then on. This was certainly true for Donnie Dampier, who, by turning 16 in December of their sophomore year, was probably the first of the class to earn that elusive driving license, but who also had a bad experience that first time out that affected his approach to driving from that time forward. On the evening after earning his license, and poised to celebrate with some of his friends, Donnie's dad, showing his trust and confidence that Donnie would drive responsibly, gave him the keys and allowed him to take out their new Studebaker, a 1952 top-of-the-line Land Cruiser. This was one of Studebaker's 100th anniversary editions, redesigned to discontinue the controversial "bullet nose" grille, which Dampier Motors used as a "dealer demonstrator" model – that is, until a customer wanted to purchase it, slightly used, at a discount.

So, Donnie gathered up some of the guys, likely Bobbie Anderson, Kenneth Booth, Larry Cameron, Jackie Wells, Frank Conyers, and Jackie Shepherd. Jock Conley had not yet arrived on the Carlisle scene. They dropped off Larry, who had stayed in town for the great event, at his home in Myers Station, then headed up a narrow, winding lane toward Smitty's Cabin, when Donnie, who was too excited and distracted to drive alertly, suddenly felt a loud "thump" and heard a horrible "screeeech" from an old fence post and broken barbed wire that was extended out into the road that the inattentive Donnie did not see in time to avoid.

"Sleepless In ---!" – After spending a fretful and sleepless night, Donnie got out of bed that morning wondering what fate awaited him when his dad would see the results of his careless mishap. Elmer was up early and walked to work, as he often did, and, still not aware of what had happened, left word for Donnie to bring the Land Cruiser to the garage by mid-day. A very anxious Donnie told his mother what had happened and took her out to see the damage, which looked even worse in the daylight, and asked her, "What should I do"? Ann looked him in the eye and said, "Joe, to be a man, you know what you have to do!" Joe, Donnie's middle name, which was what his parents, his kinfolks, and Jock Conley, called him, replied, "Yes, ma'am," and he took the car to his dad to face the "truth and consequences." After his disappointed dad studied the situation, he said, "Joe, go home and put on your old work clothes, and quickly come back – you are going to fix the damage"! So, the next couple of days, under the expert directions of Jess Back and Leon Steele, Donnie Joe did all the work by beating out the dent, grinding and sanding the scratches, which extended the full length of the passenger side, and then primed, painted and polished the damaged area, which "looked good as new" with the final inspection by his dad. Even though a potential buyer of the "Land Cruiser," could not detect that the car had been damaged and repaired, Donnie's dad discounted the "demonstrator" price to an even lower figure than he would usually sell a demonstrator model for.

"Oh, Don't Worry, Donnie Dampier is Driving!" – This very stressful, first-time bad experience of driving "legally" had such a lasting impact and influence on Donnie that he soon developed a strong widespread reputation, locally among both students and parents, of being a very safe and conscientious driver. This was so much so, that when the local girls asked their mother's permission to ride out of town to the drive-in movies, or to ball games, and when their mothers invariably asked the question, "Who are you going with, and who is driving?" – the girls knew that a quick permission to go was usually forthcoming if the answer was, "Donnie Dampier is driving." Years later, some of the girls admitted that they might have said they were riding with Donnie Joe, but in reality, they went with one of the other guys! "Can you imagine any of our girls doing that"?

Probably most teenagers of the 1950s, as well as those thinking back, would quickly associate a classic 1950s Chevy or Ford as the representative icon of that era. Not so for the kids of the Carlisle Class of 1955. For them it was the Studebaker.

Donnie Dampier, from an early age, had ready access to used Studebakers from the Studebaker dealership at Dampier Motors. He had also been taught to drive by his dad, with the exceptional and able assistance of his mother, at around the age of 14, and allowed to drive around town on errands.

In high school days, the most functional used Studebaker was the 1948 Champion "Starlight" Coupe. However, the most glamorous was the 1951 V-8 "Commander" convertible. It was the signature car for the class. It was considered as Donnie's car, yet in reality it was every classmate's car, for it was usually loaded with the girls and boys of the Class of 1955, as well as Donnie's girlfriends and other buddies of Carlisle. Some of the guys and gals liked to play on the name by labeling it as the "Stud-ebaker" or the "Stud-mobile."

The Studebaker Convertible –During the summer prior to our senior year, Donnie's dad provided a used 1951 "bullet-nosed" Studebaker convertible to drive. This was a very stylish and sexy vehicle; it was black with a white top (which was down most of the time), and was trimmed in chrome. Its most distinguishing feature was two large chrome-plated air horns mounted on each of the front fenders, which were sounded by pulling a string hanging under the dash. These horns (labeled as "goose horns" by Kenneth Booth) were so loud that the local police threatened to put Donnie in jail if they were blown in town; so, naturally the temptation was too great for Kenneth, Jock, Jackie S, Jackie W, and the other guys to refrain from pulling the string, and Donnie would have to quickly leave downtown! Donnie found the remedy for this by banning the guys to the back seat, and filling the front seat with the local girls!

The Studebaker "Starlite" Coupe – Donnie's dad provided a second set of wheels off the lot to drive during high school in a used 1948 Studebaker Starlite Coupe. This had the unique Studebaker design of that day in that it appeared to be "coming and going" at the same time! A two-door with the rear window wrapping around the back seat (the "starlite"), it was fairly small, but frequently carried five or six of our classmates and buddies around. The two armrests in the back seat opened up to reveal two hidden compartments (each with a drain hole in the bottom over each tire well), which Donnie and the gang put to good utilitarian use as "ice boxes"! Carlisle and Nicholas County of the 1950s were both "dry," meaning there was no legal sale of alcoholic beverages. However, the locations of the local bootleggers were well-known where illegal purchases of booze could be made! This provided an adventure for teenagers to sneak in to these forbidden haunts to buy a little brew! So, the guys and gals (sometimes) would put ice chunks and beer in the Starlite ice boxes (the melted ice would drain out) and drive to a secluded area for a little beer drinking! Even though Bourbon Whiskey and other "hard" liquors were available, we rarely drank anything but beer; and since we started early in the evening and didn't have a lot of spending money to buy brews, we were usually pretty sober when we decided to go home. Had Donnie's parents discovered the innovative use of the armrest compartments, his wheels would have been quickly grounded!

Donnie's access to used Studebakers came with responsibility. In addition to the requirement to drive responsibly to keep his riders safe, Donnie's dad expected him to maintain the cars (regular checking of oil, water, tire pressure, etc.) and to keep the cars in good condition for resale. The old saying of biblical origin – "The

Lord giveth, the Lord taketh away" – also applied with Donnie's dad if he had a buyer for a car that Donnie was using. Alas, such was the fate of the sexy signature car of the Class of 1955, the 1951 Bullet-Nosed V-8 Studebaker convertible with the mounted "goose horns."

Dancing In The Dark – and The Daylight

It is said that "romancing frequently follows dancing," so it follows that sometime about our sophomore or junior year the local girls decided that the boys would learn to dance! They found willing partners and an accommodating place to practice in William's Restaurant on West Main Street. There, we were allowed to push the back tables aside, dance, drink Cokes, and play popular music of the day on the jukebox. Our classmate, Barbara King, believes this was probably where many of the class heard Elvis Presley on record for the first time!

Driving 'n' dancing ofttimes connected the car to the caress. As we picked up our dates, usually the boy collected his "best girl"; then, on a moonlit night, the couple would drive to a quiet, secluded place, frequently off a country road, turn off the motor and lights, but leave on the car radio (hoping the car battery was well charged – as we were – so it would not run down) – and, while listening to the music, would romantically engage in a very slow dance beside and around the car.

Class of 1955 "Barn Dance" – One of the great party events held in late October of our senior year was a barn dance on the farm of Jackie Shepherd's parents. Many of our parents were there, not only as chaperons, but also as willing, dancing participants in the fun! It was great to see dads/daughters and moms/sons dance together! In one of our old photos, we see Barbara King dancing with her dad, Maurice, and Donnie Dampier dancing with his mother, Ann, in a square dance foursome. Kenneth was seen dancing with his mother, Mrs. Booth, while Jock's parents, Joe Frank and Katherine, both avid dancers, along with Walter and Adelade Shepherd, always seemed to be on the dance floor with varied partners. Joe Frank and

Walter made sure none of our girls sat on the sidelines as wallflowers. The evening also included an old-fashioned hayride coupled with a hotdog and marshmallow roast before an open campfire, thanks to Mr. Shepherd. Our parents were always very involved with us, but, at the same time, not intrusive!

In our senior year "class night," the class designated, as "Best Dancers," Jackie Shepherd and Marjorie Farris, our "Little Margie"; however, in dancing events, Jackie and Carol McLean would frequently seek out each other as dance partners. Some of the boys, such as Billy Vanlandingham, Jackie Wells, and Donnie Dampier, liked to add athletic lifts of their partners, jitterbug style, as part of their '50s dance routines. Donnie, in particular, incorporated these "lifts 'n' rolls" as part of his dancing style throughout high school and most of college until a slipped-disk back problem (not caused by dancing) curtailed this lifting style. Donnie and his high school sweetheart, Faye Roundtree, got quite proficient at this, which incorporated lifting Faye up on one of his hips, then down to the floor, then Faye bounced up on the other hip, back to the floor, then would jump and straddle Donnie's waist, then he would lower and slide her between his legs, then, in the finale, would lift Faye and roll her over his back, to face each other when she landed, and all of this without missing a beat!

In college, when Donnie and Pat, his future wife, first started dating, they occasionally added the "lifts," but that was soon dropped and they developed the free-form, fast-flow dancing style that they still use over forty years later. Donnie and Pat have frequently been considered as good dancers, and down through the years have occasionally won some "Back to the '50s" fast-dancing jitterbug contests at community dances. What is generally referred to as fast dancing goes by different names, such as the modern-day jive, which dance professionals say was born out of the jitterbug, influenced by the American swing of the big band era and the boogie-woogie of the war years. We, in the 1950s, incorporated elements of each into what we called '50s rock 'n' roll.

Perhaps Donnie would not have developed his love of dancing and confidence thereof if the girls of the Class of 1955, during our early high school years, had not mandated, "You boys will learn to dance … or else!" And so, without elaborating on the "or else," the boys of the Class of 1955 did learn an appreciation for the dance!

The "Briar 'n' Rabbit" Dances – Another dancing event of Carlisle was the "Briar and Rabbit Dance" that gave us the opportunity to dance to live performances of some of the "Big Bands," such as Woody Herman, Ray Anthony, Buddy Morrow, Les Brown, etc. This unique dance format brought the bands into Carlisle some two to three times each year on "off weekday" nights in between major weekend gigs at Lexington's Joyland Park or Cincinnati's Moonlight Gardens, or en route to St. Louis or Chicago. It was founded by a group of University of Kentucky Phi Sigma Kappa Fraternity brothers from Carlisle around 1948 and lasted some twenty-five years. Records are a little spotty as to who the founding Phi Sigs from Carlisle in the late '40s might have been, but the likely group would have included the Conley brothers, J. Patrick and Joe Frank (even though Joe Frank resided in St. Louis at the time, he likely was an influencing factor, with his love of dancing), the Soper cousins, John E. Jr. and John W., Ben Pumphrey, and Frank Mathias, and there were surely others who would have worked with those in Carlisle, such as Custer Blair, in forming the "Briar 'n' Rabbit Dance."

Three members of the Class of '55, Jock Conley, Donnie Dampier, and Billy Buntin, were initiated on December 16, 1956, to the Phi Deuteron Chapter as life members of the Phi Sigma Kappa fraternity, known as the "Phi Sigs" at UK, a national fraternity which, in the year of 2005, celebrated its 132 years to date of brotherhood. Jackie Wells pledged the Phi Sigs, but dropped out of UK during his freshman year before being initiated as a member. Carlisle native Donnie Lynam is also a "brother" of Phi Sigma Kappa.

Carlisle native Frank Mathais and Lexingtonian Byron Romanowitz (this twosome has musically jammed 'n' jazzed together many times to provide Big-Band sound dancing) are older Phi Sig brothers of Jock, Donnie, and Billy.

The unusual name for the "Briar 'n Rabbit Dance" was said to be an identity for Nicholas County as a place abundant in briars and rabbits. This was also fitting for people to dance to the "Muskrat Ramble" in a "Bramble" (briars) – an interesting theory!

Growing up in Carlisle during this era afforded the Class of '55 the added expansion of our social development to learn and participate in the art of expression and communication that is provided by the dance; some have proclaimed it "the rhythm of the soul," and many of our class literally "felt" the lyrics from "Sing, Sing, Sing" of the "Big Band" era, "It don't mean a thing, if it ain't got that swing." Many Big Band historians credit Benny Goodman, "The King of Swing," with ushering in the popular era of the Big Bands with a performance on July 4, 1936, filling the musical atmosphere with its unique beat and rhythm. This was the same year that Donnie Joe Dampier was born, which may explain why Donnie has always loved to listen to and dance to the Big Band sound. As humorist/author Mark Twain expounded, "On with the dance, let any joy be unconfined, is my motto."

These "Briar 'n' Rabbit" dances, as well as our junior-senior proms, were held in the original National Guard Armory on East Main Street of downtown Carlisle. Donnie and Pat frequently came back to Carlisle for these dances during the '60s, with a special memory of Donnie, from one of those years, of the dancing of a spirited polka around the floor as a partner with Katherine Conley, Jock's mother! The "Briar 'n' Rabbit" dances were great as long as they lasted, but unfortunately, they were phased out along with the great traveling bands of the Big Band era.

The old county fairs were also held there in the downtown National Guard Armory where many of us exhibited our 4-H projects, skills, and crafts in farming, gardening, and home economics.

Downtown Draws and Double-Your-Pleasure Desserts

The Carlisle Drug, located in the middle of downtown Main Street, was the favorite after-school afternoon hangout, where we gathered for friendship, fellowship, and FOOD. There was an old-fashioned soda fountain where we ordered handmade milk-shakes and malts, ice cream sodas, and Cokes. For some reason, cherry Cokes were rumored to be "illegal"! The Carlisle Drug was famous for its absolutely heavenly homemade pimiento cheese sandwiches, which we prized. We would cram six or more of us in booths designed for four. We were a close-knit group in an original and real "Happy Days" atmosphere. Doc Bradshaw, the proprietor, often tried to exhibit a mean demeanor, but really loved us. He did hate it when we tried to read the comic books and magazines at his stand in lieu of buying them! The soda fountain and the booths are long gone; however, G.C. Meyers, CHS Class of 1949, now operates and keeps the tradition and history of the Carlisle Drug alive.

The "Little House With The Big Eats," appropriately nestled downtown in the "Little Town With the Big Heart," was located on the east corner of Main and Broadway before it was torn down several years ago. The name was very fitting, for it was a small, warm and cozy restaurant that served the best burgers, split fried hotdogs, chili, and vegetable soup to be found anywhere in its day. Many of us in high school, when we were not required to eat in the school cafeteria, would walk downtown to eat lunch at "The House." Donnie Dampier loved their chili so much that he usually ordered two bowls! The Little House staff ultimately provided him with his own, special, oversized bowl that held approximately two servings, which would be taken off the shelf as Donnie would walk in and order the usual! Some of us on late Sunday afternoons, in order to give our mothers a deserved rest from preparing Sunday supper, would supply one or two quart-size Mason jars to be filled with chili or vegetable soup, or both, for takeout from the Little House. They always included a paper bag full of oyster crackers. Frankie Hughes, CHS Class of 1951, operated The Little House With The Big Eats for many years. Prior to Frankie's proprietorship, the little restaurant had been operated by Mr. "Spud" Marshall, then later by Les

Courtney.

Garrett's Restaurant, on the opposite corner area of Broadway, now continues the tradition and reputation of a great local small-town eating and meeting place in Carlisle.

Two homemade dessert treats enjoyed (in season) by members of the Class of '55 down through the years were snow cream and hand cranked ice cream.

In wintertime, when the ground was covered with at least 3-4 inches of snow, it was "snow cream time." We would take a large mixing bowl, scoop it full of snow, and bring it inside for the creation of the treat. Since most of our homes, businesses, and schools were heated by coal-burning fireplaces, stoves, and furnaces during that era, the first step was to scoop off the top layer of snow containing coal soot! Our mothers then performed the magic of converting the clean snow (we had little concern for other pollutants then) to a delicious dessert by adding sugar, vanilla flavoring, and milk (whole milk at that time) and/or cream – then, "voila ... snow cream"!

In "the good old summer time," an even greater treat eagerly awaited us, and that was ice cream made in the old fashioned, hand-cranked bucket freezer (most of us did not have the electric variety until later). The method most often used was to place a twenty-five pound block of ice into a burlap sack, then use an ax to break the ice into smaller chunks inside the sack. The ice and coarse "ice cream" salt were alternately placed in layers around the sealed container with the ice cream mix, then several of the men and boys took turns cranking, because as the salt melted the ice, causing the cream mixture to harden, the cranking got more and more difficult. The event of ice cream making was usually a double-your-pleasure activity because it was most often held in conjunction with a family, church, school, or community "pot luck" picnic. Modern-day ice cream may be good, but it does not best the old fashioned kind of our growing-up days!

Sizzling Summer Jobs and Toiling in Tobacco

Just about every member of the Class of 1955 had some sort of summer or after-school job, to earn spending money or to add to the family's finances, and if we were in between paying jobs, we all had regular chores around the house to share the burden and contribute to the family wellbeing. For most of us, that work ethic had started in grade school, just as soon as we were big enough to handle the tasks at hand, whether they be bringing in coal and wood to heat the house, carrying in water when there was no city water, mowing the yard, cleaning house, helping with meals, washing dishes (no dishwashers back then), washing and hanging clothes on the line, or other jobs that needed doing.

In high school, we frequently found jobs outside the home, but often some of us worked at least part of the time in the family business. Anna Mary clerked in the Clinkenbeard Variety Store, Kenneth in the Booths' little country store his dad operated at Frogtown, Larry at Cameron's Store in Myers Station, Billy at Buntin's Garage, and Donnie helped out at Dampier Motors. If memory serves, Barbara King worked part-time at the Carlisle Drug, while Gordon Moreland clerked at Hopkins Drug Store. Kenneth also did farm work, as did Jackie Wells, Billy Vanlandingham, and Jackie Shepherd.

Jock Conley would probably take the prize for the "most sizzling summer job" the summer he worked in Harrodsburg for his uncle, who owned and operated a blacktop contractor firm. A person watching a blacktopping operation would quickly notice that the blacktop is deposited hot and steaming, and Jock's main job was to follow the blacktopping truck – shovel, hoe, and broom in hand – and spread and smooth the hot blacktop before it was rolled. Jock would later say, "Shoot, this job was tough, but it had to be better than working for a circus, and with a similar shoveling job, follow behind the elephants in a downtown circus parade!"

Jackie Shepherd worked full time on the family diary farm on Scrubgrass Road, but there were lax times between planting, tending, and harvesting when he was available to work elsewhere. Like the time that Larry Wagoner, an MMI alumni and "cadet" classmate of Jackie, was looking for a couple of hired hands in his capacity as foreman/manager for a large Bourbon County farm operation outside of Millersburg, and Jackie graciously "volunteered" Donnie Dampier to go on the work detail with him. Mostly, this was hard, physical labor in the peak heat of the "dog days of summer." One of the assignments for Jackie and Donnie was to drive a tractor with a flat bed wagon to some fields that were being cleared of large rocks in preparation for future cultivation. Many of these rocks were so large and heavy that it took both of the strong backs of Jackie and Donnie as a team to lift them onto the wagon bed, or sometimes required that they first be broken up with a sledgehammer!

"Sucker Sickness" – As grueling as the rock removal was, it was the preferred assignment, at least for Donnie, over two other work details during the week or so at the Bourbon farm. This was the season for tobacco suckering at a time in history when this function was done by hand, rather than by chemical use implemented a few years later.

"Suckering" was the practice of removing the small "sucker" shoots from growing between the leaves and "topping" removed the flowering tops, both practices which were performed in order for the plant's energy and nutrients to be concentrated into the bottom leaves. Those who grow tomatoes (of the same botanical family) have probably also removed the tomato suckers in order to have fewer stems and leaves and produce bigger tomatoes.

Donnie had frequently worked in tobacco on the farms of his grandfather and uncles, pulling plants, setting, hoeing, housing, and stripping tobacco, but had never suckered or topped tobacco, and, once having the experience (a bad one), would never do it again. As they moved deeper into the large tobacco field, hand pulling the sticky suckers that covered the hands with gum, with mature plants taller than the average height of a man, closely enclosed by the huge leaves that allowed for little air flow, and working in heat of over 90 degrees, Donnie was getting hotter and sicker by the minute, gasping for breath, until he began to vomit and staggered to the end of a long row where he passed out! After he was revived with ice water, under a shade tree and finally out of the direct heat and away from the stifling, pungent odors of the tobacco plants, Donnie recovered but was through for that day.

The day after being overcome with "sucker sickness," Donnie came back with Jackie to give it another try, where, in lieu of working in tobacco again, he was reassigned and positioned on the back of a threshing/combine machine (over the heat of the motor), and in direct sun, to guide and direct the grain discharge chute into the wagon that was pulled alongside! When Donnie returned the next day after that, he quickly volunteered for the rock removal job again. After these two bad experiences with heat, Donnie was ready to challenge Jock for the "prize" for the most sizzling summer jobs! Meanwhile, Jackie Shepherd was observed to not only survive, but he actually seemed to thrive on these jobs!

"Measuring of Tobacco" – There was another job essential to tobacco production that some of the boys, such as Jock Conley, Jackie Wells, and Donnie Dampier, were hired to do by the Agricultural Stabilization and Conservation Service (referred to as the ASC Office, or the ASCS) of the U.S. Department of Agriculture. The boys were sent out into the farm fields to conduct a process that was called the "measuring of tobacco." Back then girls were never hired for the "field work" of measuring tobacco. However, some of our girls were occasionally hired during the summer to work inside the ASC Office. This included the duties of signing in, and checking the forms submitted by the boys. The name of the ASC or ASCS Office has been changed a few times down through the years, and, is now titled the Farm Service Agency.

This measuring process was done early in the summer growing season, before the tobacco plants had grown up to much over a foot tall, or less. The data collected by the measurers was applied to a formula by the ASC Office to determine the acreage allotment, the "tobacco base," which the individual farmer was permitted to grow that season under the federal regulations in effect. The method used to determine the tobacco growing allotment was changed from acreage, which apparently began in the 1930s, to poundage in the early 1970s, probably in 1971. To the 1950s farmer, it was very important that this required procedure resulted in a fair and accurate acreage measurement, for a shortchanged measurement could mean lost dollars in the farm family's pockets, so the guys in our class took this job seriously! For Donnie Dampier, this was a much more interesting and pleasurable job than working in tobacco itself – it kept him outside, in cooler temperatures in open breezes, with the young plants not emitting the pungent odors that felled him before, and each farm setting was a unique challenge.

Many, if not most, of the tobacco patches and fields were accessed from small country roads, farm wagon lanes, or sometimes by driving through pastures, down creek bottoms, and up and over hills. Since it often took a rugged vehicle, Donnie's dad gave him the use of a gray 1947 Studebaker, straight shift, pickup truck that was occasionally utilized by Dampier Motors for service calls. In the hills, hollows, and bottom lands (that snaked alongside the meandering streams and creeks) of Nicholas County, the measurers were more likely to find odd-shaped tobacco patches, rather than easily measured rectangles and squares, and, if we were not careful, both the farmer and the measurer could be "walked into the ground" by many trips back and forth!

The measuring method, which required teamwork, was for the farmer to take the end of the chain and walk down the row until the measure was fully extended (66 feet, or 4 rods), which was held and released, like a tape measure, by the measurer, with the farmer either inserting one of the pins or marking a line in the soft soil with his foot, then, as the farmer walked to the next length, the measurer walked to the farmer's mark, recorded the measure, then the process was repeated until the field was fully plotted.

Donnie's "Devised" Measuring Method – Donnie Dampier, recognizing the challenge that each farm and field was different, devised his own method that was welcomed by the farmer (it reduced the number of trips back and forth) and still resulted in an accurate measurement for the farmer's allotment. Donnie's method was to first study the aerial photo, then visually view the field, in order to mentally determine the geometric shape, at which time he would then sketch the shape on the clipboard. This gave Donnie the opportunity for practical applications of the principles of linear (plane) geometry that were taught in Ms. Gilley's class at old CHS, as it was often found that the tobacco patches were laid out in parallelograms, trapezoids, quadrilaterals, and sometimes triangles (especially "right" triangles) that would follow the natural contours of the terrain and only occasionally would actually be in the shape of a rectangle or square. They would then find the approximate middle row of a patch, and if Donnie, by looking over the short tobacco plants, could see where the top and bottom rows started and ended (rows were frequently not the same length), he would have the farmer make his foot mark, thereby measuring both the top and bottom rows as they walked, and Donnie would record these measurement as well as the number of chains walked to the end of the field. Then they would find the approximate middle of a side row and make a measured walk (crossing the axis) to the other side of the patch. If the patch was not too large for Donnie to see both sides, the measurement resulted in one walk through, and one walk across, which were found to be much in favor with the farmer!

Donnie enjoyed this aspect of "working in tobacco," where he ofttimes already knew the farm family or had the opportunity to meet new folks, and most of the farmers either knew, or knew of, Donnie through his dad and mother. Elmer and Ann were both well-known and well-thought-of by most of the folks in Nicholas County. Donnie occasionally received the added benefit of some welcome refreshments provided by the farmer's wife, and, if he happened to be working at the farm when the dinner bell rang, he was often invited to share a home-cooked lunch (we called the midday meal "dinner time" and the nighttime meal "supper"). Just about every farm family had a large iron bell mounted on a tall post, with a long string attached to the clapper (ringer) that could be heard across the fields when the farm wives rang the dinner bell, signaling the farmers and hired hands in for the prepared meal, and which was also occasionally used to sound an alarm. Some might think these extras were provided to influence the measurements, but there was never a thought of that – this was just good old Nicholas County homespun hospitality!

Midnight Milk Cans Pick-Up – Then there was the summer of measuring tobacco that Jimmy Shepherd (CHS Class of 1952), the older brother of Jackie by some three years, solicited Donnie Dampier to operate Jimmy's milk pick-up routes during his two weeks of National Guard summer camp duties – to which Donnie agreed, giving him the extra money of two jobs for that period. The milk pick-up job started at around 9 to 10 p.m. each evening, depending on when the refrigerated truck from the milk company arrived and was parked behind the courthouse. Jimmy had left the Shepherd family pick-up truck (probably the same one that Jackie learned to drive on) for Donnie's use to collect the filled milk cans from individual farms that had contracted to sell milk. Donnie rode with Jimmy on the last night before Jimmy left for summer camp in order to learn the location of the participating farms and their milk houses on the three or four routes out of Carlisle.

Donnie's usual routine was to sit around the front court house walls, hanging out with some of the guys, and girls, until he saw the milk company truck arrive, then he would drive the pick-up out one of the designated routes to the numerous farms on the route, fill the bed of the pick-up with the individual milk cans, return to Carlisle, unload the filled milk cans into the refrigerated milk truck, then go out another directional route to an additional list of farms, until the milk from all the participating farms was collected to complete that evening's work. Donnie would arrive home at about 2 to 3 a.m., sometimes later, frequently cook his own breakfast, which usually consisted of 2-3 fried eggs, bacon and/or sausage, fried "mush," toast, jelly, and about a half-gallon of milk. Most people nowadays are unfamiliar with mush, a cornmeal mixture similar to grits but more solid, which was usually prepared into a roll, stored overnight in an ice box or refrigerator, sliced and fried, and served with butter and sometimes syrup. As often, as not, Donnie's mother, knowing the approximate usual time he would get in, would have the table set with much of the breakfast ready, then Donnie would go to bed, sleep until 10 to 11, eat some lunch, then go out to his assigned farms (frequently, the same ones he had picked up milk from the previous evening) to measure tobacco. Donnie, due to his temporary milk job, had arranged with the ASC Office to be available only afternoons during this period. It was not unusual to be at sundown and in the dim twilight when completing the last measuring job for a day.

The double jobs were satisfying work during that summer, even though the late-night/early-morning milk routes were somewhat lonely, as no one was ever seen at the various farms during the routes, for the farm families were usually in bed and asleep by the time Donnie arrived to pick up their milk. Joe "Little Joe" Blount was good company a couple of times during the first evening route. And, since the hours required of the double jobs were hurting his love life, Donnie was especially pleased when his girl friend, Faye Roundtree, accompanied him, again only on the first route (she had to be home by around 11:00 PM). But no one wanted to stay up late enough to go with him after that first route. It really did not matter, for Donnie stayed busy enough that the nightly work passed by quickly. Even when Faye went along, which was only one or two times, there wasn't much time for romancing, except for "close conversation!"

In addition to the extra money, the process of lifting, loading, and unloading the heavy milk cans contributed toward building up Donnie's upper body for his athletic pursuits. At the end of the afternoon milking, the milk was poured into the milk cans, which, when full, weighed 100 pounds each or better. The cans of milk were placed into a holding vat in cool water, sometimes supplied from a local spring, and some with a chunk of ice – only a few would have electric cooling in those days of the early-mid '50s. In order to collect the milk cans, Donnie would lean over the edge of the container vat, lift the heavy cans straight up, turn around with the cans held chest high, and place them into the bed of the pick-up truck, which he had backed up to the milk-house door that had been propped or hooked to an open position. On one occasion, as Donnie was pulling away, before going back to close the door, a screen door popped loose, hooked on the back bumper, and was pulled off one hinge, leaving it dangling! Donnie, who really did not have anything against screen doors, left a note for the farmer, explaining what had happened, along with his name and telephone number, but the farmer never said anything about the mishap, and on the next nightly run, Donnie found the door re-hinged and good as new.

The Tobacco Culture - Growing up in both the Bible Belt and the Burley Belt (tobacco), where tobacco was king, would occasionally create a contradiction of conscience, with a little soul searching, over the propriety of "growing the weed." However, this usually passed quickly, like a little "passing of gas," with the rationalized reality that no crop known at that time could surpass tobacco economically. It helped those who were struggling with these emotional/spiritual concerns to clear their conscience in that we rarely would hear much about the health dangers of tobacco preached from the pulpits, but would sometimes receive a spirited sermon on the "evils of alcohol." Whereas, if we had grown up in the bourbon-producing towns of Bardstown, Frankfort, or Lawrenceburg, etc., we likely would have heard the reverse.

Indeed, after Sunday services, a common ritual of many of our adult men, as soon as they were outside the church doors, would be to reach inside their pockets for a package of Camels, Lucky Strike, Chesterfields, Old Gold, or Kools, etc., and light up in unison!

When there were expressed health concerns over tobacco use, the farmers of Nicholas and the adjoining counties during the 1950s should not have felt their mainstay crop was suddenly being picked on, for there were attacks, assaults and opposition, at least as far back as 1604, when King James I forbade the use of this "Sot-weed" in England, saying, that "the unsavory, filthie, stinking smoake is a vile custome," and, who knows, there probably was similar concerns and opposition heard from segments of the West Indian population, some hundred or so years before that, in Columbus's day of 1492. This was the same King James responsible for the "Authorized Version" of the Holy Scriptures – the English translation from the Greek, otherwise known as "The King James Bible. The translation was undertaken in 1607 and first published as "set forth A.D. 1611."

In Pursuit of An Agrarian Life – The members of the Class of 1955 were truly privileged to have lived and grown up in the lifestyle and environment of an "agrarian society." This could be defined as numerous small family farms, each of which usually ranged from around eighty acres to a hundred acres or so, which surrounded and embraced the many small towns of our area. The family farm is one that has usually been passed down from generation to generation, comprised of good, hard-working folks, the family farmers, who have an affinity for agriculture … a stewardship of the soil … a love of the land!

This description most assuredly fit that of Jackie Wood Shepherd. The family name of Wood – through his grandmother, Mary Elizabeth Wood, the mother of Jackie's dad, James Walter Shepherd – claims its American heritage from the state of Vermont, where the family was engaged in the manufacture of farm implements. So, it can be safely said that Jackie's middle name was "cut from, and carved out of, the Wood from that branch of the family tree," with his roots grown through the Wood family (pun intended)!

Jackie used to say that a definitive reason for entering the dental profession (which he also loves) was part of his plan to eventually earn the financial resources to enable him to reach his ultimate goal of owning and operating his own dairy farm. So, when a fine Nicholas County farm became available, located on Carpenter Pike and nestled between the point where Big Brushy Creek empties into Hinkston Creek (forming the Nicholas/Bourbon Counties line), Jackie seized the opportunity and purchased his dairying farm in three plots from 1968 into the early 1970s.

Whereas, if the Class of 1955 had taken a class poll on which of our classmates would have entered farming as a livelihood, Jackie Shepherd, of the boys, would have won hands down, with probably Kenneth Booth or Jackie Wells as runner-up, and, for the girls, we probably would have picked Carole Donovan or Martha Sue Feeback or Mary Phyllis Smith. Consequently, if our imaginary poll had predicted "the least likely to end up on the farm," we would quite probably have picked Jock Conley and Anna Mary Clinkenbeard. We would have chosen well in the case of Jock, but, wouldn't you know it, as this history is written, Anna Mary (now Hammons) and her husband, Donnie, have been full-time farmers in the Nicholas County neighboring area of Cowan in Fleming County for over forty years, and continue strong in their pursuit of the agrarian life!

VIII

Sports at a Small School – Sports for a Small Town

"The drama of sport is a big part of the drama of life. ... And, the scope of this drama is endless."
Grantland Rice

Girls Sports at Carlisle High School – "The Missing Link"

In our era of the '50s, varsity sports were limited to boys' teams only, with the girls restricted to gym class and intramurals. Many of our girls would secretly say that they got all the exercise needed by either chasing or being chased by the boys! Women's basketball had been sporadically played in Kentucky high schools since around 1904, but had been discontinued in 1932; however, the 1974 Kentucky General Assembly reinstated girls' basketball as a sanctioned varsity sport and the girls' "Sweet Sixteen" High School Basketball Tournament resumed in 1975. This discriminatory practice that denied sports participation by women has been overturned and rectified through federal law by the provisions of Title IX over the last three decades.

The Nicholas County High School Lady Blue Jackets, well coached by Barbara Kenney to feature outstanding team play and led by "Most Valuable Player" Kim Denkins, won the 1993 State Sweet Sixteen Title played in the Capital Plaza Civic Center in Frankfort, Kentucky. Kim, who went on to have a stellar four-year college career with the University of Kentucky Lady Wildcats, was honored in the year 2001 by the KHSAA in naming her as one of the Top 25 Girls Basketball Players in Kentucky History ("The Terrific 25")! Donnie Dampier of the CHS Class of 1955, who worked at the time with the Kentucky Department of Education located in the Capital Plaza Tower at Frankfort, took annual leave time to attend each of the NCHS Girls' 1993 State Tourney games, to proudly cheer the girls from his home county on to victory!

Women did make a positive impact as pioneering lady coaches during World War II while the menfolk were serving overseas. They did a great job of filling in as high school coaches of boys' basketball teams in at least three Kentucky communities:

Marjorie Wheeldon, believed to be one of the first females to coach a boys' team, led the 1943-44 Stearns High School boys to a winning season. Ms. Wheeldon, who was described in articles as "very pretty" (born out by old photos), no doubt inspired many of the young men of Stearns to go out for the basketball team! The Blue and White Wildcats of Stearns High School, which consolidated into the McCreary County System around 1959, had previously played in the 1929 State Basketball Tournament, defeating Almo, of Region 1, 18-16 in the first round before losing by the score of 29-8 in the quarterfinals to Corydon (Henderson County).

Nora Young Mahurin, another lady coach of that era, coached the boys' team at Short Creek High School (Grayson County) during the 1943-44 and 1944-45 seasons.

Anna Laura Bray, as late as the 1949-50 season, coached the boys' basketball team at Cordia High School, located in Knott County.

A very tough and strong-willed lady who preceded and probably influenced the aforementioned lady coaches was the legendary Mrs. Rhoda (Caldwell) Kavanaugh, who established the Kavanaugh Academy, sometimes called the "Annapolis of Kentucky," in Lawrenceburg during the early 1900s. In addition to founding the school, teaching numerous high-level courses, and serving as principal, she also did much of the coaching of the basketball team, even though the school had an official coach. She would walk the sidelines during games carrying an umbrella and was known to poke and whap a boy under the basket to get his attention as she shouted instructions – "Get that ball, boy," or "Guard that man" – and even boys from the opposing teams claimed to occasionally get equal attention! She was reputed to keep the boys on their toes during practice by occasionally walking through the boys' dressing room giving guidance, as she would say, "Now don't you boys worry about me coming through here, just think of me as you would your mother!" During her tenure, until her retirement in 1946, she earned the respect and accolades of coaches, players, and students, as the school was quite successful both academically and on the basketball floor. Kavanaugh played in the State Tournament four times from 1918 to 1933, advancing to the title game of 1930, where they had a disappointing loss to Corinth by a score of 22-20.

Cheerleading was an activity that provided an important way for some of the girls to directly participate in the arenas of sports competition. The practice and art of cheerleading back then was truly the leading of cheers (not the advanced athletic acrobatics of today), which stimulated the spectators – to get them involved in the game – and inspired the boys! Indeed, ofttimes the boys on the bench, to the consternation of the coach, focused as much attention on viewing the cheerleaders as they did on the game before them. This was especially evident in the close confines of basketball, with special attention of the boys given to the opposing team's cheerleaders, as well as their own! Even the older spectators, on some occasions, found cheerleading as interesting as the game itself.

The story is told of two older gentlemen who were discussing whether or not to attend a high school basketball game during the 1954-55 season, when the team was not doing so well. The overheard conversation went something like this: As the first man asked, "Say, are you going to the game tonight?" the second man replied, "I sure am. I don't have too much interest in the game, but I sure do like to watch the cheerleading!"

The cherished history of cheerleading originated as far back as the late 1880s, when the first organized and recorded yell, done in "locomotive style," was first seen and heard during a college football game on the Princeton University campus as:

"Ray! Ray! Ray! Tiger, Tiger, Sis, Sis, Sis! Boom, Boom, Boom! Aaaaah! Princeton, Princeton, Princeton!"

Organized cheerleading as we know it today officially began at the University of Minnesota (Golden Gophers) during a football game on November 2, 1898, initiated by a University of Minnesota undergraduate by the name of Johnny Campbell, as he and five other young undergraduate men led the yelling of cheers, some still in use today, utilizing the megaphone, with their goal to spur the team to victory by involving every spectator – "everybody leaves the park today breathless and voiceless!"

It is thought that the first school "fight song" also originated on the University of Minnesota campus during 1898.

It was probably around the mid-teens of the 1900s when cheerleading expanded from the college campus to the high school ranks, and it was in the 1920s when young women became active in cheerleading, breaking into the previously all-male domain. By the 1940s and 1950s, much of high school cheerleading, at least in the small schools across the Commonwealth and the country, had become pretty much the exclusive arena of young women. Two primary reasons, at least in the small high schools, were that most of the available able-bodied boys were participating on the varsity athletic fields, and, since the girls did not have varsity sports as an option, they flocked to the art and activity of cheerleading as the accessible avenue to demonstrate their school spirit and pride.

Yes, the cheerleading girls of the Carlisle High School Class of 1955, as well as their counterparts at Nicholas County High, Stearns High School, Barbourville High, and numerous other high schools across the country during the '40s and '50s, can proudly look back at their honored and respected position of cheerleader and say that they have shared this activity with some famous persons down through the years, such as former U.S. President Dwight D. Eisenhower, actors Jimmy Stewart and Kirk Douglas, and actresses Meryl Streep, Raquel Welch, and Cybill Shepherd, just to name a few.

Although no specific reference has been located as to "when and who," it is surmised that the "Cheerleading Corps of Carlisle" was formally established by the mid-1920s, providing an approximate forty-year span of cheering for the home team, until the closing of Carlisle High School in 1963. The cheerleading activity was probably in full swing and sandwiched around the December 1924 dedication and opening of the new Carlisle High School Gymnasium, and the November period of 1925, when "Homecoming" was established and Carlisle became the Musketeers. It could have been a year or two earlier, around 1921 or 1922, as this was the era when Carlisle, in its third year of varsity football, was competing well enough to generate a strong school spirit for students and fans alike. With little or no ink devoted to the art of cheering in the early 1920s (they had no "won-lost" records), it is not known by this writer who the young women were to historically perform as the first cheerleaders of Carlisle High School, but it is likely there were no boys on the squad.

The Carlisle High School cheerleaders for our senior year from the Class of '55 were Carol McLain, Pat May, and Sylva Joy Owens, along with juniors Mary Catherine Allison and Betty Vice. Carol McLain, who was always considered as very pretty, feisty, and full of energy, served four years as varsity cheerleader, and before that served as junior cheerleader. Molly Jane Flora was a cheerleader for the Musketeers for a couple of years prior to transferring to Lafayette.

Beginning with the school year of 1948-49, some of the other young women who cheered for our athletic teams included Nell Wilson, Sue Crouch, Helen Ruddell, Dolores Hamilton, Emily Van Bever, Kay Fisher (the future wife of band director Carroll Hall), Kay Flora (sister of Molly Jane), Janette Hughes, Dotty Dotson, Marietta "Marty" Hardin, Janet Mattox (sister of our classmate, Wanda), Jane Ellen Gillespie, and Wanda Lawrence (cousin of Donnie Dampier), and, no doubt, some others that were inadvertently left out.

Following the five decades' tradition of Homecoming, of which the first was held at the University of Illinois in 1910, our own Pat May was crowned 1954 Carlisle High Football Queen at Homecoming festivities during the Georgetown-Carlisle game, in the likely 30th renewal of the traditional Homecoming celebration for the Musketeers of Carlisle High School. The halftime Homecoming activities must have been the highlight of the evening, since the undermanned Musketeers were overwhelmed by a score of 0-44 to the superior numbers of the Georgetown Buffs, a consistent CKC football power of that era! Pat and her attendants, Sidney Crouch and Mary Catherine Allison, were escorted in the presentations by the football team co-captains, Larry Cameron and Donnie Dampier. As a freshman, Martha Sue Feeback had been an attendant to the 1951 Homecoming sponsor, Carol Shrout, and was presented with flowers by football co-captains Gary Flora and Jim Hughes. Martha Sue no doubt was excited, embarrassed, and blushed a bit on getting this attention from these two good-looking "older" guys!

The Pep Club was another school organization that provided important activities for several of the girls, along with some of the boys, to participate in the sports programs. The Pep Club was responsible for the buying of sweaters, letters, and other awards for the football and basketball teams, as well as selling refreshments at the games. Nationally, the first pep club was established in the 1870s at Princeton University.

The Carlisle "Coach-less Wonders"

"What counts in the final analysis is not so much if you win or lose. ... What matters most is how you played the game!"

A Paraphrase

The 1954 Carlisle Musketeer football team was reported in *The Lexington Herald* and *The Nicholas County Star* as "The Coachless Wonders of the Central Kentucky Conference" by remaining undefeated after three games, with two wins and a tie – sitting in one of the top spots in the Central Kentucky Conference standings – but without a coach! Carroll Holmes, the coach of the preceding year with a 2-5 won-loss record, had suddenly and unexpectedly not returned.

In the late summer of 1954, as the boys of the Class of '55 began anticipating and preparing for their senior year of football, the word began to spread that CHS might be forced to cancel the upcoming football season for lack of a coach! This was a devastating prospect for our seniors! Superintendent Robert Davis recognized our pending disappointment, but more importantly, saw the value to all of our class, the entire school, and the community to have a football team to identify with and cheer for. Mr. Davis, who admittedly knew nothing about coaching football, agreed to be our "official" coach in name only so we could have a team our senior year. J.W. "Bill" Shelton, assistant freshman football coach for Blanton Collier at the University of Kentucky, was brought in by Superintendent Davis and led the Musketeers for two weeks of tough, no nonsense, pre-season conditioning drills before returning to his UK duties. He was assisted by non-certified alumnus Ben Pumphrey, "Doot" Hardin, and Billy Clark (last season's starting "Muskie" quarterback), who left after the first week to join the UK freshmen football team for fall practice.

"Doot" Hardin (CHS Class of 1951), who wore numbers 47 and 56, came to us well-grounded in fundamental football, as he played varsity football each of his high school years under the tutorage of Coach Tebay Rose, the heydays of Musketeer football during the era of the late '40s through the mid-'50s. Doot, who led the team in scoring during his senior season of 1950, was a co-captain and a star performer on, perhaps, one of Carlisle's all-time finest teams that finished with a record of 6-1! With a total of 81 points scored, Doot possibly led the CKC Conference in scoring that 1950 campaign, and is one of the single-season Musketeer scoring leaders of all time!

We actually had great "unofficial" coaching for those first three games in former CHS alumni Jimmy "Doot" Hardin, and Ben "Pokey" Pumphrey, who plotted strategy as they patrolled the sidelines sending in plays and shouting instructions, which, during their brief but shinning moment, had elevated the Musketeers to a con-

The Coachless Wonders
The 1954 Carlisle High School "Musketeers"

Front Row, Left to right of the "Seventeen Good Men" (the seven seniors identified with jersey numbers): Front Row, Left to right: Charles McCarty, Jock Conley (#50), Jerry Davis, co-captains Larry Cameron (47) Donnie Dampier (#55), David Feeback, and Jackie Shepherd (49). Second Row: Roy Gaunce, Jackie Wells (51), Kenneth Booth (52), Billie Logan, Billie Gilley, and Billie Vanlandingham (#53). Row Three: Team managers, Wayne Berry and Ivan Logan, Ronnie King, Kenneth Cartmill, Billie Straw, and Billie Berry. Standing: James "Doot" Hardin, and newly hired "official" head coach John Louie Walters.

tending position for top honors in the CKC; then, as they honorably stepped aside when the new "official" coach was hired, we lost the remaining games to finish at 2-4-1!

Perhaps, if the debut of *Sports Illustrated Magazine* had been delayed until one month later, to late September of 1954, and if the editors of the now celebrated sports magazine had heard of the unique successes through the first three games of the football team of Carlisle High School, the "Coachless Wonders" might have appeared on the front cover of the very first issue of SI hitting the news stands on August 16, 1954! No doubt, the shinning faces of the seven seniors of the Class of 1955 would have been featured, but, alas, instead, the inaugural cover pictured the great future Baseball Hall of Fame performer Eddie Mathews, the left-hand hitting third baseman of the Milwaukee Braves, swinging away in front of packed County Stadium! If the Coachless Wonders had appeared on that inaugural SI cover, it would have partially explained (along with the efforts of their last four opponents, of course) their loss of the remaining games of the season, as the Carlisle Musketeers could have been the first to experience the notorious "SI cover jinx" in lieu of three years later, when the University of Oklahoma football team's record 47-game winning streak was broken the week after its 1957 "cover shot."

It was some 35-40 years after the 1954 season that Larry Cameron, the signal-calling tailback of the Coachless Wonders and now a successful high school football coach for many years in Florida, heard one of his assistants knock on Larry's office door: "Coach, you have a visitor to see you – from your past."

It would not be too difficult to imagine or visualize Larry in the role of "Coach," played by Craig Nelson, in the very popular TV series of the same name of the '90s, and, although Larry always spoke well of his assistants, with respect, he may have had one or two over the years that fit the comical mode as did Jerry VanDyke, or Moose, in the series.

To Larry's surprise, the visitor was none other than Coach J.W. "Bill" Shelton of Coachless Wonders days! There must have been a pause of several seconds as the two long-time members of the coaching fraternity eyed one another – recognizing the physical changes of each that had occurred over those many years past. Larry recounted that Coach Bill had not only remembered Larry from 1954, but he also remembered a hard-running fullback named Donnie Joe on that Musketeer team. Bill also recalled that he, as assistant coach for the UK freshmen footballers, had provided sideline and dressing room passes to one of the UK Wildcats home games for Larry and Donnie. Larry's dad, Paul Cameron, had driven the two young men to the game on November 13, 1954 - a 33-7 victory for the Cats over the Memphis State Tigers. With these special passes, enabling them to interact with the UK players, Larry and Donnie must have felt on Cloud Nine as potential recruits for UK football in this, the first season of newly hired Coach Blanton Collier, who had hailed originally from Carlisle's nearby neighbor of Paris, Kentucky.

The Season of the Coach-less Wonders

Following is a recapitulation, with reflections, of the 1954 game-by-game Musketeer football season as recalled from memories that are combined and compiled with headlines and detail game accounts extracted from the *Nicholas County Star*, *The Carlisle Mercury* and *The Lexington Herald-Leader.*

The headline of *The Nicholas County Star* that ran on Thursday, September 9, 1954, read, " 'Coachless Wonders' Will Meet Paris Friday Night In Season's Grid Opener – Carlisle Shy One Coach As Holmes Fails To Return As Musketeer Mentor!" The Musketeers had opened grid drills with 20 hopefuls, but this number diminished to a 17-man squad by the third game. There were eight lettermen carried over from the previous season which included the "fearless five" seniors of the Class of '55, Kenneth Booth, Larry Cameron, Jock Conley, Donnie Dampier, and Jackie Wells. Two very valuable additions, also "fearless," were transfers Jackie Shepherd and Billy Vanlandingham, also of the Class of '55.

As these two long-time, traditional pigskin foes were preparing for the upcoming '54 football season, there was much early anxiety in both camps that the game would even be played. In addition to Carlisle's possible cancellation of the game, and possibly the season, for lack of a coach, the Paris Greyhounds had faced the possibility of dropping football all together. It was only a year before, prior to opening the '53 season against the Musketeers, that the Paris program was so beset with problems that there was much speculation that the Hounds might have to give up football. Things looked pretty glum in Greyhound Town, but their fans and players could not have known that in a few short years, their floundering football fortunes would be led to the top of their class by none other than the now "certified" Coach Ben "Pokey" Pumphrey!

In the 1953 game, played at Paris, two classmates of the Class of '55, Larry Cameron and Donnie Dampier, were instrumental in the Muskies' winning score of 13-0. Whereas Larry had logged time in the backfield since his freshman year, this was Donnie's debut and "coming-out party" as a backfield running back. This game marked the beginning of "the team" of Cameron-Dampier as backfield mates for the remaining two years of their high school careers. As reported by *The Nicholas County Star,* "After a scoreless first half, Carlisle was not to be denied. Employing power plays through the line, Dampier carried the ball over from the three-yard line for the first score, but Clark's pass to Cameron for the extra point was incomplete. In the fourth quarter, Larry Cameron went through the line, and after shaking off the backfield tacklers, scampered across standing up. Billy Clark converted by running a play off tackle. The victory was strictly a team affair; however, looking exceptionally good on defense were Billy Logan, a sophomore, along with Clark and Dampier, and on offense, Dampier, Cameron, and senior Bobbie McFarland. Dampier, a converted lineman, showed such backfield ability that he promises to be a power house in the future." Dampier was also credited with over 150 yards rushing for the contest.

Carlisle 26, Paris 19 – at Carlisle, Ky., September 10, 1954

(*The Lexington Herald*) – "The 'coachless' Carlisle Musketeers broke a 19-19 deadlock in the final 10 seconds to defeat the Paris Greyhounds, 26-19, in a Central Kentucky Conference football thriller here tonight. Donnie Dampier, who had scored twice previously in the contest gathered in the oval on the 30-yard line as time ran out and streaked into paydirt to break the deadlock. Larry Cameron plunged across for the extra point as a formality – the damage was done when Dampier went over. Dampier opened the scoring in the opening minutes when he streaked 60 yards to tally. Cameron went through for the extra point. In the second period, the Muskies moved into a comfortable 13-0 lead on Cameron's 80-yard streak around left end. Paris closed the gap just before the half when Don Behler shot a 12-yard pass to Tommy Belt. Behler added the extra point on a plunge and it was 13-7 at the intermission. Carlisle – and Dampier – went to work in the third with the youngster going over from 22 yards out, after he first recovered a Paris fumble. The extra point attempt was no good. Paris wasn't to be outdone, despite the 19-7 deficit, and scored a TD with Bill Cassidy crashing over from the 10. Behler's plunge was cut short. Paris tied it up midway of the fourth quarter when Behler tossed six yards to Cassidy. The extra point try was stopped and the clubs battled the next four minutes with the score tied – until Dampier, the fleet senior fullback, broke the stalemate at the gun!"

The coaching duties for the Musketeers were handled under the capable direction of James "Doot" Hardin and Ben Pumphrey, Jr., but Superintendent R.E. Davis sat on the Carlisle bench – just to make it official. Donnie's touchdowns were scored from a play called "33 Trap" that had been devised by 'coach' Pumphrey to fit the Musketeer single-wing formations. The play required precise timing, faking, and effective blocking, usually from a "pulling" guard (Kenneth Booth), so considerable time was spent on its perfection in each practice session. Transfers Billy Vanlandingham and Jackie Shepherd each made impressive debuts, with "Van" playing most of the game at end (both on offense and defense). Jackie saw considerable action alternating the blocking back position with Jock

Conley, as both were also two-way performers on the defensive side as well. *The Nicholas County Star* described the impressive win that was scored by the Green and White eleven as "one of the most thrilling story-book finishes ever seen here"!

The 1954 victory was the fifth consecutive win for the Musketeers over the Paris Greyhounds. The game itself was indicative of the down-to-the-wire contests usually played between the two arch-rivals; for, in the nine-year period (beginning with the Tebay Rose era), the Musketeers had won six with three losses, but with an average score for the nine games of only 12-11!

Prior to the game, former Musketeer star Benny Donovan, CHS Class of '52, on furlough from the Navy, visited our dressing room, and, in an effort to pump us up to victory, offered a ten-dollar bill to any Muskie who scored three or more touchdowns against the Greyhounds! After the game, Benny was there to keep his word as he awarded the ten-dollar bill to Donnie Dampier, who had just scored the three TDs! Donnie, realizing his success was dependent upon the effectiveness of his teammates, happily proclaimed that he was treating the team at the Daily Queen! Upon taking their post-game showers, six or seven of the boys, along with several girls who had been waiting, loaded into Donnie's '48 Studebaker Starlight Coupe. There must have been a dozen or more celebrating teenagers crammed into a vehicle designed to transport five, or six at the most (it was a good thing we had taken those showers)! As the happy contingent was traveling across town, Donnie's girl friend, Faye Roundtree, was most surely sitting in his lap. Donnie certainly did not mind this closeness, but he was concerned over the hindrance to reaching the controls of the coupe, namely, the brakes! So, as they entered the Dairy Queen parking lot, a little too fast, Donnie barely reached the brakes in time to come to a sliding stop some 5 or 6 feet from the plate glass window, where some of the concerned inside customers had began to move aside out of possible harm's way!

Thankfully, with no harm done, Donnie "blew" the entire ten dollars (a lot of money back then) on his teammates and some of the girls! It is not recalled the method used to divide the $10 between the approximately 20 kids, but one of Ms. Gilley's math lessons must have been applied, for some got cones and some milkshakes or sundaes, all at different prices. Jackie Shepherd most likely received a milkshake, which he always got choked on, and still does to this day! One thing is certain – ten dollars went a long way at the Carlisle Dairy Queen in 1954!

Carlisle 18, Stanford 14 – At Carlisle, Ky., September 17, 1954

The Lexington Herald of Friday Morning, September 17, 1954 made the following pre-game comments about the contest: "Stanford will make their first appearance in the pigskin picture with a new coach, where Denzil Ramsey replaces Garis Ball at the helm. … Stanford opens at Carlisle, where Musketeer fans are anxiously awaiting another look-see at the 'Coachless Wonders' … and, wonder if they will stage another whirlwind finish as they did last week to nip Paris at the gun."

(The Nicholas County Star) – "The Musketeers came from behind a 14-6 deficit to defeat the Stanford Wildcats 18-14. Subbing coaches James Hardin and Ben Pumphrey once again provided the brains for the winning attack, which struck like lightning in the third quarter after a boggy start. Stanford took a 7-0 lead in the first period when Boyd Gilliam sped 12 yards around end and Edwin Darst added the extra point on a dropkick. In this era of football, the 'dropkick', where the kicker adeptly 'drops' the football, and kicks it on the bounce, was used often for extra points and field goals. Larry Cameron evened the score as he plunged over from the one early in the second quarter, but a 15-yard penalty wiped out Donnie Dampier's bid for the extra point. Stanford made it 14-6 at half-time as Ronnie Patterson picked up a Musketeer bobble on an attempted handoff deep in Musketeer territory and raced 20 yards to pay-dirt, with Tommy Grimes' pass to Patterson connecting for the extra point."

On the play leading to Stanford's second score, Carlisle was attempting to run a "buck lateral" play, with a direct snap to the fullback (Dampier), who faked a run into the line, but handed off to the blocking back (Jackie Shepherd), who had rotated and set, then he handed off to the wing back (David Feeback), who was to run the play around the left side of the unbalanced line. However, guard Wilbur Conyers got mixed up on the play (thinking a "trap" had been called) and mistakenly pulled off the line, leaving a huge gap for the defensive Stanford lineman to come through, untouched, effectively tackling all three Carlisle backs at once, resulting in the lost fumble! Needless to say, coaches Pumphrey and Hardin were not happy and had a few "choice words" for us at halftime!

"After intermission, the local lads rallied to score two touchdowns in less than eight minutes. After Cameron and Dampier had moved Stanford's kickoff to the Wildcat 35, Cameron took to the air and rifled an aerial to Billy Gilley. As the big end waited to grab the lofted pigskin a Stanford back deflected the ball into the waiting arms of alert David Feeback and the twisting speedster outran the Wildcat secondary to register a surprising TD! Moments later Gilley recovered a Stanford fumble on the Carlisle 45. A Cameron forward pass to Gilley who then executed a lateral pass to Feeback covered 21 yards to the Wildcat 34. Three plays later, Dampier 'streaked' down the far sidelines to score the winning touchdown!" For the record, Donnie was fully clothed in football uniform, thus was not engaged in the "streaking" craze of running totally nude in public that became popular in the '70s!

A factor of the game long forgotten by most of the Class of '55 is that Carlisle wore blue jerseys that were borrowed from MMI when Stanford arrived in white, the jersey color usually worn by the Musketeers. Note that due to very limited funds, we only had the one set of white jerseys (with green numbers), and did not have the alternating green jerseys that most schools would have had to designate home and away games.

Also, with this game, Doot Hardin, one of our successful "unofficial" coaches, left us the following Monday to return to UK to finish his college studies.

In the spirit of sportsmanship often demonstrated by small-town schools, the Stanford High School faculty, football parents, and cheerleaders, as well as the hometown team, hosted a post-game "hospitality" with welcome refreshments for the visiting team. The Musketeers of our junior season of 1953, as the visiting team to Stanford, enjoyed this tradition, which had apparently begun several years previously. Stanford had a good team in 1953, with a fine 4-2-1 won-loss record, finishing number 6 in the CKC standings (the Frankfort Panthers won the championship with an undefeated record of 8-0-1), and, no doubt, their boys were feeling much more hospitable than hostile, as they had socked it to us pretty good by the score of 26-0. With the distance and travel time from Carlisle to Stanford, the Blue 'n' White boys of Stanford probably felt secure that the Carlisle boys would be deterred from future infringement upon their girls. However, they could never be too sure about the adventurous spirit of those Musketeer men of the "Green 'n' White."

The Elkhorn High School Elks of the capital city of Frankfort were the next team on the Musketeer schedule of 1954. The Lexington Herald's Friday morning pre-game analysis stated: "Carlisle, taking the field for the first time this season with an official coach, steps outside the loop for a crack at the Elkhorn Elks. It marks the third straight week the Frankfort flock has opposed a CKC member and the Elks are hoping to gain their first win over a conference club after losing 27-0 to Danville in the opener and to Anderson last week, 20-6. John (Louie) Walters, former Danville High star, makes his coaching debut with the Musketeers. Stopping Donnie Dampier and Larry Cameron will be the chief problem for the Elks."

The *Nicholas County Star* chimed in to say: "John (Louie) Walters, newly named coach of the Carlisle Musketeers, will make his initial appearance as Muskie mentor Friday night at Frankfort, when Carlisle will attempt to annex victory number three at the expense of Elkhorn. Walters, who received his degree from Centre College in 1951, was on the sidelines to observe last Friday as the Musketeers came from behind to defeat Stanford."

So, officially from this point on in the season, the Carlisle Musketeers could no longer be called "coachless."

The previous year, in the 1953 season, was the initial encounter between Carlisle and Elkhorn. This also marked the opening CHS band performance of Carroll Hall's "Marching 32." Even though the home-standing Musketeers played well, pass interceptions and penalties did them in, as the Elks walked away with an 18-0 victory on a rain-soaked field. The Class of '55 members played well – Jock Conley downed an Elkhorn kickoff, Larry Cameron had a pass interception, and Donnie Dampier had some nice runs. A highlight for the Muskies was a goal line stand, from the one-foot line, with Conley and Kenneth Booth on the front line (outweighed by some 15 pounds to the man) and Dampier and Cameron at linebackers to stop the Elks in their tracks!

Frankfort was one of our longest jaunts from Carlisle, comparable in distance to Nicholasville, Lancaster, and Stanford. Some of us who were members of the football squad as freshmen in the 1951 season will remember the long distance traveling to Hazard, settled in the Southeastern Kentucky mountains. This was in Coach Rose's final season as mentor of the Musketeers, a game in which we went in with high hopes toting a 3-0 record, but lost to the Hazard Bulldogs by a score of 26-7. One vague memory of this game, other than the "drudgery drive," was that at the post-game supper at a local Hazard steakhouse, one of the varsity players could not partake due to some lost front teeth during the encounter. This must have appeared as a "hazardous journey" of long duration, with our first experiences of the mountain roads and the encountering of coal trucks seemingly around each sharp curve! Of course, Nicholas County had more than its share of hills and curves, but we had seen nothing like these!

The Musketeers and the Elks played their 1954 game on Alumni Field of Kentucky State College, the home of the Green and Gold Thoroughbreds. The field sat down below what was then a two-lane East Main Street, directly across from the campus of the all-black college, resting upon a hill that overlooks the city of

Frankfort.

For the Class of '55 players and the rest of the "Coachless Wonders" team, this was the first and probably only opportunity to play varsity football on a college football field. None of the seven members of the Class of '55 went on to play varsity football at the college/university level, and, as far as known, this was also true for the remaining underclassmen of the 1954 team.

Carlisle 7, Elkhorn 7, at Frankfort, KY, September 24, 1954

(*The Lexington Herald*) – "The Carlisle Musketeers, who marched to a pair of victories this season without a coach, had to cash in on a recovered fumble in the fourth period to remain undefeated with a 7-7 deadlock with Elkhorn in their debut here tonight under new coach John Walters. Elkhorn broke the scoring ice in the second quarter with Dickie Hullett's eight-yard dash to cap a 60-yard drive. Wayne Wylie passed to Dave Taylor for the extra point. The Elks had a 44-yard touchdown jaunt by Charles Sartin called back because of a rule infraction earlier in the period. The Muskies set up their score with a fumble recovery on the Elk 14 in the final frame with fullback Don Dampier plunging two yards for the tally. Dampier also plunged over for the tying point. Carlisle, with some good gains by Dampier and Larry Cameron, drove to the Elk 15 late in the game but lost the ball on a fumble."

Donnie Dampier especially remembers that Elkhorn had two fine, hard-hitting linebackers (whose names were never known), who were frequently there to "scissor" Donnie with clean, hard tackles on each thigh as he broke through the line of scrimmage! Dampier, who was very much in the CKC scoring race after the game, standing in third place only a few points out of first, was never able to totally recover from the bruises and soreness to his thigh muscles administered by the two Elks, somewhat hampering his performance and scoring output for the rest of the season. Combined with only minimal thigh guard protection and no whirlpools or other sports medicine techniques, players at most small high schools such as Carlisle had difficulties preventing and overcoming these types of injuries.

At the exact midpoint of the seven-game season, the Carlisle Musketeers traveled to Lancaster, the county seat and only incorporated town of Garrard County.

Carlisle 7, Lancaster 19 – at Lancaster, October 1, 1954

The Lexington Herald's Friday morning preview: "Carlisle's Musketeers hope to register their first win under their new coach, John (Louie) Walters, when they travel to Lancaster to meet Coy Dyehouse's 'hepped-up' Green Devils, who knocked Anderson from the unbeaten ranks last week, 14-13." Lancaster entered the contest with the Muskies with apparently one of their best teams in many years, at 2-0-1, the only blemish being a surprise 27-27 tie against powerful Nicholasville (if that can be called a "blemish"), in the '54 season opener for both. In previous years, Carlisle had a great deal of success against the Green Devils with seven consecutive wins before dropping the 1953 contest on the Musketeer field by a score of 7-0.

"The Lancaster Green Devils handed the Carlisle Musketeers their first setback of the season here tonight in a hard-fought contest, 19-7. Carlisle grabbed the lead late in the first quarter when Donnie Dampier went off-tackle for 45 yards. Larry Cameron tacked on the extra point with a line plunge. The Green Devils tied the score in the middle of the second period on an 11-yard pass play from Hugh McCulley to Robert Turner. Shirley Price ran the extra point over. Then late in the period the Green Devils broke the deadlock when McCulley raced nine yards into the end zone for a touchdown. The try for the extra point was no good and the half ended, 13-7. Lancaster scored again in the middle of the fourth period when Cabele Leavell tallied from 10 yards out."

This was a game in which Donnie Dampier was hardly a factor, and should not have played at all, having come into the game feverishly ill with the flu. Just as Donnie was tackled as he crossed the goal-line in the first quarter with his only scoring opportunity, he passed out and remembers little about the remainder of the game except being shocked back to consciousness a few times with smelling salts! Ronnie King, an inexperienced junior and weighing only some 135 pounds, was pressed into service in Donnie's fullback position for the remainder of the game. Larry Cameron tried, in vain, to take up the slack of his missing running mate, but Lancaster, knowing this, keyed on Larry to reduce his effectiveness. The coach played a groggy Donnie some in the second half as defensive lineman, with Jock Conley and Kenneth Booth alternating in Donnie's regular linebacking spot. The Dampiers were aware that Donnie did not feel well before the game, but were not aware of the extent of the condition until after the game when his parents admitted him to the Lancaster Hospital for overnight treatment.

Permelia, Larry's mother, was probably also there that night, as she frequently traveled with Elmer and Ann to the Musketeer away games. Permelia and Ann who had been very good friends for years, probably were drawn even closer, as the two always sat side-by-side during the Carlisle High School playing days of our junior and senior years – the "in-the-stands" counterparts to Larry and Donnie "on-the-field" – as these two "Musketeer Mates" also lined up side-by-side in the offensive backfield and in the defensive backfield as linebackers.

Carlisle 6, Nicholasville 26 – Carlisle, October 8, 1954

(*The Lexington Herald)* – "Nicholasville's Tarantulas, who probably will be knocked out of championship contention because of a 27-27 tie with Lancaster, shouldn't have too much trouble staying unbeaten. Billy Lockridge leads his Spiders to Carlisle for a shot at John (Louie) Walters' Muskies, who attempt to get back in the win column after a tie with Elkhorn and a loss to Lancaster."

Nicholasville Wins – "Nicholasville's touchdown twins, Bob Rice and Bob Stinnett, accounted for four touchdowns here tonight as the Tarantulas registered their fourth straight triumph, 26-6 at the expense of Carlisle in a Central Kentucky Conference tilt. Rice reeled off a 70-yard scoring jaunt in the opening quarter and

Stinnett plunged for the point to make it 7-0. Stinnett blasted up the middle 41-yards for a score on the second play of the second period to bring his scoring total for the season to 60 points, tops in Central Kentucky. Rice raced 72 yards around right end later in the period for his second marker and Billy Kenney recovered Rice's fumble into the end zone for the extra point making it 20-0. After a scoreless third quarter, Carlisle finally hit pay dirt by driving 73 yards for the tally, with Larry Cameron passing two yards to Billy Gilley for the marker. A pass attempt for the extra point failed. Rice registered his third touchdown shortly after the ensuing kickoff by taking a pass from Stinnett with the play covering 48 yards. The extra point failed and the final score stood at 26-6. Rice's three markers raised his season output to 43 points."

A less than 100% Donnie Dampier, still weakened by the aftermath of the flu and hobbling from frequent leg cramps from the Elkhorn game, failed to score and dropped from third to fifth place in the CKC scoring race. However, even though Donnie had frequently experienced the thrill of scoring, one of his all-time favorite football accomplishments was a nonscoring play that occurred in this game, and one that Jackie Shepherd and he still relive! In the Musketeers' third-period scoring drive, a buck lateral play was called with a direct snap to Donnie, who then handed off to Jackie. Donnie made a good fake at carrying the ball, resulting in being tackled by two Nicholasville players, the effect of two blocks. Meanwhile, Shepherd broke free from a tackle and crossed the line of scrimmage, where he found himself hemmed in by two more Tarantulas, who were positioned to apply a big sting to Jackie! Donnie, who had always been taught to get off the ground as quickly as possible to look for another block, saw Jackie's plight and made a flying, flattening block of the two surprised Tarantulas, right in front of an equally surprised Jackie, enabling him to leap the pile and advance the ball another twelve to fifteen yards, to set up Larry's TD pass play to Gilley for the Muskies' only score!

The Georgetown Garth Buffalos were the next opposition to face the Musketeers in a season that was quickly winding down.

Carlisle had had only limited success with this traditional opponent, having won two times in the last eight games; and 1954, the year of the "Coachless Wonders," would be no different. Georgetown, the town, in the 1950s was approximately two to three times the size of Carlisle, so an assumption is made that Garth High School enjoyed the advantage of the same ratio of students, and potential football players, over Carlisle High. For instance, Lawrence Stamper, a frequent visitor with his grandparents in Carlisle, was a member of the Georgetown Garth High School Class of 1949, which had 39 graduates.

In the 1953 game of the previous year, the Class of '55 members had a little better game than in '54 as seniors; we helped the Muskies at least score fourteen points. As *The Nicholas County Star* reported, "In Georgetown, Coach Carroll Holmes eleven found Georgetown's stampeding herd of Buffaloes just that as they fell before Tom Green's Buffs 44-14." The Buffs scored in the opening minutes when Duke Owens blocked a Muskie kick and fell on it for a touchdown. Other Georgetown players in on scoring plays during the game included Ray Perry, Lou Hoffman, R. C. Covington, Harry Brockman, and Joe Johnson, son of Mayor Joe Ed Johnson, a former Carlisle High School coach. George Lusby, who would later be elected as Scott County judge executive, also played in the game. *The Star's* account of the Musketeer scoring: "Billy Clark fired a short pass to Donnie Dampier and the latter streaked 65 yards behind good blocking to score. Dampier added the extra point on a run. A few minutes, Clark tossed a 50-yard scoring pass to Bobby McFarland. Larry Cameron ran for the extra point."

Future Class of '55 members Billy "Big Van" Vanlandingham and Jackie "Shep" Shepherd would have been welcome additions to the squad, and maybe helped change the outcome, but they had not transferred back to CHS as yet.

Carlisle 0, Georgetown Garth 44 – Carlisle, Ky., October 15, 1954

"Buffs Maul Carlisle – Georgetown Garth spoiled homecoming festivities for Carlisle High School tonight by romping to a 44-0 victory in a Central Kentucky Conference football tilt. Georgetown coach Tom Green's eleven were led in scoring by Billy Price and Billy Wilson who each scored two touchdowns, with Ray Perry scoring another. Quarterback Joe Johnson and Charles Grote, a transfer from the Pikeville High School Panthers, exchanged touchdown passes to each other. Charles Gibson converted for the extra points. Carlisle's only threat ended when the Musketeers fumbled after driving to the Garth 21-yard line in the final period. Donnie Dampier, Jackie Shepherd, and Larry Cameron led the Musketeer's game effort, but to no avail. All three senior boys along with Jock Conley, Billy Vanlandingham, Kenneth Booth, and Jackie Wells will be making their last appearance for the green and white, as one-touchdown underdogs, next week against Cynthiana. Cameron, who sparked Carlisle's futile running attack before being injured late in the game, was temporarily replaced by Billy Straw, who turned in a commendable performance while subbing for the CHS play-caller."

Billy Wilson, an All State performer who had returned the second-half kickoff 80 yards to pay dirt for the Buffalos, and Donnie Dampier, the Musketeer fullback, became good friends years later when they both worked in the Kentucky Department of Education.

Carlisle 6, Cynthiana 13 – at Cynthiana, October 22, 1954

"Musketeers Edged By Cynthiana 13-6 Friday Night In Last Game Of Season – A Musketeer fumble on its own four yard line which Cynthiana recovered in the third quarter proved to be the margin of victory as the Bulldogs wrote an unhappy 13-6 finish to Carlisle's 1954 football season in Cynthiana Friday night. Cynthiana, which held a 6-0 edge at the time, had driven to within inches of the Carlisle goal, only to lose possession to the stubborn Musketeers in a brilliant goal line stand. Taking over in an attempt to move the ball out of dangerous territory, Carlisle fumbled and Cynthiana's Wayne Hill added his second TD of the evening on a four-yard plunge. Billy McKee tacked on the extra point and the

Bulldogs led 13-0. Not outdone, Carlisle gobbled in a Cynthiana bobble on the Bulldog 30 in the fourth period. Taking to the air, Larry Cameron, playing with a shoulder separation, rifled a 16-yard pass to Billy Gilley to set the stage for Donnie Dampier's seventh touchdown of the season. Dampier led all Musketeer backs in the scoring department with 43 points. Carlisle finished the season with two wins, four losses, and one tie. They annexed 70 points and allowed the opposition 142 points." (*The Nicholas County Star*).

In that 1954 contest, Donnie Dampier remembers fielding Billy McKee's second-half kickoff, and at mid-field, hemmed in by Bulldogs, he saw a "looming" Billy McKee positioned for the tackle. So, Donnie lowered his head straight at Billy, and the two friendly gladiators collided with a resounding "thump!" For a few moments the two combatants lay stunned, then Donnie rolled over and said, "Tough tackle, Billy," and then Billy responded with, "Great run, Donnie!" Then, the two friendly rivals helped each other up and continued the game. Such was small-town, small-school football of the Central Kentucky Conference in the 1950s!

In the preceding 1953 season, some of the future "Coachless Wonders" and Class of '55 members were instrumental in the Muskies' 27-6 victory over Cynthiana before a large, enthusiastic Homecoming crowd at Carlisle. In a synopsis from *The Nicholas County Star*, "After a scoreless first half, bruising Billy Clark, playing in the finest fashion of his colorful Musketeer career, was joined by veteran halfback Bobby McFarland, as the two seniors teamed up to leave a lasting impression with the supporting homefolks. Dampier Registers. David Feeback, playing heads-up ball in the defensive backfield early in the third quarter intercepted a pass from Cynthiana quarterback V.D. Florence. Clark gained 21 yards, from which point Donnie Dampier, the hard-charging tailback, plowed the remaining 16 yards over tackle for the initial tally. After the Bulldogs punted to the Carlisle 11, Clark and Dampier drove to the Cynthiana 45 where Clark raced in for the second score. Once again, Feeback stole a Florence pass on the Carlisle 42. From there Clark steamed to the 25, Larry Cameron bulled to the 18, Dampier to the six, and Clark over for the TD. McFarland grabbed a Clark pass for the final score of the game and 1953 season."

Reminiscing the Replays – When two or more of those who participated in sports of bygone years get together, it is a common activity to reminisce about the past glory days (if there were any), and to rerun memorable games played, accomplished plays, individual efforts, etc, This is usually between old teammates, as has frequently occurred down through the years when former Carlisle Musketeers Larry, Kenneth, Jock, Jackie, and Donnie, either as pairs or as a group, replay and relive their days as "The Coachless Wonders," but sometimes the replays are with individuals who were not teammates, but competitors playing on opposing teams.

Such was the case for Donnie Dampier when, some twenty to twenty-five years after completing his career on the football fields of Carlisle High School, and while attending a conference social function, a casual conversation with a fellow attendee revealed that his new acquaintance had been a Cynthiana Bulldog. And the two had competed against each other in the gridiron seasons of 1953 and 1954 in both their junior and senior years. The former Bulldog began to reminisce his experiences against the Musketeers by recounting, "Oh, yes, I didn't know your name, but I remember you well. ... I can still see those bright blue eyes of yours peering out from under your helmet, positioned directly across from me on the line of scrimmage ... and I remember how strong and tough you were for me to block ... and I also remember the very tough times I had in trying to get by you to tackle your backfield mates!" Well, at this point, Donnie was basking in past glories to think that a former opponent remembered him so well as a player over two decades later, and in such a complimentary way – when suddenly, Donnie thought, "Hey, I don't have 'bright blue eyes,' and I would not have lined up on the line of scrimmage across from this fellow. ... I was in the backfield, as a fullback and linebacker those two years. ... He is not talking about me, he is remembering Kenneth Booth!" So, when Donnie revealed to the old Bulldog who he was really talking about, he responded, "Oh, yes ... so you are Donnie Dampier. ... I remember you now ... you are the Carlisle boy that my teammate Billy McKee talked about often ... but back to that Kenneth Booth ... he was one strong and tough 'son-of-a-gun'!"

So, since another decade or two have passed, and when the old Bulldog, in "replaying the reruns" of his high school football days with his former Cynthiana teammates, and now knowing the true identity, by name, of one of his strongest individual opponents, and, with a likely bit of embellishment over time, has probably by now elevated Kenneth Booth to legendary levels in his own time!

The Historical Value of "The Coachless Wonders"

Those reading about the exploits of the 1954 Carlisle High School Musketeers football team may wonder, "What is so special about 'The Coachless Wonders'?" This, of course, is a fair question since this team did not win the CKC championship, nor did it finish with a winning season record. However, in many ways the 1954 Muskies epitomized small high school football of those times and, therefore, were representative of the hundreds, perhaps thousands, of these small-town football teams and their players throughout Central Kentucky (and across the country); and, this team had the added distinction of a publicized, identifying label that provided a media measure of fame, "The Coachless Wonders."

In these small, underfunded school systems, most limited to a small pool of potential players, there must have been numerous times when small school administrators considered if they would field a team in a given season, sometimes with uncertainty about a returning coach or whether they would have enough players or available funds for uniforms, equipment, and facilities. As previously stated, Paris High School was on the verge of dropping football altogether. By late October 1954, and the last weekend of the season for most CKC teams, the Stanford Wildcats were reduced to only a 13-man squad and were worn down in a 19-0 loss to the Anderson Bearcats. The squad of the Winchester Shawnees was so depleted, and down to mostly inexperienced underclassmen, that the team forfeited the scheduled game with the powerful Danville Admirals. The success of a small school football team was seriously hampered if a key starter was out of competition for most of a game. Such was the case when Lancaster's fine quarterback, Hugh McCulley, sidelined from the second quarter on in their game with the Madison-Model Purples, had their offense stymied and lost by a score of 13-0. This was also true when Carlisle's leading rusher and scorer, Donnie Dampier, after scoring a touchdown early in the first quarter, was lost for the remainder of the game (on offense and defense) against the Lancaster Green Devils as the Musketeers lost by a margin of 19-7. These kinds of adverse situations happened over and over, year-in and year-out, to most of the small-school football teams of that era.

The game of football is a rough and hard sport to participate in. To those many young men who played the game for small high schools in the '50s, and their predecessors from the '40s, the "game" might be described as doubly tough in comparison to the modern version for a number of reasons. Most of the starters played both ways (offense and defense), so we were actively on the field the entire game – none of this playing 3 or 4 plays, then sitting on the bench for another series of plays when the ball was turned over. The era of "two-platoon" football, which was just being introduced into the game on the college level, had not trickled down to the high school game, so there were very few, if any, "special teams" that specialized in only one or two facets of the game (such as a kicking team); we did it all!

We had no training facilities or weight rooms to develop our bodies – that was done by working on the farms or construction. There were no trainers, sports medicine, whirlpools, etc., to heal our injuries – we used a lot of tape (applied by the "jack-of-all-trades" coach) and liberal application of liniment for sore muscles. The protective equipment (shoulder pads, knee and thigh pads, etc.) would be considered inadequate and unacceptable by today's standards. Benny Donovan (CHS Class of '53) is the only known Carlisle player of those times that is recalled to have worn rib pads to protect his bruised and perhaps cracked ribs. Plastic, padded headgear was just beginning to replace the old leather helmets by the early '50s. The seniors on the "Coachless Wonders" of 1954 who were on the team for four years played with leather helmets as freshmen, and only some got to play in the new plastic helmets as sophomores. And, they were not all that great, for Donnie, Larry, and Kenneth (perhaps more) had to get replacements, more than once, for helmets that cracked from contact!

Protection for the teeth and nose was nil, as there is no awareness that any of the boys wore a mouthpiece, and only the rare exception that any player had a nose guard on his helmet. As a result, there were numerous times of swollen lips, black eyes, cracked, loosened, or lost front teeth, and bloody or broken noses! It is really amazing that there were not more of these types of injuries than occurred, because we played all-out, full-force, and "hell bent for leather"! Of the "Coachless Wonders," it comes to mind that Kenneth Booth and Billy Logan lost some front teeth, Donnie Dampier had a chipped front tooth, and Larry Cameron had a broken nose (actually, a broken nose was somewhat of a "status symbol" that many of the boys, and some girls, admired). As memory serves, by looking back into the late '40s and early '50s, there were only two Carlisle High School players that played with the exception by wearing a nose guard; they were Gary Flora (Class of '52, who had received a cleat injury to the face) and David Hardin (Class of '54). David, who played with the Class of '55 when they were juniors, was a big, strong, rugged player, but had an extremely sensitive nose that bled profusely with only light contact, so he was issued a nose guard to protect against that otherwise frequent happening. Another physical characteristic that is remembered of David Hardin, who was a part of the Class of '55 during his junior year, was that he had very large and powerful hands. In football, if David made a grabbing tackle using his hands, that opponent never escaped his clutches; and no one beat David in a hand-gripping contest!

Most thankfully, athletes back in the '50s did not have to contend with the AIDS epidemic and the concerns over the exchange of blood, so when we got bloodied, we played on! The original white playing jersey (#55) which was worn by Donnie Dampier and has been saved by him to this day still shows some stains of blood drops that were received during the season of the "Coachless Wonders!"

The boys of Carlisle High School, as well as our competitors, played football because we loved the game! It made us feel that we were a part of something positive, win or lose, and most of us experienced losing a lot! It brought our classmates together as teammates, as we knew we were in there for each other; and this included our girls, who were also always there to encourage and support us, whether it was in victory or defeat! We all lived the Musketeer motto, "One for All, and All for One"!

Perhaps the participation in sports by the young men from the small towns and small schools around the country, as well as the "Coachless Wonders," is best described by the stirring words of a former president of the United States of America that have been titled "In The Arena," or which could also be titled "On The Playing Field":

It is not the critic who counts, nor the individual who points out how the strong person stumbled, or where the doer of deeds could have done them better. The credit belongs to the one who is actually in the arena; whose face is marred by dust and sweat and blood; who strives valiantly; who errs and comes short again and again; who knows the great enthusiasms, the great devotions and spends oneself in a worthy cause; who, at the best, knows in the end the triumph of high achievement; and who, at the least, if fails, at least fails while doing greatly; so that one's place shall never be with those cold and timid souls who know neither victory nor defeat.

Theodore Roosevelt

In the 1950s, most of the boys participating on small school teams did not have much expectation of playing varsity football at the next level in college, and certainly no unrealistic dreams of pro football contracts. For small-town high school students of that era, going to college was the exception and not the expected norm. Most of the boys planned to work in the local or family businesses or farm, or join the military service, while the majority of the girls, with fewer career opportunities during that time, looked to marry and be housewives.

The CHS "Coachless Wonders" of 1954 have been somewhat 'immortalized' with a copy of the labeled team photograph displayed in the Kentucky History Center as part of the Kentucky Historical Society's exhibit, Front Page Fifties: Kentucky at Mid-century, which had its run from early December of 2000 into September of 2001. The photograph of the team, accompanied by the original jersey of "old # 55," were provided by Donnie Dampier upon the Center's request. All seven Musketeer members of the Class of 1955 are pictured in the exhibit photo. On the front row are Jock Conley (#50), Donnie Dampier (55), Larry Cameron (47), and Jackie Shepherd (49); then on row two are Jackie Wells (#51), Kenneth Booth (52), and Billy Vanlandingham (#53).

Donnie, who also served as a part-time museum guide for the "Fifties Exhibit," had been asked by museum patrons on a couple of occasions questions concerning the numbers on our jerseys. Since most of the jersey numbers range in the 50s, the first question is, "Why are there not numbers identifying backfield or end positions (20-40, or 80s)?" or, "Is this a photo of only the linemen" (many find it difficult to visualize a full football team of only some 17 players) on the "Coachless Wonders" team? The speculative answer given is that Carlisle High School had limited funds for equipment and jerseys, and with a small number of players to outfit, probably were able to purchase a block of jersey numbers (such as the 50s series) at a much cheaper price.

Ben Henry "Pokey" Pumphrey – Hall of Fame Coach

It can be accurately stated that Ben Pumphrey holds a special place in the annuals of athletic accomplishments, of which he contributed in the arenas of coaching high school football at Carlisle and Nicholas County. Ben Henry Pumphrey was born on February 23, 1924, a native and long-time resident of Carlisle, and a graduate of the Class of 1941 of Carlisle High School.

Although Ben would never describe himself as such, he was truly one of the heroes in preserving our freedoms which we all cherish, as he served his community and country with distinction in numerous combat bombardier missions during WWII. These were real hard-life experiences from the fields of battle, which helped to forge the spirit of discipline, toughness, and teamwork that Coach Ben applied to the fields of football.

Apparently, the state's unenlightened certification requirements had delayed "Coach Ben" from his quest to become a high school coach/teacher and deprived the Class of 1955 from one to two years of developing and playing for one of the finest coaches ever produced in Kentucky.

Coach Pumphrey went on to a very successful coaching career at a dozen schools, which, in addition to the 2-3 games at Carlisle, included stints at MMI, Lexington Dunbar (the "all-black" original), Paris High, Belleview, Mason County, Montgomery County, Harrison County, even venturing into the mountains of Clay County at Oneida Baptist, Fleming County, Bath County, then back to become the most successful long-term coach at Nicholas County High.

In Ben's first football head-coaching position, which was at Paris High School, he took a team with only a handful of wins in the previous decade and led the Greyhounds to a competitive 2-7-1 record; then, in only his second year, produced a fine 6-4 won-loss season, their first winning season in many years. Then, in December of 1963, *The Louisville Courier Journal* named Ben Pumphrey as the Coach of the Year in the Class A Division. In that 1963 season, Coach Ben led the Paris Greyhounds to an unbeaten regular season, the first at Paris in 20 years, then Ben took his team to the semifinals in the Class A playoffs. So, from a team that had won only 4 games in 8 years before Pumphrey arrived, over the next six years, he guided the Greyhounds to 41 wins, making the state playoffs twice.

In Ben's first season, a short stint at Lexington Dunbar, he led the Bulldogs to their first-ever wins over powerful Lexington city rivals Tates Creek and Lafayette. Pumphrey 's next coaching stop was at Belleview, a northern Kentucky school that had suffered through 10 consecutive losing seasons; however the coach produced winning seasons each of the next two years. Ben then heeded the call from Emery "Little E" Clark for help at Flemingsburg, where Little E, as a practicing veterinarian, knew that Ben could produce some "horses," perhaps even some thoroughbreds, for the dismal football program previously played at the Fleming county school. And Coach Ben did not disappoint Little E's confidence, for, after a 2-9 debut, he guided the Panthers to four straight winning seasons, finishing with 8-3 records in each of his last two campaigns.

Ben, who now seemed to be circling his home town of Carlisle in his football coaching pursuits, moved on to Bath County, uncharacteristically recording two straight losing seasons, but before he had time to turn that program around, the lure to return home again was too strong. He accepted Nicholas County High School's appeal, where the coach faced a most dismal program.

When Pumphrey arrived at Nicholas County, the school, in the 12 years since it had started a football program, had enjoyed but one winning season, which was in 1964. The 1964 winning season, which was coached by Gayle Bowen, Carlisle native and CHS alumni, was achieved in the second year of Nicholas County High School football, after the consolidation with Carlisle High School. In 1969 and '70 the school went though an agonizing 21-game losing streak. In three other seasons it had won only one game. So, there was much skepticism, or, at best, very guarded optimism, on Coach Ben's chance of much success. But Ben, who had played tough-nosed high school football for the Carlisle Musketeers in the late 1930s and the 1940 season before entering the service, and who loved a challenge, expressed his confidence on returning to the community of his roots. "When I came back here all the old people I went to school with didn't think we could do it. But people found out we could win, and we weren't going to turn and run from people."

In his first season at Nicholas County High in 1975, the veteran coach guided the Blue Jackets to a 6-5 record, the school's first winning slate in the 11 years since 1964. Then, in only his second season, the 1976 Nicholas County team qualified for the Class-A playoffs with a final record of 10-3, best in the school's history, which included a District Championship and a win over bitter rival Paris during that campaign. Prior to that win, no Nicholas County Blue Jackets team had ever beaten Paris, and the last time a team from the Nicholas community had beaten the Greyhounds was the old Carlisle High School Musketeers in 1961, in the next-to-the last season of CHS football existence. So Coach Ben Pumphrey had beaten Paris High, the school that some dozen years previous was also a downtrodden program that Ben, after becoming their coach, had developed into one of the Class-A powers of Kentucky high school football. Thereby Coach Ben created his "Phoenix" (a legendary bird represented by ancient Egyptian mythology as living 6 centuries, being consumed in fire by its own act, and "rising in youthful freshness" from its own ashes)! And now, Coach Ben was well on his way to raising another program from virtually nothing to make the Nicholas County Blue Jackets a force to be reckoned with!

A "Career of Class" – Along the way, at each of the schools where he served as head football coach, Coach Pumphrey also developed successful and competitive track teams. Among his accomplishments, which demonstrated his prowess as a teacher of track, he coached Nicholas County to seven consecutive Regional Track Championships, and Bellevue to back-to-back Class A State Track Championships in 1967 and 1968. In addition to its own appeal, Ben recognized that the sport of track serves to complement and increase the skill development of the students who played on the football teams.

Those who played for "Coach Ben" will remember his conjoining words of encouragement before and during each contest, "By golly, boys, you can do this," or, "By golly, boys, get off your butts, and get after them," or, "By golly, boys, we can win this game!" Coach Ben, even as a Christian gentleman, but also being human, no doubt probably uttered a few more colorful words in the decades of trying to get "snot-nosed" high school boys to perform up to their potential; however, in all the times this writer was ever around Coach Ben, including the athletic fields of endeavor, "By golly, boys" were usually the strongest words ever recalled.

Once Ben Pumphrey got his chance, he coached as an assistant or head coach for over 45 years, covering four decades. At a variety of schools as a head football coach, he is credited with compiling a winning record of 165-142-7 in 25 years. Actually, in the opinion of this writer, Coach Ben should also be additionally credited with the two wins and a tie while he was on the sideline coaching the "Coachless Wonders," for it was Ben's leadership which made us the "Wonders." Perhaps Coach Ben's overall won-lost percentage (54%) might be viewed by some sports historians as falling short of greatness when compared to the records of other great high school football coaches of Kentucky; however, they would be shortsighted in their view. In Ben's case, without exception, he went to schools that had a previous record of futile football and, starting from the ground up, built the teams into inspired, competitive teams. In each building or rebuilding project, of which Ben seemed to relish the challenge, it was natural he would suffer through some losing seasons before he rejuvenated the team and introduced the school to winning ways. Also, Ben coached his entire career at small schools, limited to small pools of available athletes. Without the benefit of recruiting to bring in other players, he built with the material he had at his disposal, and, in some years in a small school, the talent pool would run thin.

The "What Ifs ..." – This in no way is meant to minimize our worthy opponents on the fine teams of Elkhorn, Lancaster, and Cynthiana, but these were all contests that the Musketeers were capable of winning – if we had remained as the "Coachless Wonders" with the "unofficial" coaching of Ben "Pokey" Pumphrey and we had stayed relatively free of injury and illness. After all, before the 1954 season began, many of the Carlisle faithful were touting this Musketeer edition as potentially one of Carlisle's finest in recent years.

If we could have remained unbeaten through at least the first four games, it is quite likely that the late Billy Thompson, the fine sports writer of *The Lexington Herald* during that era, would have written a feature article about our team (similar to his feature of the Nicholasville Tarantulas in the October 21, 1954 edition, in which he colorfully wrote, "The Terrible Tarantulas have caught 11 victims in the spider's web, and three others have gotten tied up in the smooth-webbing machine"). It is only speculation as to how Billy Thompson, with his way with words, would have phrased such an article. Perhaps it would have said something like, "The Carlisle 'Coachless Wonders,' the magical Musketeers, with their 'mythical coach,' have not misfired their muskets in mastering all comers so far." If such a feature article had been written, it would have solidified the historical fame of the "Coachless Wonders."

Also, to expand on the "what if" thinking, if some of the fine athletic young men, such as Bobbie Anderson, Billy Buntin, Frank Conyers, and David Odor, each of which would have been our senior classmates along with underclassman Buddy Alexander, had stayed at Carlisle High School, the 1954 Musketeers would certainly have contended for the CKC crown! Looking back, we can all identify with the memorable and famous line uttered by Marlon Brando in the 1954 Academy Award winning performance of *On The Waterfront*, when, playing the role of ex-boxer Terry Malloy, he agonized, "I could have been a contender." But all of this is speculation, with a lot of "ifs"; and, as the late Jerry Claiborne, successful football coach of the University of Kentucky Wildcats during the 1980s, was fond of saying, "That old 'if'n' game doesn't get you anywhere, and it sure doesn't win you any football games!"

A "Hall of Fame" Career – At this writing, Coach Ben has entered into his eighth decade of life but stays active with part-time coaching and teaching of math, and, despite the "legend," he has not coached and taught all of those 80-plus years – it just seems that way! It is interesting to visit with Ben, sitting around his kitchen table to reminisce, as this writer did on January 3, 2003, and give special attention to a wall in his home that is filled with plaques and citations of numerous awards Ben has received over his long and dedicated career of working with young people. Even though Ben H. Pumphrey is most noted as a high school football coach, he has also received many awards for his work in the sports of track and basketball. Ben is equally proud of his accomplishments as a high school teacher of mathematics, proudly proclaiming, "Every kid that I taught learned math, and no one ever failed in my class, nor did any of them ever fail a math course they took afterwards in another class!"

On March 16, 2004, the 17th Annual Dawahares Kentucky High School Athletic Association "Hall of Fame" Induction Celebration/Ceremony was held in the Bluegrass Grand Ballroom of the downtown Lexington Center, and, Coach Ben Henry "Pokey" Pumphrey was indeed one of the14 people who were enshrined into this hall of honor! This is a very great and well-deserved honor for Coach Ben, and there is shared a great deal of pride among the hundreds of players of several high schools who performed for Coach Ben over his three-to-four-decade career; and, especially the members of the Carlisle High School "Coachless Wonders" of 1954, who can say we had the opportunity to play for the "Hall of Fame Coach" in his very first coaching opportunity!

And, so it was, on that Tuesday evening prior to the beginning of the Boys' Sweet Sixteen Basketball Tournament, Jackie Shepherd, Donnie Dampier, and Jock Conley, the representative "Three Musketeers" for that evening, were in attendance at the banquet and induction ceremonies to honor Coach Ben.

In the final analysis, we sort of remained "coachless" during that season of 1954 without the "rudder" of Coach Ben to guide us.

Donnie Dampier "old # 55", playing from the single wing fullback position, led the Musketeers in scoring in both his junior and senior seasons, finishing as the seventh highest scorer in the CKC Conference for the 1954 season. The other senior year starters from the class of 1955 included Larry Cameron at tailback (quarterback), Jackie Shepherd at blocking back, Jock Conley at end, Kenneth Booth and Billy Vanlandingham leading the line, and Jackie Wells at defensive back. The underclassmen members of the "Coachless Wonders" were Billy Gilley, Billy Berry, Charles McCarty, David Feeback, and Ronnie King of the junior class, along with Billy Logan, Billy Straw, Jerry Davis, Roy Gaunce, and Wilbur Conyers, who were sophomores and freshmen. The average team weight of the 1954 "Coachless Wonders" was approximately 161 pounds, with the backs average at 156 (with Donnie the heaviest at 165), and the line weighing in at approximately 165 pounds!

Sports for the Boys of Carlisle High School – "The Ties That Bind"

The young men of Carlisle who were able to play their entire football careers, especially the junior-senior years (when they were physically developed), under the successful tutorage of coach Tebay Rose, were fortunate indeed. Coach Rose was able to "sell" and teach a consistent "Tight-T" system of football that emphasized the fundamentals of blocking and tackling together with good techniques of the run-pass-kick that insured a continuity of offense and defense strategy from one season to the next.

In contrast, those of us of the Class of 1955 who were on the Musketeer football team all four years of high school (Larry Cameron, Kenneth Booth, and Donnie Dampier, with a 4-year won-loss record of 11-16-1), played under four different official head coaches, each with a different system and style: freshmen (1951), Tebay Rose (our only year of participating on a team with a winning record); sophomore (1952), Bill Klier; junior (1953), Carroll Holmes; and senior (1954), John Louie Walters, including Ben "Pokey" Pumphrey for two winning games in 1954 as our "unofficial" coach. Although the three future "Coachless Wonders" of the Class of 1955 played little as freshmen on Coach Tebay Rose's last CHS team, the 5-3 won-lost season of 1951, the fundamentals of blocking, tackling, team play, toughness, and spirit of the game were permanently instilled into the minds and hearts of these "Three Musketeers!"

Mr. Tebay "Coach" Rose was the most successful CHS football coach of this era, compiling a winning 24-17 record in a six-year tenure (1946-1951), recording three straight winning seasons before leaving Carlisle to become head coach at Harrodsburg High School. Coach Rose continued his winning ways with the HHS Pioneers with a school record of 7-2 in the 1954 season, also producing that year's highest scoring team in the Central Kentucky Conference, and the tenth highest in the state. His three-year record compiled up to that point with Harrodsburg High School was 14 wins, 11 losses, and one tie. Then, in 1955, Coach Rose, with an overall won-loss record of 8-1 (6-1 in the CKC), led the Pioneers to the CKC championship under the Dickinson Rating System, with a reported "only 20 good men" on the team, in what was considered as the best "all-time" football team at Harrodsburg High up to that point. Mr. Rose later came back to Carlisle in 1957 to serve as CHS superintendent until Carlisle consolidated with Nicholas County High in 1963. Mr. Tebay "Coach" Rose died in June 1995 at the age of 77.

Bill Klier, a veteran of World War II, came to Carlisle as a coaching successor to Coach Rose, after earning a degree in biological science from Western State Teachers College in Bowling Green (now Western Kentucky University) and playing four years of college football at that school. Coach Bill Klier, with two years of high school coaching experience at Fordsville, Kentucky (Ohio County) and Middlesboro City School in Bell County, was way ahead of his time with innovative formations such as "the split T," "the flying wing," "the winged T," "the W formation," etc. It is surmised that if Coach Kier had remained at Carlisle for 3-4 seasons and given a few more players, he would surely had led the Carlisle Musketeers to some fine football fortunes. He was a good coach who loved his vocation.

As a sophomore, Donnie Dampier was given the dubious assignment by Coach Klier to memorize his considerable "play book" to be his on-the-field resource in the team huddles! Donnie, who entered that season as a 145-pound lineman "substitute" in the first two games, had worked himself into the "starting" end position by the third game, a 21-0 loss at Lancaster, but then, just as his real football career was beginning, missed the latter games while hospitalized with pneumonia. Coach Klier had utilized Donnie, with his knowledge of the entire Book of Formations, as a multi-purpose performer on both offense and defense, and, as Donnie remembers, he played just about every position except quarterback in his shortened season. Meanwhile, Larry Cameron, who had also started the season as a "sub" lineman, was elevated as the starting LH backfield position in the second game, a 7-6 victory over Paris.

After the one year at CHS in the 1952 season, with a 2-4 won-loss record, Coach Klier returned to his Louisville roots, where he had played four years of high school football at Male, to successfully coach in the Jefferson County system for many years. Coach Klier's opening opponent at CHS was a 24-0 loss against Cynthiana, which incidentally was coached by his brother! The Bulldogs, led by the big Fowler brothers – Orville "Jake," at some 195 pounds, and "little brother" Norman "Mutt," at 218 pounds – really socked it to us, with Jake scoring 4 TDs. Mr. Klier, who taught biology, physiology and physical education at the city school, will be remembered by many of the CHS girls as an extremely handsome man!

The "Big Van" – Perhaps our Class of '55's potentially best "raw talent" in terms of size and strength was Billy "Big Van" Vanlandingham, the Musketeer version of "The Big Bopper!" Billy, like most of us, did not receive a lot of early teaching in the basics of sports and was a "late bloomer." However, in the one year he played varsity sports for CHS, in his senior year after transferring back from NCHS, Billy loved both football and basketball. He especially liked playing against the "single wing" run by the Nicholasville Tarantulas our senior year when they pulled their linemen and ran around end where Billy played defensive end. He got "to meet a lot" of the Tarantulas as Billy said, "When they commenced to come at me, there wasn't so much I could do but go with them!"

Nicholasville, ofttimes referred to as the Spiders, was truly one of the top CKC football powers throughout the early to mid-'50s when the Class of '55 played them. By the end of the 1954 season they had amassed a 16-game undefeated streak (13 wins and 3 ties), which began after a 1952 season ending loss of 13-7 to the also powerful Versailles Yellow Jackets. The CKC Champion "Spiders" of 1954, with their second CKC trophy in the 28-year history of the loop, were led by the "touchdown twins" of Bob Stinnett and Bob Rice, who finished first (102 points) and third (80 points) among CKC scorers (Mack Jackson of Danville finished second with 81 points), and 265-pound lineman, Al "Big Boy" Sheely, one of the biggest footballers in the state during that era. Kenneth Booth, Jock Conley, Jackie Shepherd, and Billy Vanlandingham, always competitive and seeking new challenges, used to say they would draw straws for the right to line up opposite Sheely, who outweighed each of them by some 100 pounds or more, so "they could have a chance to whip the big guy"; or, was it the other way around, and the "short straw" had to oppose him? This is the game that Jackie Shepherd remembers the most of the "Coachless Wonders" campaign, for he continuously returned to the huddle, seemingly each time with a newly bloodied nose and/or mouth. Jackie would anguish, "I don't know who, what, or how, but they are sure doing something!" Regardless, they and the rest of the team gave the Spiders a good battle in our senior season contest; for, after a half-time deficit of 0-20, we played them tough on an even 6-6 basis the second half to lose by a respectable score of 6-26 to one of the top high school football teams in the CKC and the state!

In the beginning of the 1958 school year, Nicholasville High School, along with Wilmore High School, was consolidated into the Jessamine County System, ending a continuing football tradition and closing two more quality independent small-city schools in Central Kentucky.

Musketeer Athletes of Note - Little Carlisle High School, despite not having a large population of able-bodied boys to choose from, still had an abundance of very good athletes in the late'40s and through the '50s, during the era of the Class of 1955.

Perhaps the most noted was Emery "Little E" Clark (CHS Class of '48), who went on to be a three-year letterman (1949-1951) at the University of Kentucky, playing on teams that had a three year record of 28-8, who participated in three consecutive major bowls (the Orange, Sugar, and Cotton), and earned 1951 recognition as an All SEC performer on defense under the legendary UK Wildcat football coach Paul "Bear" Bryant. "Little E," who wore #26, was a proud member of the University of Kentucky team in the January 1, 1951 Sugar Bowl that upset the mighty Oklahoma Sooners, under equally legendary Coach Bud Wilkerson, by a score of 13-7, breaking that team's national record 31-game winning streak!

The Snow Storm of 1950 – Many football fans will remember the final 1950 regular season game played in Knoxville against the Tennessee Volunteers, with some from Carlisle and other Kentucky communities having first-hand knowledge, by experiencing the "Great Snow Storm" which engulfed that weekend of November 25, 1950. The late Louis "Stretch" Hemple of Georgetown, Kentucky, who became great friends with Donnie Dampier while they were employed by the Kentucky Department of Education and who reminisced often about UK sports with Donnie, vividly recalled that adventurous weekend with his paraphrased account:

"We left very early on Saturday morning, tickets in hand, from Lexington on the train, in a heavy snow en route to Knoxville. Due to the delays caused by the conditions of the snowstorm, we finally arrived at the game during the second half! The groundskeepers had to shovel "tons" of snow off of the playing field, leaving mounds of snow banks around the playing surface. To top it off, we lost the game 7-0, and then it took me two extra days to get back home!"

"Little E" remembered that the ground, in the 16-degree temperature, was like running on concrete; and the winning Tennessee touchdown pass from tailback Hank Lauricella to wingback Bert Rechichar was caught in a snowdrift! This game was played in the days before I-75, and many football fans from

Kentucky found themselves in near-blizzard conditions, stranded on US-25E and other routes out of Knoxville, as they strived to return home. Numerous residents along these routes, in both Tennessee and Kentucky, to their grateful credit, took in many of the stranded motorists, some perhaps from Carlisle, providing them with warm accommodations, fellowship, and hot food.

Louis Hemple also had another "Carlisle connection" by proudly proclaiming that he sometimes dated our own Carlisle native Nell Wilson during their college days. The dapper Louis, who probably got his nickname of "Stretch" due to his tall and slim physique, together with the beautiful and refined Nell, no doubt made for a striking couple, possibly remindful of Hollywood actors Jimmie Stewart and Ginger Rogers, who were also "a sometimes couple" of the '40s.

"Crashing the Gates" – As "Little E" prepared to play in the final regular season game of his career, to be contested on Stoll Field against the Tennessee "Vols" on November 24, 1951, in Lexington, there was much optimism that the Cats would finally defeat their long-time nemesis. Even though the game was billed as a sell-out, this optimism must have spread to the ticket office and the media with the widespread announcement that a large block of tickets would be available on the morning of game day.

A good friend of Elmer Dampier, of whom memory is not clear, but possibly the father of Charles Shrout, decided to go and buy tickets at the gate and invited Donnie Dampier to accompany them. The threesome arrived early at the ticket office, located in front of Memorial Coliseum (which had just been newly opened for Wildcat basketball in 1950), but the crowd of ticket seekers was already large and growing, so they were positioned some ten layers back from the ticket window. The throngs of ticket-seekers were packed in like sardines, and Donnie remembers that he and Charles were near panic, and nearly suffocating, with their faces jammed into the long hair of a couple of women. With game time approaching and no sign of anyone opening the ticket windows, the restless crowd that had now swelled to several thousand began to chant,

"We want tickets! We want tickets!"

Then, with the close proximity of McLean Stadium sitting just across the street (Euclid Avenue, which was referred to as the Avenue of Champions), cheering was heard, signaling the start of the game! And still no indication of any ticket sales! With that revelation, the huge crowd of "want-to-be" ticket purchasers rushed in mass across the avenue and began to "crash the gates" by climbing over the locked inside chain-link gate and fences. With the first dozen or so that dropped to the inside of the gates, the security personnel escorted them back outside and locked the gate again, but soon the huge numbers of "gate-crashers," both men and women, far outnumbered the ticket-takers and began to enter the stadium in mass, to find room as part of a standing-room-only crowd.

It was during this time, while awaiting their turn to climb over the fence, that Donnie and Charles, both in their early teens, were "exposed" to a first-hand and unobstructed view of the "feminine mystique" as women of all ages, adorned in their dresses and skirts, were scaling the fences, above the heads of the boys, and, as the female fans swung their legs over the fence, had "momentarily misplaced their modesty!"

Finally the overwhelmed security personnel raised their hands in defeat and opened the gates for the remainder to freely pass through!

It is probable that the official capacity attendance for McLean Stadium of over some 35,000, together with the several thousand unofficial standing-room-only crowd of gate crashers, might have combined to represent the largest crowd to watch a college football in Kentucky, at that time in history. However, all that effort of crashing the gate to get in was for naught, because the Wildcats suffered through the worst defeat by a Bryant-coached team while at Kentucky: a 28-0 loss to the single-wing formations of the Volunteers that afternoon.

Conclusion of a Great Career – The 1951 season concluded with the Cotton Bowl of 1952, in which UK beat the Horned Frogs of Texas Christian University by a score of 20-7, and "Little

E" finished his college career with an outstanding performance by catching two touchdown passes from All American Quarterback Vito "The Babe" Parilli, as well as returning an intercepted pass 30 yards, setting up the go-ahead touchdown, and did some great punt returning (Clark was the UK punt return leader for the regular season of 1951, with 17 returned for 128 yards, an average per return of 6.9). For his great final-game performance, "Little E" was named co-MVP of the 1952 Cotton Bowl with the great "Babe" Parilli. "Little E" had performed well in each of the three bowl games he played in, as he also caught a touchdown pass, a 52-yard toss from the "Babe," in the 1950 Orange Bowl, a 13-21 loss to Santa Clara University.

"Not the Size of the Dog" – Dr. Emery O'Donnell Clark, Jr., who earned degrees at the University of Kentucky and Auburn University School of Veterinary Medicine to become a practicing veterinarian for 45 years in his "adopted" small hometown of nearby Flemingsburg, probably got his nickname of "Little E" by showing that he could play the game and that size is not important when you have the heart. Despite his undersized stature (for major college SEC football) of approximately 5-feet-9-inches and 168 pounds, he did have speed, registering the old 100-yard dash in 10 seconds flat. In many ways, "Little E," a product of small-town, small-school Carlisle, could be thought of as a symbol not only of the undersized Musketeers, but also of the thousands of other small high schools across the country whose participants fought against the odds to compete and play the game without fear! In the words that "Little E's" old college coach, Paul "The Bear" Bryant, was fond of saying, "It is not the size of the dog in the fight that counts, but the size of the fight in the dog that makes a winner!"

Emery "Little E" Clark died on May 8, 2004, at the age of 74.

Other Good Carlisle High School Athletes of the '40s/'50s Era

The Class of 1955 had some good athletes who could be counted in this class ... Kenneth "Hot Rod" Booth, Larry "Wimp" Cameron, Joseph "Jock" ("Sleepy") Conley, Donnie "Dashing" Dampier, Jackie "Speedy Gonzales" Shepherd, and Billy "Big Van" Vanlandingham. While most of our senior boys lacked consistent teaching of sports basics, Larry Paul Cameron always seemed to have a good understanding of the basic fundamentals of each sport we participated in, whether it was basketball, football, or baseball. This is probably a major and justifiable reason that Larry was named "Best Athlete of the Class" and went on to become a very successful high school football coach in the football hot bed" of the Sunshine State of Florida.

Some other notables:

The Brothers Shepherd, Jackie (CHS Class of '55) and Jimmy (CHS Class of '52), both good high school athletes, came by their ability through their heritage. Their father, Walter Shepherd, a good athlete in the pre-World War I era, played both baseball and basketball at Eastern Kentucky State Normal School (now EKU), but he really gained a reputation as an excellent professional baseball pitcher who was known to occasionally pitch both games of a double-header for a Philadelphia Phillies farm club in the Triple A Carolina League. Mr. Shepherd would say down through the years that any success he had in sports was not because he was "fast of foot," but because he had "good hands."

In addition to Jimmy "Big Jim" Shepherd, the Class of '52 produced some other fine athletes in Jim "Muscles" Hughes, Brooks "Lujack" Pitman (the left-handed quarterback), and Gary "Moe" Flora, who, it is believed, received honorable mention as an All State football center in the 1951 season.

The Class of '53 had "the dynamic duo" of Kimball Booth (cousin of Kenneth Booth) and Benny Donovan. Kimball, who fit the title of "Mr. Touchdown," was also called "Mr. Tape" by his teammates due to his regular pre-game ritual of "taping" both ankles, knees, and elbows, and who knows what else! Kimball, who wore number 55, served as a "football role model" to Donnie

Dampier, so when Donnie earned the starting position at fullback/linebacker during his junior and senior years he requested the number 55 to strive to maintain the high standard as a two-way back set by Kimball (who, incidentally, was also renowned as an enthusiastic performer on the dance floor).

Kimball Booth, like his younger cousin Kenneth, matured physically in size and strength at an early age and seemed to always be on the Musketeer football teams of the late '40s through the 1952 season. He, along with his classmate and running mate, the late Benny Donovan, appeared in team photos in the 1949-1953 editions of the *Musketeer Memories,* meaning he was on the squad as an eighth grader and perhaps earlier, as he played varsity football for at least 5 years! Kimball, who wore "Number 55" each of those years, was frequently a team scoring leader as he finished second during his sophomore year, with 43 points, to Jimmy "Doot" Hardin, who led with 81 points, on the great "Muskie" team of 1950 that finished with 6 wins and only 1 loss. Then, as a junior on the 1951 team, he was the scoring leader with 50 points on a very successful season with 5 wins and 3 losses, on a fine team that would turn out to be the final edition of a Musketeer team coached by the great Tebay Rose.

In the final game of that 1951 season, in what would be the last Carlisle High School football game mentored by Coach Rose, the Musketeers upset the powerful Versailles Yellow Jackets by a score of 20-19, one of the best teams in the CKC Conference that year. It was in this game that Coach Rose again demonstrated his skill in leading his boys to overcome adversity, as Carlisle's fine lefty quarterback, Brooks Pitman, went "down 'n' out" during the game with a broken collarbone, however, the Musketeers still prevailed, despite the loss of Brooks, a good example of that wise old adage that "from adversity springs accomplishment."

Kimball returned his senior year to again lead the Musketeers in scoring with 11 touchdowns during the 1952 season, to finish as one of the CKC scoring leaders, as he and Benny Donovan served as co-captains on the first Muskie team after six years that were not led at the helm by Coach Rose.

Kimball was a classic example of the high school football star that married the cheerleader, as Kimball married his high school sweetheart, the very pretty Jane Ellen Gillespie, CHS Class of 1953, and a three-year varsity cheerleader for the Musketeers. With the couple choosing to remain in Carlisle as their lifetime home, Kimball has continued to maintain a visual presence in the community with his jovial, homespun personality, whether it be involvement in the local political scene or in exercising his "gift of gab" while sitting on his retiree's "loafing bench" on Broadway.

Billy Clark (Class of '54), the younger brother of Emery "Little E," was a fierce and talented multi-sports competitor in football, basketball, and baseball. Billy, who was not blessed with the blazing speed of his older brother, could probably have gone on to be a very good basketball player at a small to mid-level college if he had focused on that sport. During his junior year Billy demonstrated his basketball proficiency to put points on the board in January of 1953 by scoring 37 of his team's total of 44 in one game against Georgetown Garth, and in another, he scored 33 of the 47-point output the Musketeers were able to score in a game versus Cynthiana! Along with Billy Clark, the Class of '54 contributed the speedy Bobby McFarland and Eugene "Shipwreck" Kelly. At around 220 pounds, Eugene was one of the few football players at CHS to perform at that weight and was recognized as one of the best Musketeer two-way linemen ever produced during our era, a smaller, high school version of a Lou Michaels type.

Some members of the Class of '56 who played alongside the Class of '55 and were fine athletes included Billy Gilley (at 6-5 possibly the tallest performer during this era), David Feeback, and Ronnie King (brother of classmate Barbara), who, between his junior and senior year, "shot up" to gain some two inches and twenty pounds in size. Even though they were fine football performers, this trio was more noted for their basketball abilities. In one basketball game in 1955, Feeback and Gilley combined for 70 points (Feeback with 36 and Gilley with 34)! Gilley went on to earn some college basketball playing time at both Duke University (that Blue Devil) and the University of Tennessee, but, as a Volunteer, he never learned to sing "Rocky Top" very well.

Some of the great athletes of earlier years that are recalled include Charles "Dead Horse" Dixon (CHS Class of '47), Jimmy "Doot" Hardin (Class of '51), Charles "Choo-Choo" Harper (Class of '50), and two from the Class of 1949, Henry "Hoss" Peters and Kenneth "Scout" Campbell. Henry Peters could have been labeled as the original "The Natural" in that he seemed to effortlessly excel in each sport he participated in; however, Henry has never been mistaken for Robert Redford in that role! As a senior, Henry Peters led the Musketeer teams in scoring for both football and basketball, and, the Carlisle High School fullback earned honorable mention honors on the 1948 Louisville Courier-Journal All-State Football Team. In Musketeer basketball annals, Henry apparently also has the dubious record for fouling out in the most consecutive games!

There were a few of the Musketeer athletes who were considered to be very fast during their day – "Little E" Clark, "Doot" Hardin, Benny Donovan, Bobby McFarland, Donnie Dampier, and David Feeback to name a few. As a "green" high school freshman, Donnie Dampier was stimulated and inspired to run when, at a "no pads" football practice on the CHS field, he watched an "unofficial" 100-yard dash between "Little E" and "Doot" that seemed like a blur, with the twosome finishing in a very fast but un-timed dead heat! Donnie was never too sure if the 10-second-flat time credited to him in the Boy Scout 100-yard dash competition was legitimate, but it was somewhat verified when, as a freshman trying out for the UK track team, he was edged out in a practice 100-yard dash race with an upperclassman, who claimed he had previously been officially timed at 9.9 seconds. Donnie, who was still trying to overcome shin splints and strained ankles from senior year high school athletics, and also found it hard to get motivated by an uninspired and seemingly uncommitted track program at UK in that era, decided to not pursue track any further.

Bobby McFarland, a quick, smooth runner, who seemed to

glide over the ground, would probably win the title as the fastest sprinter of all the Musketeers! It was speculated that Bobby, if provided with proper training, conditioning, and equipment, could possibly have been a competitor in the Olympic games. Benny and Bobby were both also noted for their ability to sing a sentimental song in an accomplished manner!

The Central Kentucky Conference

In September of 1954, the CKC opened its 28th annual football season with a loop membership of twenty teams. The seeds were probably planted as early as 1914 that would ultimately lead to the formation of the Central Kentucky Conference when representatives from schools in Mt. Sterling, Winchester, Paris, Georgetown, Frankfort, Somerset, and Lexington organized the Central Kentucky High School Athletic Association (CKHSAA) to establish football eligibility rules, which would apply for their geographic region

The first recorded, organized high school football game contested in Kentucky occurred in November of 1893 and was won by Louisville Male by a score of 14-12 over Louisville Manual. Carlisle High School had been founded during that school year of 1892-93, with a total of 9 students, only two of which were boys, listed in their first group of graduates, the Class of 1893. From that inauguration into high school football, the Louisville Male High School "Purple" Bulldogs went on to be a consistent football power in the annals of Kentucky high school history. Entering into the 2004 football season, both Male and Manual have fielded football teams for some 111 seasons, with Male High recognized by the Kentucky High School Athletic Association as the number one "all-time" winning program, with 744 victories to their credit. There have been a number of long-time legendary high school programs within Kentucky, such as the Ft. Thomas Highlands Blue Birds, listed at number two in victories with 729, followed by number three, Mayfield (702); number four, Paducah Tilghman, at 675; and our own fellow CKC member, the Danville Admirals, with 651 victories, standing at number five all-time.

Obviously, the Carlisle High School Musketeers, in some 45 years of fielding a football team (1919-1963) with somewhere between 300 and 340 games played, fell short of joining the elite high school programs of Kentucky. It would take much time and painstaking effort to historically trace the actual number of games played, as well as the number of victories registered (a quick guess is around 150 wins) – so, this will be left for another time, and perhaps another writer. However, the Carlisle Musketeers inadvertently have the dubious distinction of contributing to the "all-time" winning totals of number-one Male High and number-five Danville. The 1940 Carlisle team played against the state champion Male Bulldogs on the field of Manual Stadium, losing by only 26-0, which was probably the only time Carlisle ever played against a team ranked as number one in the state. The undermanned Musketeers, playing 11 "iron men" (of their squad of 18), which included future coaching "Hall of Fame" recipient Ben Pumphrey at tackle, gave a good account of themselves, training only 6-0 at half-time, before the superior squad number of 72 players on the Male roster was able to take charge! In the early years of Carlisle football, the Musketeers had some winning success versus the great Danville program, but lost more than they won, which added to Danville's all-time victory totals.

By 1914, with most of the larger high schools now playing, and more and more of the smaller schools also playing football, there was becoming a need for uniform eligibility rules. Two years later, in April of 1916, this association ended when the member schools helped to create the Kentucky High School Athletic Association (KHSAA), with statewide jurisdiction.

Carlisle's Foray into Football – It appears that Carlisle High School began its initial varsity football campaign in the fall season of 1919. The Carlisle Graded School opened that fall, on September 4, counting an enrollment of some 400 students, with 76 in the high school grades. The newly organized "Athletic Society of the Carlisle High School" met on Friday, September 5, to elect the following seniors (CHS Class of 1920) as officers: Marion Insko, manager ("captain") of the football team: Henry Harper, treasurer; with Hicel Asbury elected as president of the Society. All three were players on that first-ever CHS football team.

The first-ever recorded Carlisle High School football game, contested on the field of Millersburg Military Institute (MMI) on Saturday, September 27, 1919, resulted in a losing effort of 49-6.

In the midst of the "Society Page" of an October edition of *The Lexington Herald*, a one-liner reported the game, "The prep lads of Bourbon County (MMI) tripped up Carlisle High School last Saturday with a row of touchdowns."

In *The Carlisle Mercury* edition of October 2, 1919, it was reported, "Many of the boys in the game at Millersburg 'had never before witnessed a football game.' … Frank Allen of Sharpsburg (who may be considered as the first CHS football coach), who last year played on the Centre College team, will be providing 'training' for the boys this week. … An 'order' will be made this week for some 'rigging,' which is very essential for the protection, especially the head, of the players."

Neither *The Herald* nor *The Mercury* reported the player who scored Carlisle's lone score in the MMI game, so the player credited with the first football score in history for a Carlisle High School varsity football game goes unrecorded!

Carlisle's first home game of that inaugural season was a 3 o'clock Saturday afternoon contest, which was played on Jackson Field on October 11, 1919, against Clark County High School of Winchester. An assumption is made that "Jackson Field" (also referred to as Jackson's Park) is the same site which was located at the corner of East Union Road and Moorefield Road (E. Main Street), on which the Class of 1955 also played their home football games. (Note: With the spotty references to high school football during that era, at least one account listed that first home game opponent as Winchester High). There was no well-defined "sports section" in the local newspapers of that day and time, so at this writing, Carlisle's first home game results have not been found (they might have been reported in the Classifieds or the Farm Section, etc).

The only other scores located for that start-up season were a 0-0 tie with Paris, played on November 6, 1919, and their only "found" victory of that inaugural season, a 19-0 victory over Cynthiana, on Friday, November 14, 1919, which was a home game played at Jackson's Park. It is possible that in a "start-up" season for a small high school such as Carlisle, only four games may have been played.

The history-making young men, who were the eleven starters on what is believed to be the first football team for Carlisle High School, were Fisher, Otho Gaffin, Henry Harper, Barlow and Smith – the interior linemen; at ends were Feeback and Lloyd Jackson; with the backfield consisting of Hicel Asbury at quarterback; halfbacks were Harry Tilton and Marion Insko, with Bernard Linville lugging the pigskin at fullback.

In that first varsity high school football game ever played in Carlisle, it is likely that only a handful of curious onlookers showed up to view Carlisle's second game in its history, with the status of future football at Carlisle shaky at best.

As so noted, very little attention was given to football in general, especially high school football, so it was likely that very few people in our area knew much about football, its rules, or even the objective of the game. Indeed, during that era, contained in various local newspapers, there were numerous editorial commentaries "railing against the brutal 'game' of football," some calling for its abolishment!

Carlisle High School had given little consideration prior to 1919 with the fielding of a football team, but attitudes toward many activities of life undoubtedly changed as the result of the event on the morning of November 11, 1918, as the Armistice was signed – with fighting stopped on all battle-fronts – thereby, ending WWI!

With a second season of football under its belt, continuous football at Carlisle was underway, to be played uninterrupted each season thereafter, through the 1962 fall season – until the closing of Carlisle High School in 1963.

The Beginning Years of the Central Kentucky Conference – As the popularity of high school football increased, rivalries between nearby towns and counties developed, prompting a competitive need for teams to play in a league format where a champion could be crowned on the playing field. Of the original seven schools that organized the now defunct CKHSAA, all except Mt. Sterling High School then formed the nucleus of the member schools of the fledgling Central Kentucky Conference.

The inaugural football "kick-off" season of the newly formed Central Kentucky Conference occurred in September of 1926, with the following 14 charter member schools contending for the championship (listed in order by their final finish):

Cynthiana, Somerset, Danville, M. M. I., Lexington (Henry Clay), Madison, Stanford, Nicholasville, Georgetown, Frankfort, Maysville, Paris, Lancaster, and Winchester. Conspicuous by their absence were the Mt. Sterling Trojans and the Carlisle Musketeers.

What a humdinger of a kick-off season for the Central Kentucky Conference, as the sports headlines in *The Lexington Herald* proclaimed, in the Sunday edition of November 28, 1926: "Central Kentucky Football – Best In History!" No less than four teams finished the conference slate with undefeated records, but Somerset, Danville, and MMI all played a tie game, leaving only Cynthiana standing alone with a clear record and declared as the champions. And what a season our Carlisle neighbors, the Bulldogs accomplished, finishing with an overall 10-0 record, while leading the league in scoring with 347 points scored, and, at the same time, allowing only 27 opposition points. The Bulldogs' point totals could be considered a bit skewed, as they had registered a 91-0 victory over an overwhelmed Mt. Sterling Trojan team during the season. This 1926 team, which was coached by H.D. Ingles and led by team captain Rees, along with Wilson, a first-team selection on the inaugural All CKC Team, certainly has a legitimate claim as the "greatest Cynthiana football team of all time," but it will be left up to the football historians of Cynthiana to make that determination.

Carlisle's other close-by neighbor, the MMI Cadets, known

as the "Reesmen," had a fantastic 1926-27 school year, first with their great football team (led in the backfield by Torok and on the line by Greathouse, Woodall, and Carlisle native Snelling), which contended for the CKC Championship, but an even greater accomplishment was capped off by winning the State High School Basketball Championship of 1927!

In the second CKC season of 1927, the league membership swelled to 17 teams, with the addition of Versailles, Shelbyville, and now Mt. Sterling, but Carlisle, playing good football and led by Coach Embry, even with the "unbelievable squad number of 35 players" (including 12 lettermen), still had not decided to join the league. It was another 4-team finish of undefeated teams, but the "old tie bugaboo" afflicted Georgetown, Lexington, and again, MMI, as a great Danville team emerged with the unblemished record as unbeaten, untied, and unscored-upon, not only in league play, but for the entire season. A post-season game was proposed between Danville and the Ashland Tomcats (the 1926 State Champions, and ranked with Danville as the top two, statewide in 1927), but the game never materialized. It is evident that then and now, the Danville High School Admirals almost always, year by year, field a very strong football team, which has been a consistent contender for championship honors.

In 1928, the third football season for the CKC, the Carlisle Musketeers finally joined the league, retaining their membership in good standing until the school's closing in 1963. Carlisle's entry into the conference was no doubt influenced and led by their new football coach, Hobart Walker, who had previously coached at two CKC member schools, the Maysville Bulldogs for the 1927 season and at Frankfort High during the inaugural 1926 CKC campaign. The swashbuckling Musketeers, with "muskets blaring and swords slashing," were initiated into the league in fine style, as season-long contenders for the crown, finishing in fifth place with a sparkling 5-1-1 record in league play and leading the league in scoring with 164 points, as well as number of conference victories. The 1928 CKC championship, determined under the Dickinson System, was decided on the playing field in late November, between the top two contenders, the Somerset Briar Jumpers and the Lexington High School Blue Devils.

Carlisle High School, which had played to a 13-13 tie versus the Blue Devils, had the distinction of playing the Lexington school (founded in 1904 as the first public high school in Lexington) in the inaugural year the school officially changed its name to Henry Clay High School. When the school opened for classes on September 28, 1928, having moved into new facilities on East Main Street, the school officially was renamed "Henry Clay" to honor the 19th-century Kentucky statesman, Henry Clay.

Headlines in the sports section of the November 24, 1928 edition of *The Lexington Herald* proclaimed, "Carlisle's Grid Season Best In School's History." It seems fitting here, as part of our history and heritage, to recap the highlights of the Musketeers' first football season as a competing member of the Central Kentucky Conference:

In Coach Hobart Walker's first season at the helm of the "big Green" team, overall the Musketeers won eight games, tied one, and lost one, while scoring 276 points to their opponents 27 (in which their home goal line was not crossed). They opened the season with a 25-0 win at Paris (coached by Blanton Collier, who would become the future coach at U of K during the mid-'50s), followed by a 56-0 score over Bourbon County High. In one of their best games, they tied the Lexington High Blue Devils, 13-13, on Cassidy Field, then, the following week, probably with their heads in the clouds from the preceding contest, were upset 14-0 by Madison. Mt. Sterling journeyed to Carlisle to lose 13-0, then Stanford was the next victim, by a 44-0 score. Cynthiana, an age-old rival, was defeated at Carlisle 32-0, followed by a 36-0 victory over Maysville, Coach Walker's former team. Covington, the team that had played powerful Cincinnati Hughes to a 6-6 standstill, met defeat at the hands of Carlisle by the score of 12-0. Carlisle concluded its "greatest season" up to that time with the final score of 45-0 over the northern Kentucky school of Erlanger, concluding its season with six straight shutouts! Carlisle, which was led by team captain "Little" Clark (Emery, Sr.), with a team weight average of 150 pounds, consistently defeated teams that considerably outweighed them. He would become the father of Emery, Jr. "Little E," and Billy (CHS Class of 1954). It was written of Clark (the papers rarely identified the players with their first name), "Clark, one of the greatest backfield men and field generals in Kentucky high school circles … can pass, punt and run the ball." (Note – he was also known to drop-kick extra points and field goals.)

Some of the other Musketeers on the 1928 team, who, along with Emery Clark (back), were candidates for All CKC honors, included seniors (Class of 1929) Oliver Curry (end), Eugene Kerns (tackle), and Phillip Martin (center), along with other senior performers Joe Snapp and George Scott. Harold Durham (guard) and Spencer Payne (back) of the CHS Class of 1930 were both contenders for All Conference recognition. Other players noted during this era were Crouch, Barnet, and Conley. The Conley was probably Jock's uncle, William Harold "Billy" (CHS Class of 1931), who must have been noted as a "speed merchant," for in the 32-0 victory over Cynthiana in the 1928 season, he recorded two long punt returns, one of 40 yards, the other for 50 yards, registering a touchdown in the process!

Some fine small schools that fielded football teams during the early years of the CKC but were not in the conference, yet played Carlisle and/or other CKC members and now have been closed due to consolidation and "lost in antiquity," include Stanton Academy (Powell County), Lawrenceburg and Kavanaugh in Anderson County, Falmouth (Pendleton County), Flemingsburg, and the Woodford County schools of Midway, along with the Massie School For Boys, with an enrollment of around 60 boys, located on Versailles Road some 10 miles from Lexington and (coached by A.B. "Happy" Chandler, who no one at the time could foresee would, in only seven years, be elected governor of Kentucky).

There were numerous others, including at least two Henry

County schools, Eminence and New Castle (the county seat). Henry County, which was carved out of Shelby County by the Kentucky Legislature in 1798, as the 31st Kentucky county, and named for the statesman Patrick Henry, has, as a resident, at least one former Carlisle native, Jim Hughes (CHS Class of 1952), who taught agriculture within the Henry County School Systems for many years.

The Central Kentucky Conference of the '40s and '50s – It is unusual in "basketball mad" Kentucky that the game of football, emerging from the late '20s and into the '50s, was the "sport of emphasis" for CHS and most of the other high schools in the old Central Kentucky Conference. No doubt a major reason for this was that at CHS, and probably most of the other smaller CKC schools, the football coach was the "main man" who also coached the other sports offered, primarily basketball, baseball, and track.

Carlisle was the smallest school in this conference that was primarily comprised of small-town "independent" school systems. Two exceptions to this composition were the Henry Clay Blue Devils, a big-city school in Lexington, and the Anderson (County System) Bearcats. Like CHS, many of these excellent "independent small-city" schools were lost to consolidation in the late '50s and the '60s, with a few lasting into the '70s. This included member schools that Carlisle rarely, if ever, scheduled, such as the Irvine Golden Eagles, Madison-Model Purples, Mt. Sterling Trojans, Shelbyville Red Devils, and the Winchester Shawnees. It is also assumed that Lawrenceburg Independent was a CKC member prior to consolidation, along with Kavanaugh Academy, to form Anderson County High School, in 1949.

Some of the CKC schools we competed with on a regular schedule (consolidation date) were: Paris Greyhounds, Cynthiana Bull Dogs (1962), Georgetown Garth Buffalos (1958), Stanford Wildcats, Lancaster Green Devils, Nicholasville Tarantulas, Versailles Yellow Jackets, and MMI Cadets.

Of the regular rivals, only Paris High and MMI, renamed for a short time as Millersburg Military Academy (MMA), have retained their existence and identity. The remaining active original

CKC schools still in existence, along with Henry Clay and Anderson County, include the Danville Admirals, Frankfort Panthers, Harrodsburg Pioneers, and the Somerset Briar Jumpers.

The Beauty of Basketball —A "Dream" of a Game for Kentucky

"If winning does not count as important, why do they keep score then?"
(Adolph Frederick Rupp,
University of Kentucky Basketball Coach)

Ever since that December of 1891, when Dr. James Naismith invented his new "team" game – using a soccer ball and two peach baskets – and played the first ever "basketball game," instituting his "Original 13 Rules," at the YMCA in Springfield, Massachusetts – most every school boy from that time on throughout the '50s and beyond and, in the last three decades, most every school girl as well, has had a dream of playing in the Kentucky State Basketball Tournament.

Many of the boys of Carlisle and Nicholas County, including the boys of the Class of 1955, had a basketball goal, ofttimes without a net, affixed to the side of a barn, garage, store, post, and even sometimes on the side of a tree – where they frequently honed their game in a version of solitaire one-on-one! If they didn't have a goal of their own, they knew where to quickly find one at a nearby location. If memory serves, Jackie Shepherd had a goal on the side of their dairy barn, Jackie Wells on a yard post, Larry Cameron on the side of their store, Bobby Anderson on their garage front, etc. Donnie Dampier initially had a goal, without a net, mounted on the small barn sitting on the back of their Upper Jackstown lot, where he occasionally was bombarded by falling walnuts from the nearby tree! This is now the site where Donnie constructed his "pride 'n' joy" outdoor brick barbeque grill, which still stands. Once the old barn was torn down, Donnie moved his prized possession basketball goal to the front of the garage. In most cases, the goals were above an uneven dirt "court," ofttimes with rocks or gravel, which meant we were able to learn to shoot the basket before we could develop the dribble!

Bouncing Basketballs of the Central Kentucky Conference

In that same year of the creation of the KHSAA, in 1916, the first Kentucky State High School Basketball Tournament, an invitational event for eight teams, was held in Danville, won by Henderson (still, one of only three state champions to finish undefeated) over Somerset. In 1918, the recently formed KHSAA took over the management of the State Basketball Tournament, with the present-day 16 regional system not instituted until 1932. It is uncertain as to when, and by whom, the popular label "The Sweet Sixteen" originated; however, that title was awarded its official and legal trademark in 1979.

The State High School Basketball Tournament was well-represented down through the years by teams forming the old Central Kentucky Conference, with 16 member schools making over100 trips since 1918 (a few years before the founding of the CKC). Henry Clay (Lexington High School until the 1941 tournament) was the most successful CKC member by winning six state championships and one runner-up finish. Millersburg Military Institute (MMA), in 3 trips from 1927-1952, won the state title in 1927 under the coaching of Ward Rees (the same school year the CKC was formed). Somerset (1918 and 1919), Frankfort (1922), Winchester (1925), and Anderson County (1971) all advanced to a runner-up finish.

Eight other of the CKC small schools made it into the State Tournament Record Book before they were closed by consolidation: Cynthiana, Georgetown, Irvine, Lawrenceburg, Madison-Model, Mount Sterling, Shelbyville, and Winchester.

Carlisle was joined by four other CKC schools, now closed by consolidation, that never had the privilege of playing in the State Tournament: Lancaster, Nicholasville, Stanford, and Versailles. Even though the Musketeers never played in "the Sweet Sixteen," a resident of Carlisle by the name of Taylor Snelling did play on the 1927 MMI State Championship team!

Some of the other non-CKC basketball opponents of Carlisle during the Class of '55 high school years, not mentioned before, included Owingsville, the Orangeburg Tigers, St. Agatha of Winchester, and three schools from Mason County, the Mayslick Cardinals, Minerva, and St. Patricks of Maysville. The Maroons of the little school of Minerva had an interesting history in its only two appearances in the Kentucky State Basketball Tournament. In 1927 they advanced to the semifinals, where they lost to Millersburg Military Institute, the state champions of that year. Then, in 1928, Minerva returned, only to lose to the legendary "bare-foot boys" of Carr Creek in the quarterfinals by a score of 21-11.

"The Legendary Game" – The Carr Creek Indians, a small school of only 41 students, 18 of whom were boys, then advanced to the 1928 championship game where they lost to the Ashland Paul Blazer Tomcats by a score of 13 to 11 in four overtimes, in "the most famous basketball game in Kentucky prep history." In that 1920s early era of high school basketball a National High School Basketball tournament was held on the University of Chicago campus. In a rather unprecedented move, probably due to the "Carr Creek Craze," both the 1928 state champion and the runner-up teams from Kentucky were invited to the national tournament, ultimately won by Ashland. However, Carr Creek (the "Wonder Five"), the winner of its first three games, received more media publicity than any of the other 39 participating teams, to establish a "small-town tradition" in Kentucky high school basketball lore that is still revered today. Twenty-eight years later, in the era of the CHS Class of '55, Carr Creek finally won the 1956 State Basketball Championship, then, 22 years later, in 1974, the legendary Carr Creek High School of Knott County went the way of many small schools when its doors were closed, the victim of consolidation.

The "Salvation" of Small School Successes – In 1927, when the little Bourbon County school of Millersburg Military Institute (M.M.I.) beat the equally small school of London (the Tigers?) from

Laurel County in southeastern Kentucky, it was a very significant accomplishment, much more so than basketball history has previously credited the event with. In the first nine years of the boys State Basketball Tournament, it was the exclusive domain of schools from the state's two largest cities, with the Lexington School (Henry Clay) winning the championship five times, and the other four state titles divided between Louisville duPont Manual (three times) and Louisville St. Xavier. If this dominance of the big-city schools from Lexington and Louisville had continued, it is very unlikely that the statewide interest would ever have developed, and the eventual unparalleled popularity of what is now accurately referred as "the Greatest Show In Hoops" would not have prevailed, except that in that "breakout" year of 1927, MMI and London broke the mold and opened the door for the countless "Cinderella success stories" of small schools from across the Commonwealth.

Beginning the next year with little Carr Creek playing Ashland in that "epic" 1928 game, numerous small-town, small schools emerged from diverse localities across the state to either win or play in the championship game; teams that are no longer with us due to consolidation, such as Heath High School (1929 Champion) from McCracken County; Corinth High School, the Braves of Grant County (twice in the title game, 1929 & winning it all in1930); Kavanaugh Academy (a private school in Lawrenceburg founded by Ms. Rhonda Kavanaugh); Tolu High School of Crittenden County; Horse Cave High School, hailing from Hart County; Nebo High School, the "Aces" of Hopkins County; and the following five consecutive state champions, from 1937-1941: Midway, the Blue Jays of Woodford County; Sharpe High School, the "Sharpe Shooters" of Marshall County; Brooksville High School's "Polar Bears" of Bracken County; Hazel Green High School, the Frogs from Laurel County; and Inez, the Indians of Martin County – all no longer in existence, and without another chance to win it all.

There have been countless other small schools, some of which still exist and retain their identity, which have added to the continual "David and Goliath" appeal of the boys' (and now the girls') state basketball tournament.

The Corinth High School Braves of 1930 had a star player named Henry Odor, who could have been a relative of David Odor, who was a brief member of the Carlisle High School Class of 1955 during the fourth and fifth grades. Corinth's Henry Odor was very instrumental in the Braves' victory over Kanavanugh by hitting two quick field goals late in the game to tie the score, leading to their two-point victory for the 1930 championship. This is speculation, but with the combination of Henry's age (he would have been in his mid-twenties in 1937, when David was born), the similar first name to Hubert, David's dad, and sharing the uncommon last name of Odor, Henry was possibly David's uncle.

As a nine- and ten-year-old during his Carlisle days, David Odor was remembered as a big blond kid (bigger than most of the other boys in the class), robust, rather "rough 'n' rowdy," and somewhat of a daredevil. David always wore high-top work shoes that we called "clod hoppers," and his featured daredevil stunt was to climb to the top rail of the horizontal exercise bars in the back playground, hand-walk about halfway across, then drop the several feet to the ground, a feat most of the high school boys did not try! If David had stayed with us and continued to develop physically, he would have made a great contribution to our Musketeers football teams in high school, but, alas, his father, Hubert, who worked for the Soil Conservation Service, was transferred to another locality, probably to Grant County, and we never saw David again!

The Kentucky State Basketball Tournament of the 1950s

In the 1950s, basketball had joined football with its stronghold on the boys and girls of the Class of 1955, with that dream of playing in the Kentucky "Sweet Sixteen." Unfortunately, the Carlisle Musketeers never realized that dream; however, many other small schools shared the basketball glory of "a good story."

"When Cuba Conquered Kentucky" – The "story" of the

rise to fame of the obscure, and isolated tiny school of only 142 students from far western Kentucky began with a "Story" by the first name of Jack, the Cubs coach, whose new brand of basketball – inspired by the internationally famed "Harlem Globetrotters" – enamored and inspired all who watched the team play. It was probably Larry Cameron who introduced the basketball Musketeers to the behind-the-back dribble, after attending the State Tournament and watching the great Howard "Howie" Crittenden of Cuba High School perform his fan pleasing "art of dribbling" magic on the court. Along with Howie, the Cubs' "Court Magician," with his adept imitation of Marcus Haynes, the "real" Globetrotters' spectacular ball handler, the team also featured the talented 6-7 cut-up Charles "Doddles" Floyd, their version of the Trotters' "Goose" Tatum, leading an all-white team from Graves County in the "Purchase Area" of far western Kentucky, to be a fan favorite during their pre-game workouts, by performing the all-black Harlem Globetrotters routines to the music of *Sweet Georgia Brown*!

In the first Kentucky State Tournament Championship Game played in Memorial Coliseum in Lexington, the green-and-gold clad Cubs were the 1951 State Tournament runner-up, losing 69-44 to the Clark County Cardinals (a great team with 3-time All-State Linville Puckett and Lewis Snowden), but then came back, with determination, to conquer all foes and claim the 1952 State Basketball Championship over the Louisville Manual Crimsons (led by future UK Wildcat, Phil "Cookie" Grawemeyer). In this classic match-up of the small-town "country" school versus the large "big-city" school, with Cuba prevailing by 58-52 over Manual, the story of the rise of the Cuba Cubs could easily have been substituted, in place of the inspiring story of the little Indiana school of Milan featured in the very popular movie "Hoosiers," but, if so, the catchy title would naturally have required changing, possibly to the title of the 1999 book (adeptly written by Marianne Walker), *When Cuba Conquered Kentucky*!

Other "Sweet Sixteen" champions during the Class of 1955 era of the '50s were:

1950, Lexington Lafayette Generals, 55-51 over Clark County, in the last State Tournament game played in the Louisville Armory); 1953, Lexington Lafayette again (led by All-State Vernon Hatton) over the Paducah Tilghman Tornados (with Dwain McIntosh); the 84-53 winning score, with its margin of 31 points, was the only blowout in a championship game of the '50s! 1954, Inez (led by lefty Billy Ray Cassady), 63-55 over Newport Public; 1955, Hazard Bulldogs (led by All-State Johnny Cox) over Adair County... (Ralph Shearer, who became a Carlisle resident, was a star on that Adair team and was twice named to the "All-Tournament" team, still has the championship game record for most free throws, with 15, in Adair County's 74-66 losing effort to Hazard); 1956, it was Carr Creek with 72 over Henderson's 68.

The "King" of Kentucky — Carr Creek, en route to its 1956 championship, had beaten the Wayland Wasps, in the semifinals on a 30-footer in the final three seconds, in a 68-67 nail biter, by holding the great and legendary "King" Kelly Coleman to "only" 28 points, but the big man went on to set Sweet Sixteen records for scoring in one game (68) and total points in one 4-game tournament (185), per game scoring average (46.3) – all without the benefit of the 3-point shot, nor was there a shot clock to prevent opponents from holding the ball – along with most rebounds in one game (28), marks that are still intact into the 21st century!

The "King" set his single game Kentucky State Tournament scoring record in the third-place game, a stirring 122-89 victory over Bell County. The "third-place" game was a regular part of the State Tournament for 24 years, from 1938, with Louisville St. Xavier besting Frenchburg 47-17, until 1961, when Wheelwright defeated Breathitt County 72-56, and brought down the final curtain to the third-place designation.

Donnie Dampier, in his second semester as a UK freshman and who watched King Kelly play in all four games, observed that he "had never seen a player who could take over a game as did Kelly Coleman. ... He, a big guard listed at 6-3 and 212 pounds, was truly 'a man among boys' on the high school hardwood! It is interesting to note that the "King" Kelly Coleman was figuratively crowned with his "coronation" in 1956, the same year as that other well-known "King," Elvis!

"Memorable" Memorial Coliseum – This new UK Field House, located as part of the UK campus – so named in lasting memory of and as a "Memorial of Kentuckians Killed in World War II" – was completed and open for basketball at the beginning of the 1950-51 UK basketball season. The names of each of those individuals who lost their lives in service to their country during World War II are listed on the walls of the entry ramps upon entering Memorial Coliseum. The official dedication ceremony occurred during the second game, played on December 9, 1950, with a UK 70-52 victory over the Purdue Boilermakers.

In the opening round of the March 1951 State Basketball Tournament – the first hosted at Memorial Coliseum – three teams were represented from the Central Kentucky Conference: Paris, representing our home 10th Region, lost a hard-fought 49-42 contest to eventual State Champion Clark County of the 16th Region; Shelbyville (8th Region) lost 54-47 to Auburn (5th Region); while Danville, representing the 12th Region, was successful against Caverna, of Region 6, by the score of 47-42; then, the Admirals lost out in the quarterfinals, with the tally of 71-44, to Whitesburg of Region 14.

Donnie Dampier had the opportunity to attend the State Tournament to view all games for four consecutive years, from 1953-56 – with all games of that period played in Memorial Coliseum on the UK campus – and, still considers the Sweet Sixteen in the '50s as being in its "heyday." It was in the 1953 tournament that he saw a "dunk shot" for the first time, as performed by the 6-3 Ray Mills of the Clay County Tigers in their 81-72 opening round victory over the Georgetown Buffalos. Billy Mitchell of Georgetown, who the Carlisle Musketeers had competed against in the CKC, was named to the All Tournament Team. There is no awareness of any of the Carlisle boys successfully completing a "dunk" during that era, although, the 5-foot-7-inch tall Bobby

McFarland was observed jumping high enough to place a dime on the back of the rim! Jock Conley and some of the other boys, along with some of our girls, joined Donnie in regular attendance beginning with the 1954 tourney. At the time, neither Donnie nor Jock (who, as a twosome, also could not "dunk") realized the impact some of the State Tourney "stars" would have on their lives later on.

A "Shocking UK Loss!" — It was a rare occasion when any of us got to attend a UK home basketball game, so it was an exciting time when Donnie somehow, during the 1954-55 season, had obtained a ticket to sit in the balcony of Memorial Coliseum. But, on that night of January 8, 1955, the excitement turned to disbelief and shock, as Donnie watched the heavily favored Wildcats lose to the Georgia Tech Yellow Jackets (also, called the Engineers) by a score of 59-58, ending the still-standing national record of 129 consecutive home court victories. This loss also broke UK's longest overall winning streak of 32 games (from December 5, 1953 to January 8, 1955), which still stands at this writing! Then, later in the season, the "Rambling Wreck" added salt to the wound by again beating the Cats in the return SEC Conference match in Atlanta!

Until that loss in January of 1955, the Kentucky Wildcats had not lost a home game since January of 1943, the year the Class of '55 entered first grade, a period of 12 years, corresponding with the era of the Class of '55!

During the four years that Jock Conley and Donnie Dampier attended the University of Kentucky, they saw the basketball Wildcats – on their home floor – victorious in 53 games, with only 5 losses (91%), making Memorial Coliseum truly memorable!

"First Dates" – State Tournament stars Vernon Hatton and Johnny Cox both became All American performers at the University of Kentucky and were members of UK's fourth NCAA Championship team that was labeled by Coach Adolph Rupp as "The Fiddling Five." This was very significant to Donnie Dampier as it was at that NCAA Championship game (held in Freedom Hall in Louisville on the night of March 22, 1958, and won by UK over Seattle by a score of 84-72) that Donnie and his future wife, Patricia

Disney, had their very first date!

Donnie and Pat, as well as Jock and Joanie, were part of a Final Four championship game crowd of 18,803, which at that time was the "record attendance" in the 20 years of NCAA Tournament championships! In a nightlong celebration of the victory, Donnie and Pat double-dated with Jock Conley and his future wife to-be, Joanie Weissinger, who also happened to be one of the UK varsity cheerleaders! On numerous occasions each and every year thereafter, Jock and Joanie and Donnie and Pat continued to "double-date" to celebrate their lasting friendship!

In addition to this occasion being the "first date" for Donnie and Pat, the semi-final game, which they attended the previous night, was also the "first date" for the Kentucky Wildcats to play in Freedom Hall. It was won 61-60 by the Wildcats on a last-second shot by Vernon "Mr. Clutch" Hatton over a very fine Temple University team led by the great All-American Guy Rogers.

Enter the Nicholas County Blue Jackets – This new facility of Freedom Hall in Louisville had opened the doors of its basketball arena the preceding March by hosting, for the first time, the 1957 Boys' State Basketball Tournament. This event coincided with the year and site of the only participation, to date, by the Nicholas County Blue Jackets boys' team, coached by Charles Finnell and led by the "Mutt 'n' Jeff" duo of Donnie Hillock, standing approximately 5-foot-7, and the 6-foot-9 Ned Jennings. It must have been an overwhelming and intimidating experience for our small-town Carlisle "country boys" to play in the huge expanses and crowds of Freedom Hall, for, after all, it had surpassed Lexington's Memorial Coliseum as the largest basketball facility in Kentucky and the South, as well as one of the largest in the nation at that time. Nicholas County High School, representing the 10th Region and led by the "inside-outside" combo of "Big Ned" Jennings and ball handler Donnie Hillock, nevertheless gave a very good account of themselves, losing in the final 8 seconds in the first round contest to Dixie Heights High School, out of the 9th Region, by a score of 58-55!

Dixie Heights then lost out to Lexington Lafayette, the eventual champion, which was coached by Ralph Carlisle, so, to stretch "name association" a bit, it could be said that both Nicholas County and "Carlisle" participated in the 1957 State Tournament!

Lexington Lafayette, which was led by All State Bill Lickert with their third state title of the '50s, won that inaugural Freedom Hall "Sweet Sixteen," by besting Louisville Eastern by the score of 55-52. Big Ned Jennings was honored along side of MVP Bill Lickert as a selection on the 1957 "All-State Tournament Team"!

Bobby Anderson, who was a good athlete with a preference toward basketball, had transferred, at the end of his sophomore year (1952-53), from the Class of 1955 of CHS to Nicholas County High School, which had the better basketball program. Unfortunately, Bobby, who had graduated from NCHS in 1955, missed out by two years on his dream of playing in the Boys' State Basketball Tournament. Perhaps Bobby, with his competitive spirit, had played a part in paving the way for "Big Ned" and Donnie Hillock and their NCHS teammates to follow!

IX

"Graduation's Almost Here, My Love ... Teach Me Tonight"

"Tonight We Launch ... Where Shall We Anchor?"

Senior Year At Carlisle High School – 1954-55

Twenty-two students were present to kick off senior year of 1954-55, exactly one-half the number that started first grade of 1943-44. We were quite happy to greet the return of Billy Vanlandingham to the class for senior year, after his one-year sojourn as a Nicholas County Blue Jacket. Jackie Shepherd was warmly welcomed back to be a graduate from CHS after spending one year in residence at Maysville High and two years commuting to Millersburg Military Institute (MMI).

Two of our girls who began first grade with us and were poised on the portals to walk down the graduation aisles as part of the Class of 1955 – Mary Agnes Mann and Nell Shrout – instead "Got Married In A Fever" and never walked that aisle with us, as Nell "sailed off" as a Navy wife, while Mary Agnes eventually earned her equivalent high school diploma.

Three students of the CHS Class of 1955 withdrew in January of 1955, in the middle of senior year, before completing their journey to graduation; Billy Hollar, Nell Shrout Arnold, and Wanda Mattox Moreland.

Both Nell and Wanda had gotten married between their junior and senior year. In a rather uncommon event, the Shrout sisters, Nell and her older sister, Joy, took their marriage vows together in a double wedding ceremony. According to their mother, Mrs. Dorothy Shrout, the double ring event took place on May 14, 1954 in Jeffersonville, Indiana. Nell married Gordon W. Arnold, and Joy married John Scott Meeks. Both of these young men hailed from close-by Cynthiana, and both were soon to be Navy men in the process of completing their basic training at Bainbridge, Maryland. Initially, Nell had indicated that she would stay in Carlisle and complete her schooling with the Class of '55, but shortly after her new husband received his permanent Naval station assignment, Nell felt her greatest obligation, and desire, was naturally to be at his side. Their younger sister, Judy, poised to enter her sophomore year at CHS, probably felt she had been left behind at that time!

Billy Hollar, the "old man" of the class, had turned nineteen before the beginning of the class year and probably figured he had been around long enough; so, he left to seek his way in the world. Billy Hollar had a most unusual nickname, "Hootchy Pucker," the origin of which has been lost to history. None of the girls ever claimed that he had any special "pucker prowess," so perhaps a "self-proclaimed" moniker? Billy, who was one of the few to drive to school, had a favorite antic on slick snowy days – that was to quickly approach the parking spots, hit the brakes hard on the icy surface, and do a "360 spin" into a parking spot (which he accomplished very well, if there were several open spots)! If "car spinning" had been designated as an Olympic event, Billy would have, no doubt, scored a perfect "10" on several occasions!

An interesting and unique feature of the interior of Billy's car were the spinning knobs mounted on the steering wheel, of with Billy usually had two. The spinning knobs, which were held in lieu of the steering wheel itself, were thought to be an aid for turning into tight parking spots, but were quite popular in the '50s as a decorative status symbol, more so than a functional tool. They came in a variety of colors, color combinations, and pictures, of which some were considered risqué for the times, such as the one Billy Hollar had of a girl in a bathing suit (no bikinis then) straddling a barrel!

Since there was "no smoking" on school grounds, Billy's car, along with others' became "smoking sanctuaries" during recess and lunch breaks! Donnie Dampier, who did not smoke, always tried to restrict smoking in his cars (then and now)!

It is too bad that Billy "Hootchy Pucker" Hollar, being so close to graduating, did not stick around to be one of the grads of the CHS Class of 1955. It is thought that Billy Hollar, a resident in the small farming community of Hillsboro in Fleming County, died in January of 2005.

Senior Year "Send-Off"

The final months of the senior year for the Class of 1955 were filled with numerous class activities and school events. First and foremost, we were scurrying around academically to make sure we had completed all the required credits to qualify for graduation in the spring of 1955! The junior and senior classes worked hard together over the winter and that spring to earn enough money to take us on our planned trip to Florida. A fun-filled, fund-raising event was a Community Talent Show, held on April 8 at the CHS auditorium. One of the contestants on the program featured the father-son combo of Walter and Jackie Shepherd as part of a four-man barbershop quartet that also included Harvey Gaunce and R.L. Talbert! The Lyric Theater designated two "Senior Trip Nights." One movie (*The Little Kidnappers*) was for Carlisle High School, and the second for Nicholas County High, whereby they generously donated half the proceeds from the movies shown on those nights for the school trips!

The junior-senior trip was indeed a highlight of that spring. Thirty-seven students enjoyed a trip of a week's duration that took us through the Smoky Mountain National Park, then on a tour of St. Augustine, Florida en route to our main destination of Daytona Beach! For some of us, this was a first trip out of Kentucky, and for most, the first trip to the ocean beach! The trip concluded with a stopover in Gatlinburg, Tennessee before returning to Carlisle.

The Final Music Festival – The seniors of the Class of 1955 had gotten their voices in fine tune the weekend of Friday, April 1, 1955, as they performed at the Regional Music Festival on the campus of Morehead State College, with performances that would be reminiscent of *The Sound of Music.* In what would be considered as a rather unprecedented occurrence, it is believed that the entire 19 members of the senior class performed in choir at the festival, receiving an Excellent Rating for their rendition of "Toyland"!

The mixed ensemble was awarded a Superior for their version of *Bird Song at Eventide* – in the group which consisted of seniors Carole McClain, Margie Farris, Mary Cameron, Sue Feeback, Sylva Owens, Jackie Shepherd, Larry Cameron, Donnie Dampier, Jock Conley, and Gordon Moreland. The seniors received some worthy assistance from underclassmen Wanda Lawrence, Mary C. Allison, Sid Crouch, Butch Saunders, and Ted Insko.

The Mixed Quartet, which was composed of Mary C. Allison, Sylva Joy Owens, Gordon Moreland, and Jack Shepherd, were rated Superior for *Come Unto Me*, and Sylva Joy Owens received a Superior rating for her solo of *Down in the Forest.*

The Intramural Round-Robin Basketball Tournament – This was an exciting, fun-filled school event, probably unique to the

Carlisle City School, which was contested between teams representing the top six grades (naturally for the times, all boys). The boys in the lower grades, obviously, could not match up physically to the older boys, so their team-games were fortified with faculty and older boys not scheduled to play that afternoon. Faculty members, and older boys knowledgeable of the rules, served as coaches and officials. The games were played over an approximate three-week time frame, in which each grade played every other grade at least once, in the "round-robin," then, the leaders in a double-elimination format, leading to the championship. Every class, from the first-graders, who were marched in, through the seniors, ambling their way in, were excused from regular classes to attend the late-afternoon sessions – with the occasional parent, alumnus or townsperson popping in to watch the games – providing for a noisy, packed CHS school gymnasium! Since varsity basketball teams of the Carlisle Musketeers were usually eliminated during district play and never advanced out of the regional, the Carlisle Round-Robin Intramurals served as our version of the State Basketball Tournament.

The seniors of the Class of 1955 (Cameron, Conley, Dampier, Wells, and Vanlandingham), "a pretty fair team of Musketeers" who were ably coached by senior classmates Kenneth Booth and Gordon Moreland, were undefeated throughout, and played the championship game against the "faculty" (Band Director Jack Valz, Coach Louie Walters, Shop Instructor Charlie Wilson, Custodian Junior Fuller, and Charles McCarty), with the seniors winning a "barn-burner" by the score of 23-21!

Commencement Week 1955 exercises especially filled the week with activities. First, on Sunday, May 22, the local Ministerial Association held united church services in honor of our graduates. Then, on Tuesday evening of May 24, the entire class participated in producing our senior class play, a three-act comedy called *Willie's Weekend.* Donnie Joe Dampier played Willie, with Pat May in the lead female role as Eva Woods, student nurse. On stage, Pat and Donnie danced to the beat of *Dance With Me Henry,* a pop tune of the day. And, Pat and Donnie even shared a short kiss!

Wednesday night followed with a presentation of the Senior Class Night program, entitled "Hats Off," a parody on an election campaign which was possibly inspired by the new Kentucky state law that would now allow us to vote upon reaching our 18th birthday, rather than at age 21. Donnie Dampier, the senior class president, presided as master of ceremonies in the roll of Hunky Dory. In digging through a box of some old CHS school papers which had been saved by Donnie's mother, the original Hunky Dory script was found, penned in Donnie's handwriting in ballpoint pen on two sheets of yellowed 2-ring note paper. This discovery of an "ancient" manuscript is not likely to gain the historical acclaim as did the finding of the Dead Sea Scrolls, nor does memory serve to identify if Donnie was the composer of the lines, or more likely, a combination of composers. So, on that night, of the Class of 1955, Donnie walked out on stage in his costume of top hat, cutaway tailcoat, striped trousers, carrying a slender walking stick, and delivered these lines accompanied by the entire class responding with applause and cheers, as if during a political campaign rally, or acceptance speech.

To top off the Class Night evening, the Senior Parents Club of Carlisle High School entertained with a progressive dinner served in courses at the homes of Elmer and Ann Dampier, Mr. and Mrs. Allie Clinkenbeard, and Mr. and Mrs. Walter Shepherd.

The staff of *The Musketeer Review*, the Carlisle High School Newsletter, worked diligently right up to graduation. The following nine members of the Class of 1955 served on *The Review*, led by Wanda Reid as editor and Margie Farris as assistant editor, with Pat May, Anna Mary Clinkenbeard, Carole McLean, Mary Phyllis Smith, Martha Sue Feeback, Nell Arnold, and Sylva Owens on the staff.

Incidentally, the name of the school newspaper as *The Musketeer Review* was preceded many years previous, at least through 1918, as *The Flashlight*, with the motto, "If we please you, tell others – If we don't please you, tell us!" *The Flashlight* made its salutatory entry with the first issue hitting the press on Friday, December 7, 1917, which was apparently the first attempt for Carlisle High

Willie's Weekend

The Carlisle High School "Class of 1955" senior class play. "Starring, in center stage": Pat May, as student nurse, Eva Wood, Willie's love interest, and Donnie Dampier, in the lead role as Willie Winkle.

School to publish a school paper. In deciding upon a name for the paper, a "Name the School Paper" contest was held in which the students of both the high school and grade school were allowed to take part, with the winning entry submitted by Elizabeth Cole. This bit of information was found in an old scrapbook of Mary Phyllis Smith, with four issues (December 7, 1917, April 5, 1918, May 3 and 24, 1918), which had been left to her by her father, Sammy Smith. At this writing, it is not known if *The Flashlight* was directly changed to *The Musketeer Review,* or if there were other titles in between.

Commencement exercises were held for the 63rd graduating class of Carlisle High School on Thursday evening, May 26, 1955, in the Carlisle High School Auditorium. The following graduating seniors were awarded diplomas to become the CHS Class of 1955:

Graduation Is Here, My Love
The Class of 1955, Carlisle High School

Presenting, (opposite page) from the top, left to right:
Row One: Norma Ann Harris, Jackie Wells, Margie Farris, Jock Conley, and Barbara King. Row Two: Jack Shepherd, Anna Mary Clinkenbeard, Wanda Reid, Sylva Owens, Carole Donovan, and Donnie Dampier. Row Three: Mary P. Cameron, Larry Cameron, Robert E. Davis, Superintendent, Nancy E. Talbert, Principal, Gordon Moreland, and Pat May. Row Four: Kenneth Booth, Martha Sue Feeback, Carole W. McLean, and William Vanlandlingham.

Norma Ann Harris
Jackie Wells
Margie Farris
Jack Conley
Barbara King
Jack Shepherd
Anne Mary Clinkenbeard
Wanda Reid
Sylva Owens
Carole Donovan
Donnie Dampier
Mary P. Cameron
Larry Cameron
Robert E. Davis
Supt.
Nancy E. Talbert
Principal
Gordon Moreland
Pat May
CLASS Carlisle High School 1955
CARLISLE, KY.
Kenneth Booth
Martha Sue Feebach
Carole W. McLean
William Vanlandingham
Young & Carl

Class Motto – "Tonight We Launch – Where Shall We Anchor?"
Class Flower – White Rose
Class Colors – Green and White

We did not realize the significance at the time, but, in retrospect, our class motto was a poignant statement of the mixed emotions most of us experienced on commencement night. Graduation – that time we had all worked toward, had hoped for, and, at times, thought would never arrive – was finally here – "Tonight We Launch." However, the good times we had together, with the comfort and security of home and school, were now behind us as we anxiously faced an unknown and unsure future – "Where Shall We Anchor?"

The allegory mode of transportation for our journey had switched from that of a train, with its direct track to a specific destination, to that of a ship at sea, with its unpredictable smooth sailing undulating to-and-fro in stormy weather, which is life!

At a time and place that a college education was still not emphasized, the class of 1955 had at least six of the nineteen known to continue their education to earn a college degree, a higher than average percentage of nearly one-third, with many more of the class earning college or other post-secondary credits. Of the six who earned a college degree, it is interesting to note that, in a somewhat unusual ratio, our boys (Larry, Donnie, Jock, and Jackie) outnumbered our two girls (Martha Sue and Mary Phyllis).

Martha Sue, Mary Phyllis, and Larry all graduated from Morehead State. Larry, the "old married man," focused on his studies and did not try out for varsity sports for the Blue and Gold Eagles, although, if he had, he likely could have played football, basketball, or baseball. At Morehead, upon learning of an opening in the home economics position, Larry practiced the Musketeer motto of "One for All and All for One" when he sought out Martha Sue. "Martha Sue, the home ec position will soon be open at Carlisle, so if you want the position, you had better get your butt over there pronto and apply!" Martha Sue did, and got the job, starting her on a long satisfying career as a high school home economics teacher.

Jackie Shepherd also applied himself to his studies and "grabbed the tiger by the tail" as he blitzed Georgetown College – the home of the Tigers – in only three years! Doctor Mary Wharton, esteemed professor of biological and earth sciences and chairman of the department at Georgetown College, who saw Jackie's potential in the sciences, took him "under her wing" as teacher, mentor, and guide, pushing Jackie hard to achieve his potential. It could safely be said that Mary E. Wharton "Shepherded" Jackie through Georgetown College!

To Jock and Donnie, the "flagship" University of Kentucky was like sailing into another world, as they suddenly found themselves adrift and surrounded by a sea of students – many from different backgrounds – as part of a student body on campus that exceeded the combined populations of Carlisle and Nicholas County, with Robertson County thrown in! Finally each found his focus, which enabled the two very close friends to graduate together in four years, joining their wives-to-be, Joanie Weissinger and Pat Disney, in the UK Class of 1959. We would have all benefited during that transition freshman year at UK of 1955-56 from a Mary Wharton, or UK advisors and teachers that would "stay on our tails and kick butt" as our teachers at Carlisle did!

So, Jock Conley and Donnie Dampier represented the graduates of the Carlisle High School Class of 1955 at the University of Kentucky and in their four years had many "good stories for the telling" – but these stories shall be reserved for a later writing.

Three of our boys began their post-high school careers by joining military service, with Billy Vanlandingham flying off in the United States Air Force, while Kenneth and Gordon both sailed off and entered the United States Navy, with Gordon making a long-term career of that branch of the service. Jackie Wells, the remaining boy of the Class of 1955, tried out college life at UK, but decided early on that was not the life for him, and came back to "hold the fort" in Carlisle.

The "Unsinkable" Navy Man – The front page of the

August 11, 1955 Carlisle Mercury prominently displayed a photograph of one Kenneth Booth. No, it was not a "Wanted" poster, although some of the local girls who considered Kenneth a "heart-throb," with those "Paul Newman blue eyes," might have written that on their copy! Rather, the caption read, "Enlists In Navy – Kenneth Booth, son of Mr. and Mrs. Albert Booth, is stationed at Bainbridge, Md., for his boot training.

Bobbie Gene Anderson tells this story of how Kenneth came to the decision to join the Navy. Bobbie Brady, a classmate of Bobbie Gene, at Nicholas County High School, was looking for someone to go with him to join the Navy, but since Bobbie Anderson had already joined the U.S. Air Force, he suggested that Kenneth Booth might be available and willing. So, the two Bobbies drove out to Kenneth's place in Frogtown and began blowing the horn, accompanied with hollering, in harmony (but, not as melodious as the Beatles, with their *Hey, Jude*), "Hey, Booth … Hey, Booth." After about the third time, Kenneth stuck his head out of the chicken house and responded, "What do you guys want?" Bobbie Brady then said, "Hey, Kenneth, let's go join the Navy … today." Kenneth, being a young man of action and spontaneity, reportedly replied, "You mean today … right now? … OK, let's go, but first give me a couple of minutes to brush my teeth and comb my hair!"

So, Kenneth, like the rest of us of the Class of 1955, upon leaving the safe harbor of Carlisle High School at graduation and trying to chart our future course in the sea of life, apparently took our class motto, "Tonight we launch, where shall we anchor," literally when he cast his lines for a career in the United States Navy!

With Kenneth's spirit of daring and adventure, coupled with his physical prowess – and especially hailing from the Nicholas County hamlet of Frogtown, it is speculated that Kenneth would have made an excellent U.S. Navy Frogman!

The Navy gave Kenneth Booth the opportunity to exercise his adventurous spirit and "see the world," as it was revealed earlier in this manuscript that Kenneth was the first of the class to be "exposed" to the bikini, experienced in his November 1958 travels to the beaches of the French Rivera! Kenneth resumed the routines of his interesting career in the Navy, and, as far as known, did not sink any of our ships, a la *McHale's Navy* adventures and antics!

A more important attribute of the Class of 1955 is that each one became, and continues to be, a good contributing citizen in his or her respective communities. Some of our occupations included attorney, dentist, state government administrator, retailer, small business proprietors, career military service, high school coach, teacher, librarian, nurse, farmer, and so on.

1955 – A Year To Remember

Nineteen fifty-five was a good year and times to leave the "safe harbor" of school years to make our way in the world. Under the leadership of President Dwight D. "Ike" Eisenhower, this was a period of relative peace, except for the "Cold War" with Communism. America's full entry in the Vietnam War would be approximately a decade away.

As we entered the work force there was a ratio of 5 males for every 2 females in the work place, the average income was $4,197, with the price of a new home at approximately $10,950. A new automobile could be purchased for $1,910, and we could fill it with gasoline at $.23 per gallon. A loaf of bread was $0.18 and a gallon of milk at $0.92. Although the first McDonald's restaurant had opened in San Bernardino, California in December of 1948, it was in April of 1955, when McDonalds opened a "fast-food" franchise in Chicago that began to revolutionize our future eating habits.

Life expectancy during the decade of the '50s for women was 71.1 and for men 65.6. In the twelve-year period from the time the Class of 1955 entered first grade, life expectancy had increased by 3 years for women and approximately 5 years for men. Statistical rates for the late 1990s were women, 79.1, men, 73.1, and they continue to advance, providing reasonable possibilities that some of the Class of '55 may reach the ripe old age of 100!

"We Could Now Vote" – Kentucky became the second state to lower the voting age from twenty-one to eighteen, which was in effect in 1955. So, the Class of 1955 became the "first eligible graduating high school class" to actively participate in the political process. Upon reaching that age, "we could now vote"… and have a say in the operation of our local, state, and national government. Kentucky State Senator H. Stanley Blake, a 1916 graduate of Carlisle High School, had proposed, sponsored, and successfully steered to passage, in the 1954 State Senate, a Constitutional amendment to lower the voting age to 18, a measure that was also strongly supported by President Eisenhower on the national level. Senator Blake, then the dean of Kentucky's Senate, provided a strong voice for the citizens of Carlisle/Nicholas County, as well as those in the counties of Bracken, Grant, Harrison, Pendleton, and Robertson, which comprised the 30th District of that time. Senator Stanley Blake, often affectionately referred to as "Step-and-a-Half" by his friends due to an extreme limp caused by one leg being shorter than the other, had effectively served as a statesman in the Senate since 1938 during the administration of five different governors.

Generally, political philosophies and persuasions, much like religion, are developed and influenced from our backgrounds. In the Democratic bastion of Carlisle and Nicholas County during the '50s, it was frequently commented that registered (revealed) Republicans "could be counted on one hand"; however, "on the other hand," in the Republican stronghold of Barbourville and Knox County, where Pat Disney Dampier grew up, the opposite was true! Some might have expected that when Donnie and Pat married, this polarity of political persuasions could cause trouble; however, as this twosome has deliberated and discussed each election issue down through the years, the backgrounds of their diverse political affiliations have blended together, so that it has been rare, if ever, that they canceled out each other's vote!

Much of the politics of the Class of 1955 were probably gleaned from those great conduits of communication, the local barbershops and beauty parlors, where the locals, with their respective genders, gathered and, in their discussions, were quick to identify many of the problems of the world, but there didn't seem to be an abundance of specific solutions offered, except that "they" were not doing a good job, or "they" needed to do "this 'n' that," but we as youngsters never seemed to learn just who "they" were!

At this writing, four members of the Class of 1955 are known to have practiced their participation in the political process beyond the "vote" to run for elected public office, Kenneth Booth, Jackie Shepherd, Donnie Dampier, and Jock Conley.

In the month before we graduated, on April 8, 1955, renowned and accomplished author Barbara Kingsolver, a Carlisle native, was born.

On September 30, 1955, the actor James Dean, who was only age 24, died in a flaming automobile crash. He was made famous by the only three movies in which he starred: *East of Eden, Rebel Without A Cause,* and *Giant.*

Senior Year Movies and Entertainment

As we entered our senior year, some of the hit movies of 1954 that were showing in theaters across the country (there were no home videos or VCRs back then) were: *Bad Day At Black Rock* (Spencer Tracy), *Blackboard Jungle* (with the sound track of *Rock Around The Clock*), *Lady and The Tramp, Mister Roberts* (Henry Fonda), Hitchcock's *To Catch A Thief* (Cary Grant and Grace Kelly), *Country Girl* (Bing Crosby and Grace Kelly), etc. Other influencing movies of our time were *Picnic* (William Holden and Kim Novak), with its romantic theme song of *Moonglow, On The Waterfront* (Marlon Brando and Eva Marie Saint), Brigitte Bardot, who was "very revealing" in *And God Created Woman,* and *Rebel Without A Cause* (James Dean and Natalie Wood). Donnie Dampier still has a red, James Dean style jacket that is well-preserved from high school days! Even though James Dean, Marlon Brando, Marilyn Monroe, Sophia Loren, and other movie stars of that day were "icons" that we, as teenagers, tried to imitate, we were not rebels against our parents, teachers, authority figures, or society in general; rather; we grew up with immense respect for our elders and for our community!

Some of the novels that were blockbuster bestsellers of the '50s were *Hawaii* by James A. Michener, *Lolita* by Vladimir Nabokov, *Doctor Zhivago* by Boris Pasternak, *Kon-Tiki* by Thor Heyerdahl, *The Caine Mutiny* by Herman Wouk, *Exodus* by Leon Uris, *Only In America* by Harry Golden, and *Peyton Place* by Grace Metalious, among many others.

Since television was not made available for the home market until around 1950, most of us did not have a television set at home until late high school, and some not until afterwards. This was probably a blessing since our minds were not influenced and controlled by TV and we developed more independent thinking and better one-on-one communication skills. Since we were no "couch potatoes," we created our own entertainment, such as seeing how many we could cram into a car at the drive-in movies during our junior/senior years when we became old enough for a driver's license! A favorite drive-in of the time was the Judy Drive-In located in Montgomery County.

This brings to mind that around this time there was a basketball player for Bourbon County High School named Max Judy, who reportedly married a young lady with a first name of Judy! If they attended that drive-in it would have been "Judy Judy at The Judy!" Sounds like a Cary Grant line in one of his movies!

The first drive-in movie, which was invented by Richard M. Hollingshead in New Jersey, opened on June 6, 1933, showing the movie *Wife Beware.* In 1948, there was a reported 820 drive-ins, and by the mid-'50s, the heyday of the Class of '55, the number had peaked to some 5,000 drive-in theaters nationwide. Many of the movies shown were sci-fi and horror, designed to cause the couples to cuddle or snuggle up to feel safe and secure from the creatures and monsters on the screen! The drive-in movie was an integral part of our culture, so it would not be unusual that many of us, as married couples, still enjoyed the occasional drive-in movie, with maybe a chance to slip in a snuggle or two with our spouse!

As part of our entertainment, we were still listening to our favorite radio shows that we grew up on, such as Fibber McGee and Molly, George Burns & Gracie Allen, Amos and Andy, Lum and Abner, The Shadow Knows, The Lone Ranger, Jack Benny, and on and on!

Also, a few of us no doubt sneaked in some late-night listening to "black" music, considered risqué and raunchy by '50s standards, played on Randy's Record Shop from station WLAC in Nashville!

Bob Hope, who had his first personal tour to entertain the troops in 1942 at a military base in Alaska, was a longtime favorite on radio, TV, and movies.

Some of "our music" included Al Hibler's *Unchained Melody*, along with Bill Haley and The Comets' *Shake, Rattle 'n' Roll*, and *Rock Around The Clock*, which ushered in a revolutionary new dance style. Bill Haley, who grew up in Michigan, was musically influenced by his Kentucky bloodline (his parents, both musicians, were from Western Kentucky) in developing his "rockabilly" sound and style!

Another musical group with Western Kentucky ties was The Hilltoppers, who had taken their name from the college sports teams and were right for the times, having originated their unique singing style while students at Western Kentucky Teacher's College in Bowling Green, Kentucky. This vocal group, who had been voted as either number one or number two on the hit charts of 1952 through 1954, was very hot on the jukebox selections and record purchases, for the Class of 1955 as they were completing senior year. From the Hilltoppers' first hit recording of *Trying*, which landed them on *The Ed Sullivan Show* in October of 1952, to their biggest hit of *P.S. I Love You* and yet another exposure on national TV with an appearance on *The Perry Como Show* in 1953, along with another of our favorites released in 1955, *Only You (And You Alone)*, the quartet of lead singer Jimmy Sacca, along with Billy Vaughn, Don McGwire, and Seymour Spiegelman, presented music well-suited to our ballroom "belly-rubbing" slow-dancing styles of the 1950s!

Of course there was Kentucky-born Rosemary Clooney (a native of Maysville/Augusta), who came a long way since the attractive songstress started her career in music singing to help her grandfather win mayoralty races at Maysville. Rosie would follow her grandfather after he had finished speaking and give out with a song or two to the delight of the crowd. All this at the age of three!

Other favorites of our day included Teresa Brewer, Kay Starr, Patti Paige, Peggy Lee, along with the McGuire Sisters, The Platters, Fats Domino, Pat Boone, Harry Belafonte, Doris Day, and Perry Como, with many more.

With just a little "play on numbers," Perry (Mr. "C") was age 43 (the year we entered first grade) in 1955 (the year we graduated).

The Ed Sullivan Show, a very popular TV variety show in our day, ran on CBS every Sunday night at 8:00 p.m. It is remembered that many of us, with our parents, rushed home from Sunday evening church services so as not to miss any of "The Show." The show was originally titled *The Talk of The Town*, but in 1955, the name was changed to *The Ed Sullivan Show.*

Yes, these were good times! Classmates of the Class of '55 were blessed to grow up and mature with a good group of kids at a quality small school in the small town of Carlisle. As the lyrics of the old song, *Heart of My Heart*, states, "We were rough and ready guys (and gals), but oh, how we could harmonize!" There is no recollection of us doing a lot of singing on the Court House wall; however, several of the guys were frequently seen *Standing on the Corner Watching All the Girls Gooo By*, while most of the girls were sitting on the other corner wondering and humming *Where the Boys Are*!

Our "harmonizing" was being in harmony with each other!

Racial Integration at Carlisle High School (1955-1956)

One year later – after the Class of 1955 graduated – in the 1955-56 school year, Carlisle High School became one of the first schools in Kentucky to integrate by accepting Negro high school students from the all-black old Booker T. Washington School in Henryville, adjacent to Carlisle. The front-page headline of the August 25, 1955 edition of *The Carlisle Mercury* read, "Colored To Attend Carlisle High School; County Board Undecided On Desegregation." This was accomplished by a unanimous vote of the Carlisle Board of Education after hearing statements from the colored children's parents and various civic and religious organization leaders, all of whom were in favor of the move, and in recognition of the decision handed down by the U.S. Supreme Court which declared that segregation of colored children from white children in schools was unconstitutional and discriminatory. The Kentucky state attorney general had also declared that the Supreme Court decision nullified the old Kentucky "Day Law," originally passed in 1904, which had prohibited colored and white students from studying in the same classroom." The Carlisle community and Carlisle High School can be proud that this transition occurred quietly, smoothly, and without incident, which could not be said for many other communities and schools across Kentucky and the Southern states, some of which required National Guard intervention.

The *Louisville Courier-Journal*, in the Passing Show section of September 18, 1955, published a detailed full-page article concerning statewide integration of Kentucky public schools, which had its beginnings with that fall school term of 1955-56, under the heading, "Integration Trial Balance," by writer Allan M. Trout, *Courier-Journal* Frankfort Bureau. Mr. Trout led off the article by stating, "All factors considered, Kentucky has made a stumbling but substantial start toward ending segregation of white and Negro pupils in the public-school system." Some statistics of the times that were cited by the article indicated: Only approximately 200 Negroes, out of 43,361 of school age, are enrolled in white public schools in Kentucky; only 12 of the 182 districts with Negro children have taken the first actual step toward desegregation. There are no Negro children of school age in 42 districts. (Note that the 244 public school districts of 1955 have now been reduced to 177 due to school consolidations.)

The Carlisle City School System received prominent attention by *The Courier-Journal* article. In a sub-section 3 titled, " 'Splinter compliance' with order to desegregate has taken various forms across Kentucky … 10 Pupils Admitted," it reported: "Ten Negro pupils have been admitted to Carlisle High, a white school, rather than ride a bus to the Negro high school at Paris. The census of Carlisle lists 47 Negro children and one teacher."

Barbourville, the hometown school of Pat Disney Dampier, Donnie's wife, also received mention in this section:

"In the field of 'splinter compliance,' two Kentucky districts have desegregated at all levels. They are Walton-Verona, in Boone County, with a Negro census of 10 children, and Barbourville, with a census of eight. In these two cases, the abolition of compulsory segregation automatically meant the integration of both races in the same classrooms. Neither district had a Negro school or a Negro teacher. Walton-Verona pupils have been attending Negro schools of Boone County, and Barbourville pupils have been attending the Negro schools of Knox County."

In a companion article of this *Courier-Journal* issue, "Calm Acceptance Marks Most Integration Moves … Here are some glimpses of integration highlights in various Kentucky areas, written by Courier-Journal staff writers and special correspondents," Carlisle High School was again featured as one of five experiences selected from across the state. The following is the verbatim reproduction of the article, titled "It's Color of Jersey That Looms Largest":

"Carlisle – 'Give me a hamburger,' said the Negro boy. The clerk looked at the boy, who had entered the restaurant with a group of white students from Carlisle High School, then prepared the sandwich. He handed it to the boy and quietly said: 'Please take it outside.' The boy paid for the sandwich and took it out. Thus were ended whatever hopes he might have had that integration in Carlisle High School had lowered the bars against Negroes elsewhere in the Nicholas County town." (Note: This previous sentence was an italicized editorial comment by the reporter.)

The boy was one of ten Negroes who had enrolled at the high school earlier in the day. All of them were assigned to white classes without incident. In past years, the Carlisle Board of Education had paid tuition and transportation costs to send Negro students to Western High School at Paris, operated only for their race.

The Class of 1955-56 had the distinction of being the first Musketeer class in history to have black players as teammates to participate on the athletic teams, since this was the inaugural year that black students were allowed to attend Carlisle High School. The CHS football team of 1955-56 included four black players, which may have brought the rooster up to only some 15 players (as indicated in the pre-season team photograph), meaning that this team was even more shorthanded with manpower than the 1954 "Coachless Wonders" with 17 teammates! The four black players, "who made history" as the first to play football for the CHS Musketeers, were W. H. Farris, Asbury McGuffy, Ronnie Wilson, and Gayle Wilson. Several years later, David McGuffy, the son of Asbury, capped an outstanding football career at Nicholas County High School, under the coaching of Ben Pumphrey, by playing football on scholarship, and earning a degree, at Notre Dame University in South Bend, Indiana.

The ease with which four of the Negro boys were accepted as members of the Carlisle football team is illustrated in a happening a few days before school opened. During a football practice session with the white boys, Coach Ed Wells told them Negroes were expected to enroll at the school. He asked the boys how they felt about Negroes coming out for the team. Finally one of the boys replied, "Well, Coach, we don't care about the color of their skin as long as their jerseys are green." A few days later, the four Negro players led the Carlisle team to a 19-0 victory in its season opener against the all-white Paris High School eleven." (By James Goble)

Carlisle High School was further featured by the *Courier-Journal* feature story on integration, dated September 18, 1955, with a large news photo (4-1/2 inches by 7-1/8 inches) taken inside the Carlisle Musketeers ("Green and White") football locker room, which showed the four black players (W.H. Farris, Asbury McGuffy, Ronnie and Gayle Wilson) laughing and cutting up with four of the white players (Billy Gilley, Billy Straw, David Feeback, and one other believed to be Ronnie King). The caption under the Courier-Journal photo by Thomas V. Miller Jr. read, "Racial integration in sports is nothing new; and as a result, it has been accepted without any furor at the Carlisle (Ky.) High School. With five Negro boys enrolled, four play on the varsity football eleven."

The seven black students who made Carlisle history in that fall of 1955 by breaking the bounds of educational segregation, and then went on to graduate and become alumni of Carlisle High School, were Betty Jean Ledford, Betty Jo Stevenson, Betty Sue Williams, and Gayle Wilson, of the CHS Class of 1957, and Norma Jean Blount, Asbury McGuffy, and Ronnie Wilson, who graduated as part of the CHS Class of 1958.

Race relations for the CHS Class of 1955 were practiced as a "product of the times in which we lived." Since there were very few visual or public problems between the black and white communities of Carlisle/Nicholas County, there appeared to be a prevailing attitude of "live and let live." In this benign atmosphere, few of us at the time recognized the need to get on our soapbox or campaign for improved conditions for our black neighbors. Back then, the reference to "black" or "African-American" was never used. In our era, a reference of respect was "Negro" or "colored"; "darkies" was less respectful, and, of course, the hated "N" word was considered as demeaning and derogatory. Actually, it is not recalled that the "N" word was used in that manner very often in Carlisle, but was a somewhat "casual" reference. If an arbitrary "Race Relations Rating" system (with a score of 10 the highest, and 1 the lowest) had been in effect during that time, Carlisle might have scored a 6 or 7 in some areas, whereas many other communities might have scored below 5 and some a 1 or even 0!

This is certainly not to say that conditions were as they

should have been; there was, even in Carlisle, vast need for improvement. Blacks owned homes, but were mostly segregated in Henryville; they frequently worked side-by-side with whites, sometimes with comparable pay, but employment and career opportunities were limited and restricted; they shopped with the Carlisle merchants and grocers, but could not eat in the restaurants (they had their own); they went to movies at the downtown Lyric Theater, but sat segregated in the balcony, etc. The black people worshiped separately from whites in their own churches; however, occasionally, the congregations would join together for "special occasion" services. And, of course, they had been segregated into their own all-black elementary school taught by black teachers, with the high school students transported to all-black high schools in Paris, such as Paris Western. It is assumed that their black teachers were just as competent and dedicated as ours were, but their facilities would have been very limited for funds, teaching resources, and even basic supplies that severely restricted their educational opportunities. In the *Courier-Journal* article of September 15, 1955, titled "Integration Trial Balance," writer Allan Trout noted, "And nobody knows yet what is to become of the 1,386 Negro teachers who, as a class, possess higher academic training and longer experience than do white teachers as a class."

So, the Supreme Court ruling of May 17, 1954 was immensely important to opening doors of equal opportunity for all in all facets of life, that should have always been there, and society is still working toward today. Carlisle, with its positive attitudes and actions in the transition period of the mid-'50s, could have served as a model, albeit imperfect, for other communities across Kentucky and the country to follow.

The Evolutionary Entry of Elvis

And then, there was Elvis with *Love Me Tender, Hound Dog, Ready Teddy,* and *Don't Be Cruel!* Elvis, after cutting his first record in 1954 – a single under the label of Sun Records that featured

That's All Right, Mama with the flip-side of *Blue Moon of Kentucky* – was well on the way in 1956 to his coronation as "The King" with the release of *Heartbreak Hotel* and his first national appearance, on September 9, 1956, "from the waist up," on *The Ed Sullivan TV Show*, watched by 60 million viewers, which, at the time, was the largest single audience in TV history! "Elvis the Pelvis," as he was rather unkindly referred to by those who took poetic license with the rhyme of his name, was "discovered' by the late Sam Phillips (died July 30, 2003 at age 80), the founder of Sun Records of Memphis, Tennessee, in 1952, who helped to launch the career of Presley, and together they were key figures in ushering in the birth of the "Rock 'n' Roll Revolution" of the '50s!

The first recorded personal appearance on stage for Elvis was in Memphis in 1954, but it was his personal appearance in Louisville's Jefferson County Armory two years later that brings back personal memories to Donnie Dampier. Excerpts from an article taken from *The Lexington Leader*, of August 18, 1977, written by Don Edwards, and titled "He Shook Up A Generation," describes the setting and the culture back then very well:

"They were the kids of the '50s, who traded Butch Wax for Brylcream, flat-tops for ducktails – and split from their parents to follow a 'pied piper' with sneering lips and swiveling hips. In Central Kentucky one day in 1956, they hitched up their pegged pants with the narrow suede belts, grabbed the girls who wore their high school rings wrapped with fuzzy pink angora, piled into sweet-growling, three-deuce, four-in-the-floor cars filled with 30-cents-a-gallon gas and drove over a two-lane highway to Louisville's Freedom Hall.

"Presley was the reason. It was his first Kentucky appearance. He was 'king' of the new music – their music. They called it 'rock 'n' roll.' It sold millions of 45-rpm records spun on suitcase-sized portable players lugged to basement and backyard parties where kids 'dipped' when they slow-danced, shook when they fast-danced, sneaked drinks of gin-spiked 'purple passion' from paper cups and smoked nothing stronger than Pall Malls.

"It was sexy music. And in those 'pre-Pill' days, on that night at Freedom Hall in 1956, girls wearing penny loafers and pony tails threw panties on stage and carried cans of Band-Aids to protect forever any spot where Elvis might touch them. The King was special here."

Note: The columnist, Mr. Edwards, in looking back to a period twenty years earlier, probably made a natural assumption the setting was in Freedom Hall, however, Donnie's old checkbook kept from that era (and, miraculously found), verified his on-site memory of the setting of the Elvis stage appearance in Louisville, with his recorded check, dated November 11, 1956, and written to: "Jefferson Co. Armory (Elvis Presley)."

Donnie Joe Dampier, a little over a year removed as a graduate of Carlisle High School, was there that November night of 1956 in Louisville to greet Elvis in his first Kentucky concert, and, as Jock Conley would later say, "It was fitting that he be there, for Donnie was considered as the 'unofficial' president of the 'unofficial' Elvis Presley Fan Club of the Class of 1955." Donnie was in attendance with Carter Fields, his new friend and roommate at UK, as Carter, from nearby Fern Creek, was somehow able to find, or finagle, the availability of two tickets, which cost only $10 a piece, to the Jefferson County Armory for the performance. It is remembered that in that November time of the year, it was cool enough for Donnie to be decked out in his red "James Dean jacket," which was worn not because he ever tried to emulate the late James Dean (tragically killed in an auto accident in 1955), but hopeful it might draw the attention of some of the scores of girls at the concert.

For the two young men, who were part of an overwhelmed male minority that night in Louisville's Armory, it was an unusual and humbling experience, as they were frequently pushed and jostled aside by the multitudes of young women trying to position themselves to get closer looks at Elvis! Now Donnie and Carter had experienced the excitement of young women throwing panties their way during the occasional "panty raids" orchestrated at the University of Kentucky, but not the volumes of "pitched panties" that night, and from observing the gyrations of some of the young women before tossing them to the stage, it was surmised that some, perhaps many, were panties that had been worn on their person! Despite the distractions, Elvis "The Pelvis" Presley put on a great show, and, looking back, those in attendance that night under "The Blue Moon of Kentucky" were historically part of the party leading to the coronation of "The King!"

Jock was correct in his so-called "fan club" assessment, for Donnie, as a true fan, was drawn to the musical presentations of Elvis almost immediately and, believe it or not, actually could relate to Elvis with several shared similarities. … As age-wise contemporaries, both were winter babies, with Elvis born on January 8, 1935, followed by Donnie on December 11, 1936. They were both raised as an only child (although Elvis had a stillborn twin named Jesse Garon) … growing up in a very small town, south of the Mason-Dixon Line, with the unique distinction of a nearby neighboring community called Shake Rag, located just down the road … in their childhood days, each lived in a small modest house, warmed by a fireplace, without electricity, or running water with indoor plumbing (both were well-versed at running to the outhouse). There were some shared physical characteristics as well, as both had natural light brown hair (before Elvis dyed his black for his movie role in "Loving You" and kept it that way); but the most shared and distinguishing physical similarity, identified by both Jock and Donnie's wife, Pat, which they have frequently observed and noted down through the years, was and is Donnie's trait of unconscious leg jiggling (one or the other, or both), especially when listening to rhythmic music with a beat. Donnie's mother used to say, "Son, you've got the hee-bie jeebies" (this was an old fashioned term for "can't sit still"). Musically, influenced by both Brando and Elvis, Donnie rhythmically banged out beats on the bongo drums … but at this stage, any further similarities ceased.

What was it about Elvis Aron Presley, know by most as just "Elvis," that grabbed, galvanized, and endeared the King's "subjects" to him, not only in his heyday of the '50s, but among those who have remained intrigued and loyal to his mystique for over two decades, and still counting, after his untimely death at age 42 on August 16, 1977? To this writer, there certainly are a number of factors that came together to create a legend, one of which one had to be the "timing of the times."

The generations of high school teenagers of the mid-'50s, including the Class of '55, could be characterized by an "emerging restlessness," described as the "Depression Descendants" generation (born during "The Great Depression" years) who were experiencing the new freedoms from the peace gained from the ends of two major wars in our young lives, with more money, of which some could now be spent on frills other than day-to-day survival, and, with the access to the availability of the automobile, making us a more mobile society, ready to expand our horizons. We were ready for, and in need of, a "Pied Piper" who would lead us to spread our wings wider than ever before, and enable us to soar from the nest, rather than to merely climb over the edge or fall out, into the "same-old-same-old" as before. That person to lead the '50s generations, and those to follow, was Elvis Presley, who, at age 21 in '55, had just come onto the scene!

Aside from the timing of his emergence, from that of a truck driver to exciting entertainer, the characteristics of Elvis, the person and entertainer, which made him such a popular and engaging personality, were numerous. First, he had a great voice, with range and style, that was smooth and compelling in rendering a romantic ballad, such as *It's Now Or Never,* or, emitting racy, sexy tones, which suggested the risqué, as in, *I've Got a Woman Way Across Town,* he was always sensuous, appealing to both women, who wanted to be with him, and to men, who wanted to be like him!

The quality and strength of his voice were well-demonstrated when Elvis, who also loved singing spirituals, gospels, and church hymns, would occasionally richly render his renditions of *Amazing Grace, How Great Thou Art, Nearer My God To Thee, Just A Closer Walk With Thee, The Battle Hymn of the Republic,* and many others, "a cappella," without instrumental accompaniment.

Elvis had a powerful physical presence, both on and off the

stage. He was good-looking, not a soft baby face, nor too rough looking – a face that women adored and men aspired to look like. His body, in his '50s peak, on a 6-foot frame, was trim and sleek, athletic and agile – and, he knew how to wow the women in the audience. We were moving out of the "age of the crooner" represented by the wonderful talents of the late-and-greats Bing Crosby, Frank Sinatra, and Perry Como, who held the microphone, while standing or sitting on a stool, as they mellowed out their music. But Elvis, sometimes referred to as "Mr. Swivel Hips," with legs jiggling and pelvis pulsating, grabbed the mike and its stand, dancing, while dipping it back and forth across the stage, cradling it as if he had transformed the mike stand into one of the women in the audience – but, which woman? To each woman there, they likely had projected themselves on stage as the woman to take the place of the mike stand – to be the object of Elvis's affection! The King, sweating profusely during his performances, would take his "trademark" sweat-soaked silk scarves and, after tantalizing and teasing, tossed them to lucky ladies up close and, in return, panties, displayed by holding aloft, would be flung in Elvis's direction, both of which were symbolism of the sexually charged evening!

Elvis, "The Pelvis," a reference he despised, quickly drew the scorn of parents, preachers, and politicians alike, the latter always looking for "a cause," but even though there was some cause for concern, the adults, by and large, "wore blinders" to the many qualities and value systems that Elvis possessed. He publicly expressed love and respect for his dad and his "mama," politely and respectfully responded with "Sir" and "Ma'am" when giving interviews, was not known to use profanity in public, and, even though he was no doubt presented with many opportunities, he was not viewed as a womanizer, nor did he smoke or drink, and it was only in the last years of his short life that he was associated with using drugs. There did not seem to be overwhelming concern on the part of the parents of the CHS Class of 1955, primarily because we were all considered on the verge of adulthood with our graduation from high school, and, besides that, at least four of our girls were already married and "beyond corruption." Even though Elvis was still in the early stages of his remarkable career in 1955, he definitely had a long-term cultural impact on our class, and the classes to come after! Popular performers and public personalities who die young, such as James Dean, Marilyn Monroe, JFK, etc., are frequently elevated to legendary status, but none higher than Elvis Presley, "The King."

"The King Is Dead, Long Live The King!"

X

Sex ... Romance ... Love And Marriage

Love and marriage, love and marriage ...
Go together like a horse 'n' carriage ...

As we sang with the birds and gave attention to the buzzing of the bees, we realized romance was in the air ... and then there was sex. ...

Sex – That "Sense-sational" Word

Ah, yes, there is "sex!" Any history of high school teenagers would be incomplete without a discussion of the three-lettered "S" word! To members of the Class of 1955, sex was just as important and interesting, and had just as much compelling curiosity, as it did for any era, including modern times. A major difference between now and then is that we were not continuously bombarded with frank and explicit media presentations of sex and sensuality in movies, television, magazines, advertisements, etc. It was much more subtle and with a "touch of mystery!" Another allure in which we were able to develop and exercise our vivid imaginations! Most of us, girls and boys alike, were into our junior or senior years before we really "began to know the score." When the boys talked of "scoring," it was usually in reference to football touchdowns or basketball baskets made!

As to the boys, we could, and we did, look, and often – so we could relate to "Standing On The Corner, Watching All the Girls Go By … Brother, you can't go to jail for what you're thinking!"

"Sweater Girl … Sweater Girl" – In the 1950s, both the girls and boys paid notice that we were now into the period of "the sweater girl," a time which enabled our girls to "put their best front forward" by wearing a variety of well-fitted knit sweaters, a time which was embraced with open arms by all the boys! And, in the view of the boys, the community "embracing" Carlisle was well-blessed with the well-endowed!

One of Bob Hope's favorite risqué routines of the 1950s showed a beautiful, voluptuous, and well-endowed young woman standing next to Bob – in a tight knit sweater – when she says, "Bob, I just don't understand why all the boys are so interested in 'Sweater Girls' " – to which Bob responds, "I don't know either, but I sure would like to 'unravel' the mystery!"

This was an era when the open presentation of female cleavage was pretty much limited to the movies by such well-endowed actresses as Marilyn Monroe, Jane Russell, and Sophia Loren, to name a few, so the stylish knit sweaters of the '50s were a welcome substitute for presenting the beauty of the female form.

"Pillow Talk" 'n' Pajama Parties – Throughout the high school years the girls occasionally got together in each other's homes for an overnight sleep-in called a pajama party! They no doubt played many of the musical artists of the '50s mentioned above (and more) on recordings of 78, 45, and later, 33-1/3 rpms on a home phonograph player. There seemed to always be a preponderance of photos, taken by the girls of each other, which they sometimes used to "treat 'n' tease" the boys with. The pajama parties were intriguing and always a curiosity to the boys as they wondered, "What are they doing?" and "What are they talking about?" or, "Who are they talking about?" and "What do the girls look like in their pajamas?" So, the boys would sometimes try to invade these female fortresses in hopes of getting a glimpse, especially of those girls who might be in "shorty" pajamas, but their attempts were usually repelled (particularly by the mothers!).

Condom "Cotillion" – It was at this "coming of age" that most of the class boys engaged in a "comical ritual" of trying to purchase condoms (we called them rubbers) at the local drug stores. The ritual was like a well-choreographed "two step," side-stepping dance during a cotillion as we tried to avoid being waited on by a female clerk, usually an adult who had known us since childhood and who knew our parents well. In those days, things of sex were rarely spoken or displayed to adults of the opposite gender. When one of the boys finally got the male druggist off to the side (usually Mr. Alan Hopkins or Doc Bradshaw), we would speak in a soft voice and ask to "purchase a package of prophylactics," whereupon the druggist would reach under the counter (they were not openly displayed), slip the package of contraceptives into a brown paper bag, then, with a wink and a sly smile, they would tell us to "be careful!" They came in packages of three, with exotic brand names of Trojan, Sheik, or Peacocks, with one usually placed in the young man's billfold (which formed a recognizable outline) –this became "a status symbol." Another was placed in the automobile glove compartment (if it was sure the parents would not find it), with the third one hidden at home, as a "safety reserve!" These locations were where they usually stayed – in the proud possession of many a young man – for there was only the rare occasion to fulfill their intended use!

Our boys, and perhaps the girls as well, would frequently make joking remarks about the Trojans of Mt. Sterling High School. These references were not about the Trojan War of Greek mythology between the cities of Troy in Anatolia (modern-day Turkey) and the Greek city of Sparta (the Spartans) over the seduction and abduction of Helen of Sparta, described by Aphrodite (the goddess of love) as the "the most beautiful woman in the world," who became Helen of Troy when she eloped with her intended lover, Paris, the "Trojan!"

Perhaps Mary Phyllis Smith (blessed with some beauty of her own) and Jerry Cameron recalled this story of *Helen and Paris* and were inspired by its romantic adventure as they were planning for their own elopement…

The Elopement – Mary Phyllis began our senior year as a Smith, but ended it as a Cameron! Mary Phyllis, who was usually considered as quiet, reserved, and studious, surprised and excited us by her grit, courage, and resolve at her "coming out" when she and Jerry Cameron (Larry's older brother) eloped during our senior year!

"Oh, What A Night," the subtitle and most recognizable lyrics from the popular song, *December 3, 1963*, the 1972 recording by The Four Seasons, would surely describe the events of their elopement night! Mary Phyllis had revealed her intentions to only a few of the girls, such as Martha Sue, Anna Mary, Wanda, and Barbara (probably at one of their pajama parties), but probably few others, for fear her nuptial plans would be prematurely revealed. As far as is known, none of the boys of the class, including Jerry's brother, Larry, knew of their intentions. A few weeks prior to the event, in home economics class work, Mary Phyllis was making a dress, which she quietly told some of the girls was special, for "it would be her wedding dress." It was intended by her parents, Sammy and Lula Smith, as well as her three aunts, the Botts sisters, that Mary Phyllis would go to college, so a marriage before high school graduation, especially an elopement, would be met with strong disapproval! As parents of teenage girls of the '50s were prone to do, Mary Phyllis was raised by loving parents, but in a strict environment, and as one of the girls would say in later years, "They would hardly let Mary Phyllis do anything, except under close scrutiny and observance!"

So, on that "elopement night," Mary Phyllis was "supposed" to spend the night with Martha Sue, possibly as part of a slumber party, or that is what her mother and aunts thought! Meanwhile, Jerry was trying to find someone to drive him and Mary Phyllis to Jeffersonville, Indiana, where they could be quickly married. This twosome had a severe transportation problem to overcome, for you see, neither of them had a license to drive, nor knew how to drive an automobile, and especially Jerry, for he had been blind since early childhood! So, Jerry asked his longtime good friend (then and now)

Wayne Gaunce to take them to their wedding site. However, Wayne thought their elopement plans were ill-advised and tried to convince Jerry to wait at least until after graduation; also, Wayne was fearful that they would "be found out" and the Smiths might send the sheriff after them! Jerry and Mary Phyllis were committed and persistent, and convinced Wayne that "somehow, someway" they were going to their wedding bed that night, so Wayne agreed, with some reservations, to drive them to their destination.

For some reason Wayne did not have access to his own car that night, so he asked his brother-in-law if he could borrow his brand new automobile, without telling him the intended purpose! Wayne's brother-in-law finally relented, but Wayne was not to drive it beyond the Nicholas County line, so when Wayne, accompanied by Pat May, delivered Jerry and Mary Phyllis to the Louisville shore of the Ohio River Bridge, he accomplished something, overnight, that one hundred and fifty years of legislative action could not do (reducing the number of counties by extending the size of some), "Wayne surely extended the Nicholas County line to the Ohio River!" Wayne would not drive them over the state line, but made the couple walk across the bridge, which, in their anxious state, was akin to walking the plank, where, once across, they had prearranged transportation to a justice of the peace.

For Mary Phyllis, thinking back to that elopement night of October 28, there was so much excitement and anxiety, plus she was in such a fog that she hardly remembers where they spent their wedding night, but for Jerry, he surely thought of Mary Phyllis as, "What a woman, what a night – Oh! What a night!"

Classmate/Classroom Romances – Over the years, there were not many serious romances between our classmates; by being so close to each other all those years, we were more like brothers and sisters. Therefore, there was not a lot of in-class dating; however, we seemed to watch out for each other and did a lot of running around together as friends. However, there were occasionally some attractions and infatuations between our classmates, that seemed to "run in a linear line" without connecting, as, for instance, Barbara King seemed to always be "stuck" on Kenneth Booth, but Kenneth was stuck on Carole McClain, while Carole was more interested in several others. As for awhile, between the occasional connections of Kenneth and Carol, Donnie D. and Carol M. had a brief "fling;" or, for a short while, Donnie Dampier was "stuck" on Jane Flora, but Jane was crazy (her mother's words) about Billy Buntin, while Billy was focused on "who knows!" And, there were certain to be some "unsaid or unrevealed" love interests!

The Attraction To The Older Man – Four of our girls married "older men" who were previous alumni of CHS: Pat May to Wayne Gaunce, Class of '51; Sylva Joy Owens to Gary Flora, Class of '52 (older brother of Molly Jane); Mary Agnes Mann to Charles Carter, Class of '53; and Wanda Mattox to Milton Moreland, Class of '54. With the romance and marriage of Wanda and Milton, the "transplants took root," as Wanda had been transplanted to the soils of Carlisle in 1951, followed by Milton, who transferred in from Paris High School prior to the beginning of the 1952-53 school year, and just in time to be a significant member of the 1952 Musketeer football team.

The "Altar Burning" – Carole Donovan and Gordon Moreland were the only classmates of '55 to marry each other. Carroll Hall, former band director at Carlisle High School, tells a true story about a "happening" during Carole and Gordon's wedding. Since Gordon and Carole had been former band students of the "Maestro" Hall, he and his wife, Kay Fisher Hall (CHS Class of 1951), decided to come back to Carlisle for the wedding, which was held at the Carlisle Christian Church, and conducted by the resident Reverend J. J. Whitehouse, who, by the way, was a third cousin of President Abraham Lincoln.

Now, Carroll and Kay were running late, barely arriving before the "wedding march down the aisle," and, since the sanctuary was nearly full with all the back seats occupied, they had to be seated on the side front row. Most of you know the routine, if you get to church late, you have to sit up front! At the conclusion of the marriage ceremony of Carole and Gordon, Reverend Whitehouse asked everyone to bow their head, and close their eyes, for the closing prayer to bless the newlyweds. Carroll related his story thusly:

"Since they had been rushed in, he decided to keep his eyes open and raise his head to look around from his angled side front seat, to 'see who all was there.' As he glanced back toward the still praying 'J.J.,' he saw a flaming piece of the lit candle drop from the candelabra onto the carpet of the elevated alter. Carroll then realized that the carpet was beginning to ignite, so he nudged and alerted Kay by his side (who had her head bowed, and eyes closed), then quietly slipped up the two steps to the burning candle, which was beginning to burn a spot in the carpet. Carroll scraped the candle to the side and stepped on it to extinguish the smoldering candle and carpet, at which time he slipped back to his seat."

Meanwhile, the unaware Reverend Whitehouse, head bowed and eyes tight shut, was still deep in vocal prayer! Those of us who attended the Carlisle Christian Church during his tenure were quite familiar with his long prayers, and congregational "watch watching" sermons.

At the conclusion of the service, Carroll did not mention the happening of the nearly disastrous fire, because "he was supposed to have his head down, and eyes closed during that prayer time," and Carroll then related, in telling the story, that "no one else in the church mentioned it either," even though some were sure to have witnessed it – because they also were supposed to have their head bowed and eyes shut!

Carroll Hall admits that his "story" sounds almost unbelievable, especially since no one in attendance during the wedding ceremony, would admit to observing Carroll's fire extinguishing act, so he has kindly asked any doubters of his story to verify the event with his wife, Kay, as to its truthfulness…

Sometimes, the Lord seems to act in mysterious ways!

Just Parking 'n' Petting – As the saying goes, "we were no angels"; we frequently participated in parking and petting (the older folks still called it sparking). Scrubgrass Lane (out beyond Jackie Shepherd's place) was a favorite and noted "parking area" (except probably for Jackie, who sought a location farther from home). Martha Sue Feeback Taylor now resides on Scrubgrass; so, if she visited the area during high school, it could have been to look for a future home site? During our teenage era of the '50s, there were strong deterrents in place that encouraged us to "practice safe sex." There was a legitimate fear of unwanted, premarital pregnancy (this was before "the Pill") and even though AIDS was an unknown in the '50s, we were aware of other serious sexually transmitted diseases, such as syphilis and gonorrhea. The birth control pill, not introduced for public use until 1960, was initially restricted by pharmacists to married women only, which prompted some sexually active unmarried women to borrow wedding rings to enable them to purchase the pill.

Virtues of Virginity – The Class of '55, along with our peers across the country, lived through our "coming of age" period in what some historians described as "the cult of virginity." Unmarried females were supposed to protect and "value their virginity," while, on the other side, males (in their "macho manner") were expected, and even encouraged, to "sow their wild oats – by doing the deed!" This "double standard," naturally, led to much frustration, confusion, and sometimes conflict, for both boys and girls, which, no doubt, contributed to the so-called celebrated "war of the sexes!" Some statistical studies of the times indicated that, on the national level, over 50% of females married before age 19. The Class of '55, primarily due to the long-standing closeness of "our family," adjusted well, and made it through this major period of our biological development, with our psyche largely unscathed, as we moved into adulthood.

The overall attitudes toward sexual expression by the general public appeared to change with each generation leading to the sexual atmosphere of the '50s when our class moved though those teenage years. Notwithstanding the teachings of our churches, which almost always strongly preached "total abstinence from sex before marriage," the so-called socially accepted practices of sex that prevailed on the national level seemed to waffle from one extreme to the other based on major periods and events engulfing our nation. For instance, as described in generalities, the "cycles of sex" ranged from:

The restrictive Victorian views of the early 1900s – to …

The "anything goes" of the Roaring '20s – to …

The "depressed" sexual urges (caused by economic and emotional reasons) during the "Depression Years" – to …

A resurgence of sex in "the Recovery Period" – to …

The girls "saving themselves" waiting until their men returned from service during the World War II years – to …

The "welcome back home" sexual frenzy upon the return of our service men and women at war's end (producing "the Baby Boom") – then …

A return back again to the more restrictive period imposed during the '50s that the Class of '55 grew up in.

Amazingly, this view of sex of the '50s was apparently proliferated by powerful politicians on the national level (seeking re-election "causes") – and fueled by a national paranoia of Communism "that regarded 'sex' as a Communist's conspiracy that they preached would lead our youth to moral decay; and therefore, weaken our nation that would lead to its eventual overturn from within!" Our Class of 1955 did not for a minute buy into that hogwash.

On the more positive side, there were the "social morals" (learned from our parents and community) of that day that provided us with guidance for our actions; and, there was an underlying respect and consideration for the sensitivities of the opposite sex. This "system of sex" was not limited to the Class of 1955, but to a generation of young people (that included other small towns across Kentucky, as well as Carlisle) that spanned some two decades – then, things of sex began to change, considerably, in the late '60s and beyond!

The Art of Loving – Via Place Name - The "Fine Art of Lovemaking" can well be illustrated, and, serve as a guide, through the chronological use of some of the colorful, unusual, sometimes unique, but ofttimes imaginative and descriptive "place names" of numerous Kentucky small towns and communities – so, the reader is asked to "play around" with your imagination, and perhaps, filled with a bit of fantasy, "follow along":

The "Alpha" begins with "Wisdom" to recognize and appreciate the "Beauty," the "Wonder," and "Joy" of our "Lovely" partner, a "Guy" or "Princes": it may begin with the words to "Hug Me Tight" and "Kiss Me Quick" – a kiss to the "Nuckles" and "The Mouth" while admiring the "Dimple" – on to the "Shoulderblade" and then down the "Backbone" and on to the "Ankle" and back up – at this point, the lovers are getting "Fisty" (Frisky) but not too "Rowdy," and may say "Why Not?" – let us not "Wait," and they "Go Forth," but avoid the "Rush," in order to "Pinchem Slyly" on their "Mossy Bottom."

If they feel they still "Needmore," then is the time to enjoy the "Sugartit," and find the "Hot Spot" which will, in their "Confluence" and with their "New Hope," then will bring the "Tidal Wave" of "Climax," and then, alas, with some "Humility," surely leads to "Limp" – a few months later, a result could be the "Joy" and "Miracle" of an "Embryo" – for the more "Subtle," as the loving partners at "Sunset" say "Goodnight," feeling "Keene," and in the "Pink," the loving concludes with "Pleasureville," but, for some, they will think they have entered "Eden," and found "Paradise!"

Those of Nicholas, who enjoy their romantic activities at "Sunrise," will think their sexual expressions, while "Barefoot," have led them through the "Pleasant Valley" to glow in a "Morning Glory!"

Some will say all this romantic lovemaking is only for the young, those of "Twenty Six," but why "Stop" before "Seventy Six," for the "Torchlight" can still be "Red Hot" for lovers at age "Eighty Eight" and beyond!

So, to conclude this little ditty, it could be said that "Shakespeare" would have had little "Difficulty" in writing even those "Troublesome" themes of romance if he had had access to Kentucky's imaginative and colorful "Place Names!"

In our modern-day times, national statistics indicate that over 50% of first-time marriages will dissolve in divorce, so, by comparison, it is noteworthy that such a high number, and percentage, of the Class of 1955, are still married, after all these years, to their original spouse. This revelation is not meant, in any way, to denigrate any of our classmates or anyone else who has had the misfortune to experience the trauma of divorce, for it would be rare that any of us have not felt, firsthand, the pain of this disruption in our lives, as well, with our own family members or close friends.

Marriage itself might be looked upon as a mystery, in that it poses the age-old question of what is the unique attraction that draws two people together, "forsaking all others." A satisfying marriage that has endured for decades may be viewed as magical, with some saying this-or-that marriage "was made in heaven," implying perfection and easy sailing, but they are misled, for there is no "magic" in a good marriage, but there is a "work ethic." Marriage is work, not the drudgery kind, but conscious and ongoing, requiring attention and effort. There is initial and continuous commitment, compromise, cooperation, consideration and companionship, honor, respect, trust, friendship, daily affection and attentiveness for our partner, and, yes, some sex mixed in – all of which spell "Love and Marriage!"

It is expected that each of the Class of 1955 who has been blessed with a long and satisfying marriage shares all of these work-in-progress traits. Of the 21 students who began the Class of 1955 senior year together, there are at least 10, and possibly 11, classmates who have been married to their original spouse for forty or more years, with five of those married over 45 years. At least four more of the class lost their original spouse in death. This high success rate is not necessarily unique with only the Class of 1955, but could also be true with other Carlisle and Nicholas County couples of this era, as well as other small town, small school students across the country. The value systems we grew up with in the '40s and '50s, our attitudes toward courtship, love, marriage, and sex, and the role models we observed in our parents, as well as other adults we were close to, all contributed to our own sustaining marriages.

For a few of our classmates, the attractions that fired and fueled "some fine romances" that led to lasting, long-term marriages were found in high school, and had to look and go no further than our hometown of Carlisle. Some of these robust romances were revealed in the May 24, 1955 edition of *The Musketeer Review*, as found and so noted in the "When Seniors Are Gone," the "Junior-Senior Gossip," and "Songs" columns:

"Never hear Martha S. talking about a Nicholas County boy"; "Martha Sue is going to be mighty lonesome now that Ralph is on his trip. You won't know how to act not waiting on him on Saturday nights"; and "Sue to Ralph – 'I Want You All to Myself' " (Martha Sue Feeback and Ralph Taylor);

"Anna Mary, what is this I hear about you starting a hope chest? I hope this isn't serious. When is the wedding date?" and "Whither Thou Goest" (Anna Mary Clinkenbeard and Donnie Hammons);

"Now that both Jewel K. and Wanda are graduating, wonder when the wedding date will be," and "Wanda to Jewel K. – 'Goodnight Sweetheart, Goodnight' " (Wanda Reid and Jewel K. Vice);

"What's Gaunce going to do when Pat leaves for nursing training? I guess he will keep the road hot from here to St. Joseph," and their song, "Pat to Gaunce – 'Someday' " (ChaPatCha "Pat" May and Wayne Gaunce).

For some, *The Musketeer Review* revealed that some of our classmates were pre-occupied with other interests in high school, and it would take awhile to settle on their "fine romance" of one true love at a later time and another place:

Jock Conley – "Never see Jock sleeping study halls away, and even classes," "Jock, you should try going to sleep at nights, so you won't have to sleep in class," and his song, "To Jock – 'Lazy Bones' ";

Jackie Shepherd – "Never see Jackie S. coming in late,"

"Shepherd, why don't you let that masculine appearance capture some girls heart? We Carlisle girls haven't had a chance!" Shepherd's song, "To Shepherd – 'Money Burns a Hole in My Pocket' ";

Donnie Dampier – "We'll never hear Donnie Joe bragging about his dates," "Donnie, which one is it going to be, Faye or Judy? You're keeping us all guessing. One time you see him with one, and the next time you see him with the other, and sometimes you see him with both! How do you rate?"? And, his song, "Faye to Donnie – 'Two Hearts.' "

The Values of Small Towns and Small Schools

Cities and metropolitan areas certainly have much value and provide advantages in economic and employment opportunities, educational pursuits (colleges, libraries, museums, etc.), entertainment (movies, live theater, music concerts from classical to country, etc.), medical facilities, sporting events, a variety of services, shopping, and fine eating, etc. In order to enjoy the benefits, city residents and visitors must also endure the disadvantages of crowded conditions, heavy traffic congestion, pollution, noise, crime, homelessness, and the overall lack of an atmosphere of friendship that is prevalent in our small towns. Actually, most of our small towns provide for some of the city amenities (on a smaller scale) while devoid of most of the disadvantages. Perhaps the ideal home place is to reside in a small-town atmosphere, but live in close proximity of a large city to enjoy and take advantage of its assets. Actually, this "ideal" can still sometimes be found within the city metropolitan areas in the older well-kept neighborhoods, with nearby shopping "in walking distance," that quietly evolved prior to the post-war rush to quick housing.

Growing up in the slow paced confines and environs of small-town Carlisle and Nicholas County, the Class of '55 was hardly aware of a major phenomenon of demographic change which began shortly after WWII and was rapidly transforming the character and livability of large cities in Kentucky and across America.

That is the rapid development of shopping centers (the beginnings of the decline of downtowns) and the population movement to the new concept of "leapfrogging" residential subdivisions – the creation of suburbia. Houses quickly sprung up in this setting by expeditiously utilizing the mass production techniques introduced by Long Island builder Abraham Levitt in lieu of the skilled hand-built individual craftsmanship exhibited in most small town settings. There was little attempt at architectural or artistic creativity, which led to "suburbia sameness!"

At least three major elements that contribute to "livability" were missing: 1) mature trees (for cooling, pollution control, sound absorption, privacy, habitat for many of the creatures of nature, and beauty), 2) the support and security provided by long-standing friends and neighbors, with close-by family ties, and 3) "the front porch." These elements were considered as 'a given' by folks living in Carlisle and other small-town communities, and therefore most of the Class of '55 would have taken them for granted. The absence of these basic livability elements caused subdivision residents to retreat indoors, or, if they came out, to the back yard! Surrounded by people they did not know, and without a sense of place or identity, many began to feel isolated! This was especially true of women, who were relegated back to housewife status when their men returned from WWII needing jobs, and were not yet accepted as equals in the workplace of the cities, so basically were confined at home as homemakers. This was not true of the women of Carlisle and other small towns and rural communities, who still often worked side-by-side with their men in the stores, businesses, and the farm fields!

The front porch and front porch swing, usually with a rocking chair or two, represented a marvelous conveyance of friendship, communication, and neighborliness that said, "welcome to our house!" There was hardly a time of day, in nice weather or rainy days (when it was especially cozy), that residents of Carlisle would not be found sitting, swinging, rocking and relaxing on the front porch, from housewives taking a break, to retirees no longer bound with work requirements, or local business people rejuvenating themselves during lunchtime. Late afternoons and early evenings were especially popular when folks gathered to discuss the events of the day. People during those days loved to wave to folks driving by (whether they recognized them or not) and friends and neighbors walking by, and it was frequently heard, "Come on up and visit a spell!" On those occasions, the lady of the house would ofttimes excuse herself and, a few minutes later, miraculously return with homemade cookies or cake, with lemonade or iced tea or fresh brewed coffee to wash it down! On numerous occasions, in "the good old days" of small-town Carlisle, various members of the Class of '55 would enjoy the marvel of the front porch, socializing and "shooting the breeze" with classmates. Yes, the front porch is the calling card for small towns across America, Kentucky, and towns like Carlisle, and hopefully, for those people so blessed as to have one as a feature of their home, it will not be underappreciated and taken for granted.

Small schools rarely match their large-school counterparts in terms of funding, facilities, varieties of curriculum and program offerings, the volumes of students available for band, chorus, and athletic activities, etc.; however, small schools across America and Kentucky have attributes and advantages that, on the other hand, large schools have difficulty matching. The Carlisle City School System, the home of the Class of '55, exemplified all these attributes to produce excellence in education for its many students down through the years of existence! There was a continuity of teachers, with rare turnover (except as previously mentioned with our band and athletic programs), so, that after first grade, we just knew who our teachers would be for each succeeding grade, which provided us with a sense of security, well being, and confidence. Also, our teachers knew most of us well (sometimes from birth), as well as our parents and family, which provided a teaching advantage by knowing something of our background, interests, and experiences.

Since all twelve grades were housed in the same building, we were not isolated and grouped by age, but always in the company of kids both younger and older, giving us life experiences in the human behavior of various ages. When we were younger, we would learn from the older kids, and ofttimes considered them as role models, mentors, and sometimes protectors; then, when we reached the upper grades, we found ourselves in the reverse roles for the younger kids below us to follow. With the small school coupling to the small town of Carlisle, we had daily contact and interaction with adults, not only our teachers and parents (who were always nearby), but also the townspeople who owned and/or worked in the shops and businesses. There were little of the "we (kids) verses them (adults)" attitudes, since we were acclimated into the adult culture along the way, as we grew up, enabling us to communicate with and cultivate a respect for our elders.

Old-Time Discipline and the Occasional Prank – Discipline at the Carlisle City School, for most of us, was administered as a two-edged sword, that is, whatever was received at school, we could expect at least as much corrective action when we got home, to be added again by our parents, who were very supportive of our teachers! With the deserved respect and confidence earned by the educators of the Carlisle City School System, discipline was not only accepted, but was also expected, and, at no time did our parents threaten any of the Carlisle staff with a lawsuit or bodily harm, as is seen so often in modern times (especially in the larger schools). In those days, paddling was an accepted part of the process, if deemed as warranted based on the indiscretion of the student, and there was the fear of the dreaded "paddle of punishment" displayed prominently in Superintendent Davis's office. However, since most disciplinary action was verbal, combined with additional work assignments, the paddle was mostly symbolic, but if occasionally used (on both boys and girls, indiscriminately), it was never applied in public to humiliate, but in private to instruct. So, for the kids at Carlisle City School, as well as for the Class of '55, discipline, when needed, was applied as part of the overall teaching process!

Pranks played on one another have always seemed to be an important part of growing up, and strange as it may seem, the process has always been a factor in developing and expressing friendships. During grade school and into early high school, these pranks were mostly played on one another and other kids; however, when we entered junior/senior years, we got brave and extended those harmless pranks to include our teachers! These were not done out of a disrespect toward the teacher, but, rather a showing off for our classmates and an opportunity to see what we could get away with. There were a couple of pranks that would resurface every couple of years that seemed to be a tradition at Carlisle High School, and probably for many other small schools in rural communities.

One of those pranks would be instigated on snowy or rainy days when many of the kids wore galoshes (we called them "overshoes") to school. Some of the boys who lived in farm settings, such as Kenneth Booth, Jackie Shepherd, or Jackie Wells, would deliberately walk through "fresh" cow manure that morning, then, upon arriving at school, remove and place the boots (with the excuse of drying them) beside the steam radiators that heated the school. This would further activate the "farm-fresh aroma" around the room, getting the teacher's attention! However, in lieu of showing anger or disgust, the first period teacher, usually Ms. Nancy Talbert, would merely express a comment, such as, "It seems that someone forgot to wipe their boots before coming in the room – either that, or someone removed their shoes who has not washed their feet in a week!" Then she would request that the soiled boots be removed to the cloakroom, so class could resume.

A second "traditional" prank was pulled during warm weather by putting a live snake in the victimized teacher's top desk drawer before class. But our teachers were wise to the ways of the CHS pranksters, and instead of jumping in fright upon opening her drawer, would quietly close the drawer, then comment something like, "It appears that an unwanted visitor has taken up residence in my drawer. Would some of you brave students come up and remove the creature?" At saying that, some six to eight kids would come forward to view the intruder, then, the perpetrator of the prank (without admitting guilt) would usually be the one to take the snake outside, becoming the hero for the day!

These types of pranks rarely resulted in any steps of discipline from our understanding teachers, although they probably had a good idea who the pranksters were; there was no real harm done!

Besting The Bullies – Bullies and bullying have always been persistent problems for kids to contend with at all levels of school and the growing-up process, and the Carlisle City School was no exception. To learn early on how to deal with this problem was, and is, an important part of the educational process, for, if you think about it, bullying continues though out our adult lives as well in the form of aggressive drivers exhibiting "road rage," adults expressing anger at little league games, spouse abuse, bosses or co-workers seeking control in the workplace, etc. Bullying is not restricted as a male malady only; however, for boys, it will often result in physical force, resulting in bodily harm or being beaten up. For our girls, it was less likely to be applied physically, but no less troublesome; however, the girls of the Class of '55 appeared to stand up for themselves very well! The best way to handle a bully is to avoid him and walk away if possible, but since this is frequently not an option, there were some methods available to the boys of Carlisle.

One of these was "the Charles Atlas Approach." During the '50s, contained in comic books (such as "Joe Palooka") and other magazines, were advertisements (displaying the very well-developed Charles Atlas holding "the world" on his shoulders) to send off for the "Charles Atlas Body Building Courses." The advertisements were a comic strip of a "97-pound weakling" on the beach with a beautiful girl, then this big, bad bully comes up, pushes the "97-pound weakling" to the ground, kicks sand in his face, and walks off with his beautiful girl, while the weakling watches, powerless to act! Then the strip showed the positive results of a few weeks of following the Charles Atlas Course, as the "97-pound weakling" was now muscular, with a well-developed physique (no steroids used) that is shown walking up to the bully, pushing him to the ground and kicking sand in his face, as the new hero walks off with his girl back on his arm! This was not very flattering to women, implying that they were fickle females whose loyalties could be easily changed by big muscles. It is not known if any of the Carlisle boys actually sent off for the "Dynamic-Tension" course (that required no equipment), but the message and attitude was stimulated by the "Charles Atlas way" to build yourself up physically and practice self-defense skills, such as boxing, to feel good about yourself and develop the confidence to face off against a confronting bully.

Another "bullying control" was prevalent in the small school atmosphere of Carlisle where kids of all ages intermixed each day. In this environment, even though the older kids would kid around with the younger kids in fun, the older student would frequently step in on behalf of the smaller, younger kids that were being harassed by bullying tactics. This would often diffuse a bully when he or she had lost their advantage of size, strength, or surprise. When those of us in the Class of '55 advanced to the higher grades, with possible past experiences of being sometimes bullied ourselves, we found that we were looked upon as protectors by many of our younger buddies, and we accepted that role. In the larger schools in the '50s, where the high school and grade school facilities were separate, and, especially, in the modern day mega-sized schools, kids frequently walk the hallways surrounded by some 1,500-2,000 students, or more, and still feel isolated and alone, and, therefore, without any kind of "support system," when confronted by bullying. This was rarely the case in our small schools!

Growing up in Carlisle and Nicholas County in the '40s and '50s, there were a number of influences that helped to stimulate our mind-set and help prepare us to overcome bullying. At the Saturday afternoon movies, our cowboy heroes that we emulated were always overcoming bullies who were threatening the ranchers and townspeople. There was a strong spirit of patriotism that prevailed in our community that recognized that the dictators of the world, such as Hitler or Stalin, were bullies that had to be thwarted and defeated! Then, there were the parents of the Class of '55, who foremost taught us consideration for others and not to be bullies ourselves, but also, if confronted, to stand up for ourselves against those who would try to control us.

We, without realizing it, were following the philosophy of

the 26th president of the United States, Theodore "Teddy" Roosevelt, when he advised to "speak softly and carry a big stick!" Theodore Roosevelt, who served two terms from 1901-1909, was noted for his charge of the Rough Riders up San Juan Hill in the Spanish-American War, and being the first to set aside land for the National Parks System. He was immortalized as one of the four presidents, along with George Washington, Thomas Jefferson, and Abraham Lincoln, to be carved on the face of Mount Rushmore. A visit to Mount Rushmore is one of the many trips that Donnie and Pat, and Jock and Joanie, have taken together over the years. Ironically, Teddy's favorite expression was "bully, bully," but he used the phrase to express "excellent" or "outstanding," rather than a reference to "bully" as one habitually cruel to others weaker than himself.

The old adage and truism, "It takes a village to raise a child," was in full evidence and practice for the CHS Class of 1955 as we were growing up in small-town Carlisle and rural Nicholas County.

XI

The Ending of a Good School …
The Ending of an Educational Era

The Closing of Carlisle High School

Eight years after the class of 1955, in 1963, Carlisle High School (1893-1963) closed its doors for good with consolidation into Nicholas County High School; then, eight years after that, in 1971, Carlisle Elementary also closed, ending an era of 78 years of quality education. *The History of Nicholas County* recorded that there was an earlier Carlisle city school that began around 1851, but was equipped to provide only a minimal education, until 1887, when the Kentucky General Assembly passed an act that authorized an organizational change, with increased funding, that declared the

Carlisle city school as an "independent city school district," which was then chartered in 1888 as District #26.

The Eventful Years of 1962 and 1963 – "Those Were the Years" that encompassed the last school year of Carlisle High School, were the transition years that began to usher in a new era of cultural change in our society, much of which would have a lasting effect on Carlisle and Nicholas County. As the Class of 1963, 14 members strong, that comprised the final graduating class of Carlisle High School, approached their senior year during the summer of 1962, it was still much like the times depicted in the very popular movie of 1973, *American Graffiti*, with its time setting in the summer of 1962. The attitudes and activities shown in *American Graffiti* could well have been about 1954, for very few cultural changes had occurred from the years of the CHS Class of 1955 until 1962. The movie was described as the end of "The Age of Innocence," a period of time that roughly covered the years of 1952 (after the end of the Korean War) throughout the '50s and into 1963. This had been a period of increasing prosperity, relatively free from war, characterized as a good time to live, with new freedoms of mobility, sexual expression, a breaking-out period, as it were, to seek expanded opportunities, much of which was brought about by the peacetime production and marketing of the automobile, etc.

The "Last Class of Carlisle High School" in 1963 was crossing the threshold of a transition in history, especially for women. The birth control pill was becoming more available, providing for greater freedom of female sexuality; and who could know, in 1963, that just down the road, scores of women from across the country would be removing their bras, some in public, for "bra burning" demonstrations as an expression of newly found female freedoms in all avenues of life. Some would describe this action as a release from the "booby trap." Events that would begin in the 1962-63 period would alter the so-called "Age of Innocence" of the '50s into what would lead to a time of political and social unrest, which would become an "Age of Protest" of the '60s and the '70s!

While the members of the "Last Class of Carlisle High" were

listening to *Blue Velvet* and *Blue On Blue* (Bobby Vinton), *Blowing in the Wind* (Peter, Paul & Mary), *Be My Baby* (The Ronettes), and *Candy Girl* (The Four Seasons) or watching *The Fugitive* begin his run on TV or, going to the movies to see the Oscar winners of their era – *The Apartment* (1960), *West Side Story* (1961), *Lawrence of Arabia* (1962), and *Tom Jones* (1963) – there were other significant happenings of 1962 and 1963.

In 1962, "James Bond, Agent 007," the suave, sexy, super-hero creation of British novelist Ian Fleming, made his screen debut in *Dr. No*, with co-stars Sean Connery (the best Bond of them all) and the seductive Ursula Andress. This was closely followed by *From Russia With Love* and *Goldfinger*, with part of the setting at Ft. Knox, Kentucky. Forty years later, with new, updated storylines for the times introduced with "Bond ... James Bond," a succession of different "Agent 007s" are still popular at the box office!

Just as the Class of 1955 had ushered in rock 'n' roll with Elvis, the Class of 1963 was on the verge of being a part of yet another major musical wave – "The Beatles," made up of four young men with the strange hair cuts and Cockney accents, John Lennon, Paul McCartney, George Harrison, and Ringo Starr. Originally, this small group, who were destined to eventually be the first British rock band to achieve worldwide prominence, called themselves the Quarrymen (around 1957), then, in 1960, the Quarrymen changed their name to the Silver Beatles, quickly dropping the "Silver" to become just "The Beatles." Their recording *I Want To Hold Your Hand*, stormed to the top of the U.S. charts within weeks of its release by Capitol Records on December 26, 1963, and with the Beatles' television appearance on *The Ed Sullivan Show* in February of 1964, the British invasion of "Beatlemania" was launched!

On February 20, 1962, Marine Corps Lieutenant Colonel John Glenn, piloting the spacecraft Friendship 7, became the first American to orbit the earth, launching the USA up to par with the Soviet Union in "the space race." Up to this point, our concepts of space travel came from reading science fiction, and even with the orbit, we no doubt had skepticism with the President Kennedy pledge to land a man on the moon within the decade. But, with American ingenuity and resolve in full evidence, it did happen, and only six years after the "Last Class of CHS," when, on July 20, 1969, we were watching on live television as space flight Apollo 11 (piloted by Commander Neil Armstrong, USAF Colonel Edwin Aldrin Jr., and USAF Lieutenant Colonel Michael Collins) arrived at the moon. Then shortly after the announcement from the lunar lander, "The Eagle has landed," Commander Neil Armstrong stepped foot on the surface of the moon, and with his announcement, "That's one small step for man, one giant leap for mankind," the American astronaut became the first man to walk on the moon!

It was shocking news on August 4, 1962, that Marilyn Monroe, an enduring legend, had died. Marilyn, whose real name was Norma Jean Baker, was an icon of female sexuality and the female sex symbol of the '50s, and has been described as a premiere movie star of the 20th century, and one of the most famous women in the history of Western civilization. Forty years later, the sordid circumstances of her death are still shrouded in mystery and controversy.

It was in 1962 that a more pleasant event occurred, with the invention (by the City Beer Company) of cans that can be opened with tabs. Thus began the eventual phase-out of a status symbol of the 1950s, young men carrying their personal beer can opener (some quite decorative), known as the "church key," on their key chains!

On October 22, 1962, the nation and the world "held its breath" as Present John F. Kennedy, in a televised speech, informed the American people of the "Cuban Missile Crisis" – with nuclear war threatened – then, on October 28, 1962, a "sigh of relief" was heard as the Soviet premier, Nikita S. Khrushchev, ordered the removal of all Soviet missiles from Cuba, so that the immediate threat of nuclear war was past.

Governor Edward T. "Ned" Breathitt was in office when Carlisle High School was closed in 1963.

On August 28, 1963, the Reverend Martin Luther King Jr., at a civil rights march before over 250,000 people gathered at the Lincoln Memorial, in Washington, D.C., which included the supporting likes of Judy Garland, Marlon Brando, Burt Lancaster, and Bob Dylan, and viewed by President "JFK," delivered his famous "I Have a Dream" speech. He was murdered on April 5, 1968, in Memphis, Tennessee, just five years after his "I Have a Dream," and five years after the closing of one of the first high schools in the South to integrate its classrooms without incident, Carlisle High School, in the 1955-56 school year.

There were many events that occurred in that last calendar year of the existence of Carlisle High School, but none so tragic as the one that happened on November 22, 1963, that shocked and saddened America, and the world, when our president, John F. Kennedy, was assassinated while riding in a motorcade in downtown Dallas, Texas, and, then, only two days later, Lee Harvey Oswald, the man charged with the Kennedy assassination, was himself murdered at Dallas Police Headquarters by a Dallas nightclub owner named Jack Ruby. The youthful and energetic image of President John F. Kennedy had seemed to symbolize the optimistic attitude that was emerging in America, but the optimistic spirit of Kennedy's concept of the "New Frontier" seemed to die with him, and the turbulence that would mark the rest of the decade of the 1960s had just begun, thus ending the "Age of Innocence" of the 1950s.

The activities at Carlisle High School during the first half of the 1962-63 school year would indicate a decision to close the school had not been made, nor were there any expectations that consolidation was soon imminent. At the beginning of school, and prior to the opening home football game, some CHS alumni, led by Kimball Booth, erected a new scoreboard and installed 1,000 new seat bleachers at the athletic field: also, the six Carlisle High School cheerleaders displayed their new look with the purchase of new uniforms for the 1962-63 season; and, at a January 1963 meeting at William's Restaurant, the Carlisle Band Boosters made plans for the Spring Pantomime Show, a major fund-raising event with the goal of obtaining new uniforms for the CHS Band.

However, the Carlisle Board of Education, at its regular monthly meeting in April of 1963, decided that due to the reduction in their staff, this would be the opportune time to submit a proposal for merging the two school districts. It is not certain which actions spurred the other, but the April 11, 1963 headlines of *The Carlisle Mercury* read, "Rose, Leedy To Leave Carlisle School." Tebay Rose, superintendent of Carlisle City School for the past six years, returned to Harrodsburg as high school principal, and, William Ed Leedy, coach of the Musketeers for the previous six years, accepted a position at Henry County High School as head football coach and science teacher. The headline of the May 9, 1963 edition of *The Carlisle Mercury* read, "School Boards Merge Quietly," with the storyline that at separate special sessions of both the Nicholas County Board of Education and the Carlisle Board of Education, held on May 3, 1963, a proposal was adopted for merger of the two districts, effective at the end of the 1963 school term, thus sealing the closing of Carlisle High School.

The last year of football for the Green and White Musketeers of Carlisle High School was played out on the athletic fields of the 1962 season. Coach Bill Ed Leedy, who was the last football coach" led a typical-size squad of some twenty gridiron Musketeers, and they were poised to begin that last season with a nine-game schedule ahead. The kickoff of the season was against Paris High School, the Musketeers' traditional opening opponent, which resulted in a 35-0 loss to the Ben Pumphrey-coached Greyhounds. Carlisle still retained some of the traditional rivals on the schedule, such as Stanford, Lancaster, and Georgetown, which, at this time, had held off their eventual closing due to consolidation. Carlisle's long-time foe, the Cynthiana Bulldogs, had now been replaced on the schedule by the Harrison County Thoroughbreds, the school into which Cynthiana had merged with in 1958. Along the way, the Musketeers were now playing the Irvine Golden Eagles, the Mercer County Scotties, the Kentucky School for the Deaf (KSD), located in Danville, and the Mt. Sterling Trojans. In the

KSD game, the Musketeers inadvertently helped the KSD Colonels to retain their fine season of undefeated and unscored on, with the Musketeers' late season November loss of 20-0. The last team of football-playing Musketeers of Carlisle High School lost all nine games in what would be the final football season at Carlisle High School, but the players on that team continued the tradition of small-school, undermanned football teams by giving their best on the gridiron, and played the game, win or lose!

Actually, as it turns out, this was not the last season for football-playing Musketeers, for in the first football season ever for Nicholas County High School, the football team retained the "Musketeers" as their nickname for at least that inaugural kickoff season of 1963. In the first-ever varsity football game of the newly merged high school, played on the Carlisle Athletic Field and coached by Carlisle native Gayle Bowen, assisted by Donald Burton, the now Nicholas County Musketeers lost to the Fleming County Panthers by a tight score of 13-7.

As the ten boys and four girls (where did all the girls go?) of the Class of 1963 looked forward to graduation day, with commencement held on May 23, 1963, they surely gave some thought that they would go down in history as the last class of Carlisle High School, similar in name to the popular movie *The Last Picture Show.* Just as any class might wonder what lies ahead, or what will the future bring, the more perceptive members of the class possibly were observing the political storm clouds that were gathering in Southeast Asia, that would soon blow in the winds of war of Vietnam.

Thus ended the excellent educational pursuits of a grand old school … the Green and White Musketeers of Carlisle High School.

The Carlisle City School building, which housed many of the Class of '55 for most of the twelve years, would have been considered as one of the most prominent buildings in Carlisle during its era, second only to the Court House. There was a reference to some dates on the school sidewalk indicating that the original building was started in 1889 and completed in 1893, at about the same time as the Court House, which was completed in 1894, and dedicated in July of that year. The original school building was apparently constructed of wood, for it was completely destroyed by fire in May of 1903, at the conclusion of that school year, and, since available historical accounts do not indicate the cause of the fire, perhaps, there was "too much celebration" over the end of that school year? The Carlisle City School, which became locally known by the 1950s, as the "old city school," was immediately rebuilt after the fire, this time with walls that were five bricks thick, with the new structure reopened for the eager Carlisle students in September of 1904, amazingly, only some 15 months after its destruction. From that 1904 version of the brick building, increased enrollment and space needs called for an enlargement of the facility, so that in the early 1920s, a three-story addition was constructed on the south side, resulting in the final version of the building that the Class of 1955 will remember, as well as most surviving alumni! Situated at the corner of School and North Streets, on the crest of what was known as "College Hill," one of the many hills in Carlisle, it was a most imposing sight, indeed!

Most of the Class of '55 will fondly remember that North Street was one of the two favorite hill streets designated for sleigh riding on those snow-packed winter days, the other being the Christian Church Hill (Chestnut Street). The city would sometimes block off the streets for two or three hours, when folks could not travel much anyway, so we could safely sleigh ride without automobile traffic. The Christian Church Hill was the longest course of the two, with our most triumphant ride occasionally taking us two blocks, all the way to Sycamore Street! North Street was much steeper, providing a shorter and speedier descent that produced a much more harrowing adventure!

Sadly, the old school building that provided so many lifetime memories and was the "seat of learning" for the Class of '55 and countless other classes that attended the Carlisle City School System, is no longer there, razed over a sixteen-year period from

1972, when the building was purchased by an alumni of Carlisle High School, Mr. Bill Hilander, to its final destruction in 1988, and now replaced by homes on the site of "hallowed ground." In the seventy-year period (1893-1963) that the "old city school" building site was in service, there were 71 graduating classes totaling some 1423 high school graduates, for an average of 20 per year. Fortunately, many of us were able to acquire commemorative bricks of the old building, thanks to the generosity of Mr. and Mrs. Hilander, that were saved as a memento of the place where we spent so many years of our lives, and sold for the benefit of the Carlisle High School Alumni.

The City School Building was well laid out, efficient, and comfortable to accommodate some 400-plus students, teachers, staff, and administrators each school year during its existence. In any given school year, the lower eight grades had around 300 students, with the high school of grades nine through twelve accommodating some 90 to 100 students, with approximately two dozen faculty and support staff. The dimensions of the "old city school" were 80 feet by 180 feet, five levels high, with over a half-million bricks constructing the outside structure walls, which ranged from three to five bricks, a veritable fortress! The very durable bricks, made in the brick kilns of Maysville, Kentucky in the mid 1880s, were found to be some 20-25% larger than modern bricks.

In describing the building itself, a first time visitor of the 1950s, upon entering, would likely be struck and surprised at the polish and shine of the floors and stair-rails, and the overall cleanliness of the building. Superintendent Davis, our teachers, and staff, who encouraged our students to believe in ourselves and strive for excellence, believed that our seat of learning, a visual brick-and-board school building, should also reflect that idea, and be a tangible place that we could all be proud of!

The first floor was reserved for the elementary kids of the first six grades. The second floor contained the administrative offices, the library/study hall, and, the auditorium (for general assemblies, plays, choirs, and graduation commencement, etc.), along with the high school classrooms. There was even a third floor, more like a clean attic, with some classrooms, such as Mr. G.B. Leonard's "agriculture" class. The basement was always a hub of activity, housing the school cafeteria/lunch room, a lounge/recreation area, and the "school store" (a place to purchase refreshments and supplies, operated by the students, with the profits to be applied to school functions).

The basement also was the respite for the boys and girls restrooms, which were also utilized by faculty and staff. The basement was also known for the "mysterious tunnel" that supposedly provided a hidden link and passageway between the boys' and girls' restrooms. Each year, there was a ritual, sort of a rite of passage (pun intended!), whereby the older students (both boys and girls) made a point of informing the younger students just entering high school of this "secret and seductive" tunnel. It could not have been very much of a secret, since its intrigue was well-disclosed! If memory serves, there was a small opening, about shoulder high, in one corner of the boy's restroom, but this writer is not aware if there was a similar opening in the girls section. If there was such a linking tunnel, it was unlikely that anyone ever ventured within. It was dark, requiring a flashlight (for this reason, our teachers were wary of any student carrying a flashlight to school), and reputed to be inhabited with numerous varmints, including snakes, rats, bats, and spiders – a real-life Indiana Jones "Temple of Doom!" But, wouldn't be fun to imagine the "mayhem" if a venturous boy or two, while groping in the dark tunnel, surprisingly encountered a girl or two coming from the other side?

The Building of the Carlisle High School Gymnasium

"We need a big gymnasium" was an appeal to community leaders and the Carlisle school board and administrators which appeared in the Carlisle Mercury pre-school issue of September 7, 1916. Primarily, due to the WWI concerns, the appeal was put on the back burners; however, the refrain, "We need a big place to play basketball inside," was echoed again by CHS students in a 1918 issue of The Flashlight, as the Carlisle City School's first newspaper was called back then. The issue of the need for a school gymnasium stayed alive from that point on – probably encouraged and justified with the urging appeal of, "Build it, and they will come" – until a modern brick building was erected and opened for athletics and basketball events, with the "formal dedication" of the sparkling new Carlisle High School Gymnasium on Friday, December 4, 1924, to coincide with the opening of the 1924-25 basketball season for Carlisle High School.

Local newspaper articles of 1924 chronicled the progression of the building of the new CHS gym, beginning with a January 31, 1924 issue of *The Carlisle Mercury.*

"Carlisle Has A New Gymnasium Building ... In Carlisle, where a new gymnasium is now being erected in a vacant lot adjoining the high school building, work on the new gym is now proceeding rapidly – the foundation is complete, and the walls are up. Carlisle, a town of 2,000 inhabitants, having less than half the population of Maysville (which had no such facility, at the time), raised the money for their new gymnasium by a bond issue of $30,000."

A companion article in the same issue, issued in a bulletin of the State Parent-Teacher Association, praised the Carlisle City School "penny lunch room" as a model operation: "Carlisle is on the map! Their school lunchroom is used as a model for Cynthiana, Millersburg, and Flemingsburg, who have adopted their methods, and menus, in their schools."

There must have been much concern felt by the citizens of Carlisle when, before the new gym had even its first use, *The Carlisle Mercury* of August 28, 1924, reported:

"New Gymnasium Damaged By Bolt – Lightning Tears Hole In Roof of Building Sunday Night... The roof of the new gymnasium at the Carlisle City School was considerably damaged when struck by a bolt of lightning during the severe rain and electrical storm Sunday night. A large hole was torn in the roof, letting the water pour into the building. Fortunately, the building did not ignite. The damage is entirely covered by insurance, and has been repaired."

A large crowd attended the formal dedication exercises of the new Carlisle High School Gymnasium (Athletic Building) on Friday, December 4, 1924 – the largest crowd ever to witness a basketball game in Carlisle. It was reported, "The building contains a splendid hardwood floor, and there are comfortable seats to accommodate a large crowd. Discomfort experienced at former games here will be eliminated by the fact that the building is heated, and seats are provided!"

Basketball at Carlisle City School got its "jump-start" with the opening "tip off" of the new gym. In the Mercury article for opening night, it was reported, "This will be the first basket ball played here for two years, and the first ever played in school property." An accompanying article, titled "Rules For Basket Ball," written by Joe T. Embry, Carlisle High athletic director and coach, gave a detailed explanation of the rules and objective of the "game of basket ball" to a population which, in that day and time of the mid-'20s, had little previous exposure to the sport.

Appropriately enough, the first-ever games contested in the new Carlisle Gymnasium, on dedication night, were played between Carlisle alumni and current Carlisle students. In the first game played, the high school girls (yes, there were girls' games back then), coached by Miss Dorothy Fick, music teacher and physical culture director, defeated an alumni team by a score of 13-1. The alumni boys defeated the high school boys – described as the most thrilling ever seen here – by a score of 22-20.

In the following week, on December 11, 1924, in the first games played in the new gym that counted on the CHS record – against outside opponents – Carlisle's junior high team defeated the Little Rock team in the first game, by the score of 20-13. In the second game, the varsity quintet of Carlisle High School defeated Mayslick High by the score of 23-9. The varsity players who made history by playing in the first official games on the new Carlisle High School Gymnasium were: Hutchings, A. Cook, Clark, Poe

(Captain), W. Cook, and Hughes. The Carlisle junior team playing on that historic nigh, consisted of: Kerns, Crouch, Ham, Nixon, Clark, Martin, and Barton.

On March 6 and 7 of 1925, Carlisle High School, with its sparkling "state of the art" new gymnasium, was awarded, for the very first time, the distinction to serve as the host school for what was then the 11th District (Region) Basketball Tournament – for both Boys and Girls teams. Nine high schools from five counties of the area were represented: Augusta and Brooksville of Bracken County, with Germantown (split on the Bracken/Mason Counties line), Ewing and Flemingsburg of Fleming County, Maysville and Sardis from Mason County, Mt. Olivet from Robertson County, and, of course, Carlisle, representing Nicholas County – each school was represented by both a boys' and girls' team, except Germantown and Sardis, which sent only their girls' team.

The teams of cagers from Carlisle High both competed very well in the single-elimination tournament, with the boys losing to Augusta 26-16, which then lost out the following night in the championship game by the score of 26-16 to Brooksville of Bracken County. The Carlisle Girls fared even better, as they beat Germantown 11 to 8, before losing out, by the score of 13-10, to Flemingsburg, the eventual girls' champions (Flemingsburg 11, Brooksville 7).

The Carlisle Mercury of March 12, 1925, reported large crowds of near capacity for each of the 14 games played, filling the new Carlisle High School Gymnasium at each session, with the largest crowd present during the championship games on Saturday night, when it was estimated that over 1,200 people were crowed into the building! "Combined with the gracious hospitality exhibited by the Carlisle citizens, whereby many various Carlisle homes opened their doors to entertain, and sometimes provide lodging, to the visiting teams and coaches, and, the fine facilities of the new Carlisle High School Gymnasium, each of the towns represented, expressed a desire to return to Carlisle for the Region Tournament for 1926!"

At the same time the new gymnasium was unveiled, an even more significant event transpired – of greater lifetime importance to the Class of 1955, as well as all other companion classes of the Carlisle City School – with the announcement in *The Carlisle Mercury* edition of November 20, 1924 … "AA Rating Given Local High School – Carlisle High School Admitted To Membership in the Southern Association of Colleges and Secondary Schools – Effective December 1, 1924 … Carlisle School Superintendent M. Erle Lier revealed that for the first time ever in the history of the school, Carlisle High School achieved the high rating of 'AA,' qualifying them for the esteemed membership in the Association." At this time in Kentucky, there were 363 academically accredited Class A high schools, with more than that number rated as Class C, but only 35, now including Carlisle High School, had ascended to the level of AA to qualify for the distinctive membership in the SACSS – a source of great pride for all of Carlisle, by putting the small school academically in the same status as high schools in the larger cities.

By Carlisle High School meeting the exacting academic and facility standards of at least ten requirements annually for continued membership in the Association, it meant, among other advantages, that the graduates of Carlisle High School were effectively academically "certified" and, thereby, entitled to enter any of the larger colleges in the United States without a qualifying entry examination. Almost three decades later, as the Class of 1955 entered its high school years, the administration and faculty exhibited their pride of accomplishment, as CHS had annually achieved the rating of AA, to continue, uninterrupted, to maintain the school's membership in the Southern Association of Colleges and Secondary Schools – a feat continued throughout the existence of Carlisle High School.

When the Class of 1955 participated in basketball games in the mid-'50s, the by-then "thirty-something" year-old gymnasium building was still quite functional, well cared for, and adequate for a small school, but with numerous small schools already closed into bigger schools, and, with the statewide popularity of basketball continually on the rise – building much more spacious playing facilities – the old CHS Gym was now counted, along with numerous other small school gyms, as a small "cracker-barrel."

In its time of the mid-'20s, the well-constructed gymnasium of Carlisle High School could have been considered as "state of the art," at least for small schools! The gym, of which accounts of its first season of operation indicated, had a seating capacity which would accommodate up to some 1,200 "well-packed-in" spectators, had a regulation, full-length hardwood floor, high ceilings, and hanging light fixtures, large windows above the balcony to let in natural light, and which opened for ventilation, and regulation 10-foot high basket rims (with adequate stopping space between the backboard and the back wall), and the facility provided dressing rooms with welcomed hot showers.

Another interesting feature of the Carlisle High School Gymnasium – which must have been considered as innovative for its day – was a heating plant fueled by a coal-burning furnace located in a partial basement, producing "steam heat," that not only provided heat and hot showers for the gym, but the steam heat was also piped several yards to provide the same amenities for all floors of the Carlisle School building, as well!

By contrast to the Carlisle Gym, in many other small schools across the Commonwealth during this era, the kids, and their teams, played their basketball games in makeshift, multipurpose facilities, such as an upstairs auditorium, a converted barn, or, in an otherwise smaller playing space; or, some, such as the celebrated Carr Creek team of 1928, having no gym, practiced on outdoor courts, ofttimes on an unlevel surface, and in all kinds of weather – playing their official games against opponents that had an inside gym! The boys playing the game ofttimes had to focus a part of their concentration away from their opponents, and the game itself, to adjust to the playing facilities, such as a hot stove looming at one end of the court; a wall to face just as soon as an underneath shot was released, causing the boys to "prepare for a sudden stop"; the sudden surprise as their outside shot hit a low ceiling, light fixture, or rafter; and then, some of the facilities, suffering from a lack of space, dictated that their floors were shorter than full-length regulation, with overlapping lines on either side of the center circle (which provided for regulation size half courts) causing much confusion on "over-and-back" calls to both the boys, and the referee (usually only one officiated in this day and time).

During the period of the '50s, when the boys of the Class of 1955 left the cozy, comfortable confines of the Carlisle High School Gym (which, by that time, it also was beginning to be considered as outdated), they would still occasionally find some of these distracting elements of short floors, low ceilings, close confines in some opponents' home gym, although it is not recalled that any looming pot-bellied hot stoves were still around.

Amazingly, the old CHS Gymnasium, built 20 years after the school building, is now, in the year of 2004, into its 80th year, still standing in its accustomed and familiar location on the original school grounds, hopefully, to continue standing as a visible, and tangible, historical marker of the Carlisle City School! Much of the outside of the old building is now covered by ivy, not the type of ivy of "the hallowed halls of ivy," but poison ivy, nonetheless, a welcome sight!

Amazing Alumni Associations

The Carlisle High School Alumni Association, founded in 1915 – in the view of this writer, for many years – has served as an amazing accolade in tribute to the love and loyalty placed by its graduates upon this little quality school in the small town of Carlisle, Kentucky. This is demonstrated by the ongoing, annual CHS Alumni Banquet, which continues to be truly a remarkable phenomenon in that from a small school, closed since 1963, with no new graduates added to the mix in over 40 years, still has over 100 graduates attend each year! The one exception in its membership requirements that has provided for a small increase in the alumni numbers was initiated a few years ago when some former students of the Carlisle school system, who were in the lower grades scheduled to be future grads when the school closed, petitioned to join, and were warmly received, into the CHS Alumni Association.

In the Thursday edition of The Carlisle Mercury of May 13, 1915, a headline proclaimed, "C.H.S. Alumni Organize." At a May 7, 1915 meeting, with about 20 "alumni" present, at the home of Elizabeth Rice (CHS Class of 1898), the initial organization of the Alumni Association of the Carlisle High School was effected. The first officers of the association were: President, Mrs. Taylor B. Mathers (the former Bertie Dallas), one of the nine members of the very first graduating Class of 1893; Vice President, Mr. F. C. "Frank" Taylor, Class of 1895, at which time the institution had been designated as a "graded high school"; with Miss Gladys Bryson, Class of 1913, elected as Secretary-Treasurer. Committees on Membership, and an inaugural banquet were established with James Parker, CHS Class of 1900, appointed as the first chairman. (He went to work right away with an announcement in the next edition of the Mercury: "Whether a member of the committee sees you, or not, you are expected to join the association, if you are an alumnus of the school!")

And, so it was, on the Friday evening of May 21, 1915, the very first of what became a continuous Annual Meeting Banquet of the Carlisle High School Alumni Association, was held in conjunction with, and, following the graduation exercises of the 23rd graduating class of CHS, to honor the Class of 1915. At this time in the history of Carlisle High School, there were only a total of 208 eligible alumni, counting, also, the 10-member class of 1915. Included in this initial membership of the CHS Alumni Association were at least three future teachers of the Class of 1955: second-grade teacher Miss Mary Frances Fisher (Class of 1906); fifth-grade teacher Miss Earl Botts (Class of 1914); and Miss Nancy Talbert (Class of 1915), who would serve us for many years for English and literature, and as the school's principal. Joining Miss Earl in this inaugural membership were her sisters, Ethel (Class of 1912) and Ina Botts (Class of 1915), with the three Botts girls being aunts of Mary Phyllis Smith

Cameron, of the Class of 1955.

In the modern era of mega-sized high schools, many high schools have more students enrolled in one year, as did Carlisle's cumulative totals for seventy years! In Carlisle's first 33 years, there were a cumulative total of 356 graduates, with the Class of 1925, with 21, the first class to reach 20; then, the following year, the Class of 1926, with 35 graduates, became the first class to break the "thirty barrier." The nineteen-year period of 1926-1944 was the heyday in terms of the number of graduating seniors, compiling a cumulative count of 668, an average of 35 per year. During this heyday period, the Class of 1932 achieved the still-standing distinction as the largest graduating class in CHS history, with a total of 47.

The History of Nicholas County offers an explanation for the nineteen "peak" years of CHS graduates, during 1926-44 era. Of the several "county" schools located in all directions outside of Carlisle (East Union, Ellisville, Moorefield, Myers, Parks, etc), apparently only Headquarters (sometimes referred to as Headquarters High) was designed to offer "high school" classes; however, due to an agreement with Carlisle High School, very few high school students out in the county attended Headquarters during this period – most of them seeking a high school diploma, attended, and graduated from Carlisle High. However, beginning with 1945, this arrangement ended, with an immediate reduction in the number of CHS graduates after 1944.

Thus, beginning with the Class of 1945, with 28 graduates, the average dropped to slightly below 30 for the 5-year remainder of the'40s, with the 41 graduates of 1948 (one of only four CHS classes in history with 40 or more) keeping the average as high as it was. In 1952, with the opening of the sparkling new facilities of Nicholas County High School, located on the western fringe of Carlisle, few students from out in the county enrolled at Carlisle High, and with no new influx of population into the city, the old school began to creak as a sinking ship about to be lost in the sea of education. The 10-year period of the '50s saw the average number of graduates drop to slightly below 20, with the Class of 1955 one of only five in that decade to list as many as 20 graduates; then, the four years of CHS existence in the sixties saw the average number drop to 14.

Nostalgia must have filled the hallowed halls of the old Carlisle school on the evening of May 23, 1963, as 248 souls raised their voices to the refrains of "Auld Lang Syne," in honor of the Class of 1963 (the 71st graduating class of CHS), in what was described in the billing as "Carlisle High's last official banquet." To the 194 alumni in attendance at the event, which also recognized the CHS Alumni Association's 49th year of existence, there was a sad sense of loss, with perhaps a few in the audience temporarily harboring thoughts of abolishing the alumni organization, since there was no longer the attachment of an active Carlisle High School. However, any such thoughts of disbanding quickly vanished, for if anything, the alumni became even more resolved that in order to preserve the cherished memories they all felt for their alma mater of Carlisle High School, the CHS Alumni Association must "keep the eternal flame burning."

So, in the year of 2005, when the Class of 1955 gathers at the Annual Banquet to celebrate their 50th anniversary as Carlisle High School graduates, it will also be the 91st year of active, continuous existence for the Carlisle High School Alumni Association – and still ticking –Truly, an amazing Alumni Association!

The Alumni of Barbourville High School, a small independent city school system located in the southeastern Kentucky small town of Barbourville, are found to be one such group, well-known by this writer, that also demonstrates this continual caring companionship that is comparable to the Carlisle Alumni. This is the hometown school of Pat Disney Dampier, Donnie's wife, who also is a graduate of the Class of 1955. Even though BHS is still an open high school, it has an alumni group that, like Carlisle's, will not add to its numbers, and that gathers together every two years for a "Back To The '50s" Reunion that is usually held the first weekend of August at Cumberland Falls State Park. Pat and some of her very close BHS friends, Gloria (Knuckles) Compton and her husband, John (a graduate of Neon High School), along with Jim and Ann

Bays came up with the '50s idea and have organized and coordinated the gathering for each bi-annual event.

The "Back To The '50s" Reunion of BHS began about 1988 and was so popular that the alumni of the classes of 1947-49 asked and were warmly welcomed to the group, including the class of 1960, so, effectively, the reunion is open to all BHS alumni! The Barbourville City School of this era of the late '40s into the early '60s, which was only slightly larger but comparable in size to the Carlisle school, amazingly draws between the range of some 130 to 200 plus participants at each bi-annual gathering! The Barbourville and Carlisle High Schools were also alike in that they both housed all 12 grades together in the same building, so, when the '50s alumni and the 1948-49 grads are there together, it is like 'reverting back in time' when they were all in the school building at the same time!

Donnie, who, every other year, has missed some of the CHS Alumni Banquets by accompanying, and assisting, his co-coordinating wife with the Barbourville "Back To The '50s" reunions, has developed some close friendships with Pat's BHS alumni. Donnie knew he was well accepted by the Barbourville boys when, at one of the reunions, he was standing with a group, listening to them reminisce, when a couple of the guys put their hands on his shoulders and said, "Don, do you remember that time back in 1955 when we all got together and we did … so-and-so?" It just goes to show that all of us growing up in a small-town, small-school atmosphere could easily be interchanged into another like school and community.

XII

A Long Look Back ... Some Reminisces

Following are some of our favorites in a recalling of some of our school days experiences and antics that are often told and retold as "a good story" at the Class of '55 reunions and gatherings:

The Skeeter – The Great Railroad Caper – Kenneth Booth's first set of wheels was a jalopy that he called his "skeeter"! It consisted of an engine, covered by a hood, a bench front seat, and a flat bed covering the rear axle, the description of which would fit the dictionary definition as, "a dilapidated old automobile." With Kenneth's inquisitive mind he discovered that the "skeeter" fit on the local railroad tracks and would basically steer itself once positioned. After work-closing time of the nearby businesses, he would occasionally place his vehicle on the tracks by Buntin's Dodge garage and ride the rails through Dorseyville and get off at East Union Road on his way home. At both the entry and exit locations, the track was even with the blacktop parking lot and street, making it easy to get the vehicle onto the tracks. Before the afternoon of the caper, Kenneth had introduced a few of the guys, and possibly a girl or two, to this new excursion, or mode of transportation. One late evening, as some of the boys were hanging out on the courthouse yard wall, Kenneth said to Donnie, "Come and ride with me, I want to show you something, and then I'll bring you back to your car." This was possibly the first time that Kenneth revealed his new found adventure to anyone else, as he gave Donnie a fun and invigorating "ride on the rails" in the open-air "skeeter" on a moonlit night, on Kenneth's route across from Buntin's through the back streets of Carlisle and Dorseyville, then off the tracks at East Union Road, and back to the courthouse.

It was one Tuesday afternoon after school, that Kenneth invited several of us guys to "ride the rails" with him to Myers Station to visit Larry Cameron. Kenneth had always observed the train schedule, and assured all his riders that the I & N Freight had already passed through. Except, on this fateful afternoon, there was a new engineer who was coming through at a much later time to get used to the route; and, thankfully, at a much slower speed! You can imagine the shock of Kenneth and crew, and the engineer, when they saw each other rounding a sharp bend, about 3 miles from Carlisle, and, a short ways past Scrubgrass Road! Kenneth immediately cut off the track and up a steep bank, dropping the occupants in a ditch with the "skeeter" falling crossways over the ditch, and partly onto the tracks, which James Horton, the train brakeman said the train only cleared by approximately 4 feet! The headlines of the local newspaper read, "Rail-Riding Jalopy Encounters Train; One Youth Hurt!" Thankfully, none of the riders was seriously hurt. Bill Conley, Jock's younger brother, still has a scar from a deep gash on his leg, which prompted him to ask the engineer to drop him off at the Nicholas County Hospital by the tracks. This probably also gave the engineer a chance "to change his pants" from the shock of this encounter! In addition to Kenneth, those on the ride included Jock, Bill, Bobby Henry, and, according to the news account, Jackie Wells. Some of us who watched as the group left from in front of the courthouse yard thought that it was also Billy Straw and Joe Blount who went with Kenneth. Jackie Shepherd and Donnie Dampier would have been on "the caper," except both had been instructed by their parents to do their chores that afternoon. Jackie, from his farm next door, had observed the train stopping at the hospital, but did not know what had happened until school the next day. Donnie had to clean out the doghouse.

The next morning at school, as the mixed chorus was rehearsing, under the direction of Mrs. Pittman, on the stage of the auditorium, suddenly, the double doors at the back of the room burst open, and, in walked Superintendent Davis, Joe Frank Conley, Jock's dad, and, two strangers, dressed in suit and tie, and peering out from under their felt fedoras. Donnie, who was standing next to Kenneth, heard him take several deep breaths, then Donnie began to feel the wooden stage shaking under their feet – caused by the nervous twitch of Kenneth's powerful leg muscles! In a few moments, Kenneth was shaking all over, and by then Jock, upon viewing his dad in the group, had probably joined in the vibrations of the stage floor. Reminiscent of the famous line spoken by actors Paul Newman and Robert Redford in the very popular 1969 movie *Butch Cassidy and The Sundance Kid*, in the scenes where they were being relentlessly pursued by railroad detectives, Kenneth turned to Donnie and whispered, "Who are those guys?" By that time of morning, in the little small-town school, word was quickly beginning to be spread around that "something big had happened last night," so the rest of the choir began to join in the whispered chorus, "Who are those guys," which effectively ended the rehearsals for that day. As it turned out, Kenneth, with his "bright blue eyes," could have played the part of Butch (portrayed by blue-eyed Paul Newman) for the two ominous-looking strangers were indeed "railroad detectives" there to investigate the "Great Railroad Caper!"

Joe Frank Conley, there to legally represent his sons, Jock and Bill, as well as Kenneth, and the other riders, skillfully negotiated a settlement with the railroad officials to avoid prosecution. It likely helped the cause of Kenneth, and his crew, in that the officials of the I & N Railway Line did not want much publicity of the caper, with concerns that it might start a trend of rail-riding!

The Dog House – Donnie Dampier and his parents bred and raised pure-breed boxer dogs; this was the dog house, located in the back part of their garage, that Donnie had to clean in lieu of going on the caper. In addition to raising boxers, Donnie was also interested in becoming a "boxer!" Kenneth 'Scout' Campbell, CHS Class of '49, the assistant scoutmaster to Everett Smith of Boy Scout Troop No. 15, had taught us some boxing fundamentals from his experience of fighting in the Golden Gloves. A section of the doghouse was also Donnie's "gym," which consisted of a 100-pound set of barbells, a full-length mirror which aided the practice of shadow boxing, and a punching bag, used to build him up for boxing, football, and other sports. Actually, most of our physical development was achieved from physical labor in construction and on the farm!

Some of the other boys would occasionally come to the gym to try out some of Donnie's meager equipment, and on one afternoon, Billy Straw (CHS Class of '58), an underdeveloped freshman at the time, came to work out. After Donnie had demonstrated some lifting techniques with the barbells, he left Billy for a few minutes to go into the house for some soft drinks. As he returned to the garage, he heard a faint and moaning cry for help from Billy! For you see, in Donnie's absence, Billy had managed to lift the barbells about waist high – his legs crumpled – and Billy was laying on the floor, with one leg under him, and the barbells across his chest, leaving Billy virtually helpless! When Donnie lifted the weight off of Billy's chest, nothing was hurt, except a little pride! So, Donnie took some of the weights off the set and worked with Billy to gradually build up to the full size weights, but Billy learned a valuable lesson in the process, that it is wise to start slowly and have a partner present when lifting!

Donnie's bodybuilding activities were recognized by the class as he was named "best physique"; along with Norma Harris who was "best female figure!"

The Magnetic Mouth – The magnetic personality of Jock Conley has long been recognized, but in high school and college he seemed to also have a "magnetic mouth" for he was continually being punched in the mouth! Jock was always in the wrong place at the wrong time like the time he and Donnie D. attended the State High School Basketball Tournament in Lexington. It was in the old Lafayette Hotel (now headquarters for Urban County Government), a popular hangout for the kids, that Jock went to the men's room in the basement to use the facilities, when a "drunk" walks up and asks Jock to please pull his "out-of-joint" finger, upon which the drunk promptly punched Jock in the mouth! You might say that Jock was "punch drunk!" Then on the junior-senior trip some of the guys decided to cut the "duck tail" hairstyle of one of the junior boys who was a good friend of fellow junior Charles McCarty. About that time Jock walks in the room behind a "very upset" Charlie who turns quickly and punched Jock in the mouth, knocking him over an easy chair, causing it to fall over backward! After we realized that Jock was not hurt, except for the swollen lip, it was a humorous sight with all of Jock "out of sight," except for his feet that were straight up in the air!

Ring of Fire/Ring of Friendship – The long time rumor that Jackie Shepherd started smoking at age four is simply not true; however, Jackie was well into smoking by his mid-teens. Jackie frequently went to great lengths to hide the habit from his mother! One of those instances happened one afternoon during high school with Jackie, smoking as usual, and Donnie Dampier walking down East Main Street when Ms. Shepherd suddenly drove up! Jackie, quick as a cat, said, "Donnie, here take this!" When Donnie took the cigarette to hide it in his cupped hand the lit end was against the palm of his hand! While Ms. Shepherd was taking an excruciatingly long time to tell Jackie to "Get home and do your chores," the lit end of the cigarette was burning a ring in Donnie's palm! It can be said that this "ring of fire" was also a "ring of true friendship!"

The "Jack Tales" – Throughout the Appalachian region and down through the ages, a series of folk stories called "The Jack Tales," have been told and re-told. These are stories that most modern American children have never heard, but in the Southern Appalachians, these were common family stories, verbally recounted, even into the early 1950s when television likely diminished their appeal. They centered on a single character, an irrepressible fellow named Jack who roamed the hills looking for adventure, getting into and out of scrapes and situations by using his wits. Those who have known Jackie "Jack" Shepherd for a long time would agree that this description of the folk character fits Jackie in an apt way; therefore, the Class of '55 has its own version of "The Jack Tales!"

Jackie's (Jack's) approach to life – as a youngster was known as "Speedy Gonzales" – would seem to parallel the words of David Glasgow Farragut (1801-1870), a U.S. admiral who won fame as a Union Naval Officer in the Civil War Battle of Mobile Bay, who, in the heat of action, was quoted as saying, "Damn the torpedoes, full speed ahead!" It was within this spectrum that Donnie Dampier had to be tough growing up as best friends to Jackie.

In addition to the "ring of fire" previously described, there were numerous other incidents that led to bodily injury, such as the time in grade school that Donnie was riding shirtless on the back of the bicycle that Jackie was flying down the highway, hit a chug hole, throwing Donnie off on the pavement which ripped the skin off his bare chest! Or, there was a similar incident during high school days when Jackie and Donnie entered the "human wheelbarrow race" on a Saturday morning during the Blackberry Festival. Donnie turned out to be the "wheelbarrow," which meant that Donnie "ran" on his hands while Jackie ran while holding Donnie's legs. They won the race, but Donnie paid the price by badly skinning his right hand on the hot, sandy pavement, which then became infected! The following day, Jackie and Donnie left for Boy Scout Camp Offutt, where Donnie spent time each day with the camp nurse getting his hand treated and re-bandaged.

Ring of Fighting – Boxing was a popular activity during this era at Camp Offutt, and Donnie who was into boxing at the time did not want to miss out, so he entered the ring to box Jackie one-handed. He was able to fend off Jackie with his left hand only for a couple of rounds, but his one arm wore down, and Jackie then pummeled Donnie "unmercifully!"

The next year at Boy Scout Camp Offutt, the two Carlisle boys resumed their inter-Scout-troop boxing careers, as, Donnie, with both hands healthy, boxed against three Boy Scouts from Lexington who were successful Golden Gloves performers. These boys were tough inner-city delinquents whose Scoutmaster and trainer was a no-nonsense Lexington police officer, and even though these boys spent much of their days as gym rats, Jackie and Donnie (both probably fighting in the upper weight range of the welterweight class of 136-147 pounds) more than held their own against their better-trained opponents. In three matches with these boys, Donnie won two matches: one against an opponent of his size, and, the second win against a bigger boy, with about a 10-15-pound weight advantage, but then, feeling confident, was surprised as he lost to a young man some 15 pounds lighter, but very well trained, skilled, and conditioned, who gave Donnie an important "boxing lesson!" Donnie would say in later years that this was one of the best lessons learned, for it led him to decide that boxing as a potential professional vocation was not for him!

In two other "Jack Tales" that involved Donnie, one was filled with anxiety and embarrassment, the other with a near disaster. The two boys spent many a day in their youth by hiking "cross-county" through woods and farm fields, and the many hills and hollers of Nicholas County.

"Scrotum Scare" – On one occasion when they were about thirteen or fourteen, and while hiking across some fields near Myers Station, they came upon an old rusty barbed wire fence tacked to some equally old locust posts. Just as Donnie was attempting to straddle the fence, Jackie stepped on the fence, pulling a post over, and snapping a strand of the barbed wire, which then flew up hitting Donnie between the legs, full force! The rusty barbed wire ripped a tear in the crotch of his pants, penetrating through his underwear into his scrotum, with the laceration drawing considerable blood! It must have been quite a sight with Jackie helping a bloody, limping Donnie into Paul Cameron's country store, seeking a telephone. No doubt, Larry was there, along with the usual number of locals loafing a spell, and wondering what had happened. Any mother would understand the alarm that Ann, Donnie's mother, must have felt with Donnie's "call for help" to bring him a change of clothes, and take him to the doctor because he was hurt and bleeding in "his private area!" She possibly had anxious thoughts that her desire for eventual grandchildren, through her only child, might be lost due to this accident. All males would certainly relate to the concerns of a young man, who, having recently gone through the changes of puberty, and beginning to understand and appreciate his newly found manhood, might have done lasting damage to himself. Thankfully, most of the bleeding was due to cuts on his inner leg, with only superficial wounds to the main area of concern. And, in later years, Donnie came through (with the able assistance of his wonderful wife, Pat, naturally) to provide two loving grandchildren (Debbie and David) for his parents, Ann and Elmer!

"Butt Bouncing" – On a summer day in late high school, Jackie and Donnie, on another cross-country trek, decided to hike to Camp Blackhawk. The normal way to the camp was by way of the railroad track that ran right by Blackhawk, but on this day, they picked a more adventurous route along the cliffs above the tracks. The two boys came to a cliff with a small ravine, where the only way to negotiate was on hands and knees, holding onto branches of a dead tree that had long ago fallen across. Jackie went first, and in so doing, broke off most of the dead branches and also made the sandstone slippery. About halfway across, Donnie began to slide to the edge, and when grasping for the last branch it snapped dropping Donnie some six to seven feet to the next level. On the very steep slope, Donnie was not able to retain his balance causing him to land on his butt, bounce, and do a backward flip! Upon landing, he again did a "butt bounce" and backward flip; then, on the third landing was stopped with a hard "kerplunk" against a large tree, leaving Donnie sitting against the trunk looking up at Jackie on the top! A helpless Jackie had been watching and wondering if his friend would survive, hollered down, "Donnie, are you hurt bad, are you OK?" After a few moments of Donnie feeling around and, after determining that nothing was broken, he responded that he thought he was OK and joked, "As Elvis would say, 'I'm All Shook Up!' " At that, when he was sure Donnie was all right, Jackie burst out in that boisterous laugh for which he is well noted, and that probably reverberated some distance up and down the Licking River, which was down the bank just a few yards from where Donnie landed! He would say down through the years that it was one of the funniest sights he had ever seen with Donnie bouncing and flipping, bouncing and flipping, down that slope! As said earlier, Donnie had to be tough growing up with Jackie as a best friend, and being part of "The Jack Tales!"

Messing With Moonshiners – Billy Straw, CHS Class of '58 and close-by neighbor of Jackie, was another willing partner in the

"Jack Tales." Billy is the son of the late William T. Straw, the long time County Extension Agent for Nicholas County and Carlisle. During their grade school days, Billy, who was some three years younger than Jackie, loved to tag along on Jackie's adventure hikes. One of their favorite excursions was to hike down Scrubbgrass Road, or the railroad tracks, in the direction of the Cassidy Creek area, and cut through the dense woods in search of "moonshine stills." "Moonshining" (illegal home distilling) has been practiced in Kentucky since the Whiskey Rebellion of 1791, which was brought about when farmers protested paying imposed federal excise taxes on their corn product. The practice of "shining" increased through Prohibition (1920-1933), and continued in the more remote areas of America, including Nicholas County, until it began to decline considerably in the 1980s, when it was said to be replaced by a "new moonshining" (marijuana). When Jackie and Billy happened upon an unattended "still" (short for "distill"), or a vat of fermenting "mash," they loved to leave obvious, telltale marks for the returning operator to see that someone had been there! In May of 1952, the Carlisle Mercury reported that seventeen moonshine stills, each with a capacity of 50 gallons and 700 gallons of mash, were destroyed in the Myers Station area. Spokesman for the Federal Alcohol Tax unit said the Nicholas County moonshiners had devised an innovative labor-saving method of handling the mash, not heard of anywhere else in Kentucky, by building a rock furnace around each drum and therefore, setting up a separate still for each barrel. Perhaps these small operations had previously been "discovered" by this twosome!

"Hog Wash" – Down through the years, Jack's favorite story of one of their 'discoveries' was the time that the two of them came upon a vat of fermenting corn mash, contained in an oil drum, in which all four feet of a hog were sticking straight up out of the mash! Apparently, a wild or semi-wild sow had wandered onto the vat, and stimulated by the aroma as something good to eat, had somehow gotten up to the edge of the barrel, began to eat, got intoxicated, and fell in and drowned! This can be said to be another incidence of where the excessive intake of "strong intoxicating drink" can have devastating results! Jackie Shepherd's lovely wife Linda, a long-time teacher in the Scott County School System, enjoys the story so much she retells it each year to her biology and science classes!

The NCHS Window Breaking Incident and Donnie's Favorite Story of His Dad – Early in senior year, a surprised Donnie Dampier was called out of first period class to report to the principal's office! Upon entering the office there stood Superintendent Davis, Ms. Nancy Talbert, Donnie's dad, and the sheriff! Donnie's first reaction was a fear that something terrible had happened to his mother, but was much relieved when the sheriff said, "Donnie, last night someone broke out all the windows in the back of Nicholas County High School, and you were seen leaving the scene about 9:30 p.m.; and, we think you were involved!" On a double date that night, Donnie, with his date, Faye Roundtree, and Billy Vanlandingham with his date had parked for awhile beside the high school, then left and stopped at the Dairy Queen at 9:30 before taking the girls home at 10:00. Back then, the girls usually had to be in by ten on school nights; and, were allowed to stay out until eleven on non-school nights (midnight on special occasions). Donnie's dad, Elmer, listened for awhile without saying a word during the sheriff's questioning; then said, "Sheriff, can I speak to Donnie privately?" The sheriff agreed, and Mr. Davis provided his private office. Inside, Elmer looked Donnie in the eye and asked, "Did you do this, or do you know anything about it?" Donnie could truthfully respond "no" to his Dad's questions. They then went out and Elmer looked the sheriff in the eye and said, "Donnie said he knows nothing about this incident, and I believe him." The sheriff then responded, "If you say so, that is good enough for me" – and that ended the incident for Donnie!

The many years of teaching and living the values of truth and trust by Donnie's parents were now firmly impressed upon Donnie from that day forward; especially, the pride of seeing the immense respect for his Dad's word and reputation with the community; and Elmer's faith in his son! Donnie has used this story many times with his children, Debbie and David, and his grandchildren, Afton and Justin to teach them these values for living.

It was many years later at one of our reunions that some classmates finally revealed themselves as perpetrators who did break out the windows at NCHS that night! It is felt that since the damage was apparently paid for, and the statute of limitations is surely well past, that the initials of KB, BAK, JWS, and JGW (there may be others?) can now safely be revealed!

The Kenneth K(C)hronicles – Few high school classes can claim a more interesting or unique personality than Kenneth Booth. At just about any reminiscing gathering of three or more classmates some of Kenneth's high school tales are told:

Kenneth would occasionally claim to be a descendant of Daniel Boone, possibly because of the similarity of names; however, the characteristics of "bold and fearless, with a sense of adventure and strong survival instincts" exhibited by explorers such as Kit Carson, Jim Bowie, and Ol' Daniel fit Kenneth very well in high school days! We always thought that Kenneth was just kidding around (as he frequently did) with his kinship claims, however, it turns out he was correct, so verified by no less an authority than Kenneth's cousin, Kimbal, who, in his extensive family genealogical research, has made the Booth family connection to the family of Daniel Boone!

Who knows, if Kenneth had not been "born 200 years too late," in our more sedate times, we might have been reading about "the adventures of Kenneth Booth" in our history books!

We used to think of Kenneth as being nearly indestructible by surviving all his mishaps without serious injury. In addition to "the great railroad caper," Kenneth again turned the "skeeter" over in a ditch, this time off the highway at Myers Station. He was also riding in an automobile with Wayne Gaunce returning home one night that was involved in a rollover accident, with both walking away unhurt. Then, there was the time that Kenneth "borrowed" his brother's car for an afternoon adventure of playing hooky from school (with Carole McClain, Barbara King, and Donnie Dampier), that somehow, ended up driving up a creek bed with water coming up through the floor board!

On another occasion, Kenneth was the driver, along with Donnie Dampier, Jock Conley, Jackie Shepherd, and possibly a couple of the other guys, to a destination outside of Nicholas County, when Kenneth suddenly said, "Oh boy, a three-lane highway," so Kenneth passed a slower car, and sped up the hill in that third lane, then, as Kenneth topped the hill, all of a sudden, we were bouncing all over the place on the rough shoulder, and in and out of the roadside ditch, as Kenneth struggled to return the car back to the pavement, which he managed to successfully do, but not before his carload "was all shook up!" This third lane was, of course, a passing lane, which is common nowadays, but that Kenneth had not seen before in Nicholas County.

Then, the story is told of the time that Kenneth had in his possession some fireworks. On that chilly night, Kenneth, who was a passenger riding around with some of the guys, decided to scare some kids walking down the street, by throwing a string of 45 lit firecrackers at their feet. This was a string that when the fuse was lit, it would start a chain reaction by lighting each one in rapid succession. So, Kenneth ignited the fuse and quickly tossed the lighted string of firecrackers in the kid's direction, however, Kenneth, in his eagerness, forgot to roll down the car window! For a few moments, all hell broke loose in the cramped car, and "a hot time was had in the old town that night!"

Kenneth was also thought to be one of the eight boys crammed into the 1930s "classic" car owned and operated by Bobbie McFarland that overturned on the concrete in April of 1954. With the boys packed in like sardines, which had the same protective effect as modern day seatbelts and airbags (not available in automobiles at that time), no one was hurt, but Bobbie's car was severely damaged! To the Class of '55, Bobbie (Class of '54) was considered as a true gentleman and "older man" by our girls, but to the boys he was just an older guy that we ran around with, even though he was the same age as many of us. Sadly, Bobbie "Mac" McFarland passed away in June of 2001, but he remained a gentleman and good friend to us all until the end.

Jackie Shepherd also drove one of the old 1930s classics for a while. In another incident on the concrete, Jackie (with Donnie Dampier on board) was driving his car "lickety split" (as usual) toward Carlisle. Just as they topped the hill at the juncture of Miller Station Road, Jackie's overheated radiator cap blew off sending steam and hot water shooting up like a geyser, and, at the same instance, Donnie was alarmed to see his dad and mother standing on the side of the highway at the scene of an accident! They had been on a Sunday afternoon drive, a common activity of those days, and had come upon a wreck scene that had happened shortly before, and stopped to give assistance to the persons involved.

While most of the folks of Carlisle and Nicholas County were quite used to driving on dirt and/or gravel roads and blacktop, the approximate four-mile stretch of State Highway 36, from the West Carlisle city limits to the intersection with US 68 was unique to the area. Constructed of concrete, which gave it a distinctive sound of "ker-thump, ker-thump, ker-thump" each time the cars passed over one of the many seams, it has always been locally referred to as "the concrete." It was also one of the few stretches of straight, level road of over a mile in length in Nicholas where a person could try out their automobile!

There was at least one of Kenneth's mishaps, which occurred during our junior year, which landed Kenneth in the local hospital for a few days. It was after school that Kenneth and Donnie Dampier were walking down School Street toward downtown that Kenneth spotted David Hardin driving his pick-up truck in their direction. Kenneth, always one to challenge how close he could get to danger, stepped into the middle of the street, with his butt out and his back to David, with intent to side step the truck "bullfight style." David playfully cut toward Kenneth, but in turning away neither he nor Kenneth took into account the length of the extended side rear view mirror which hit Kenneth with a mighty force knocking Kenneth on his face gasping for breath! It took a few seconds, when Kenneth began turning blue while gasping, that Donnie realized that Kenneth was not kidding around, but was having serious breathing problems. Donnie then used a technique learned in football when the breath was knocked out by rolling Kenneth over on his back and gently pulling him up by the belt until Kenneth was breathing freely again. A very frightened and concerned David Hardin then put Kenneth in his truck and drove him to the hospital. Thankfully, the only fatal casualty was David's rear view mirror that was completely destroyed!

And now, in the manner of famed radio personality Paul Harvey, "the rest of the story," as told then by Kenneth. While Kenneth was lying in the hospital with a couple of broken vertebra in the upper back, a nurse came in requesting a urine sample. Kenneth, who was unable to accommodate her at the time, filled the sample jar with sweetened tea he had in the room, with a later analysis by the hospital that Kenneth also had "sugar diabetes!" Of course, we all believed the "rest of the story" at the time!

The Road To Mt. Olivet – In a similarity to "Charlie Brown," the focal character in the lovable and popular *Peanuts* comic strip, written by the late Charles Schulz, Donnie Dampier somehow met and became infatuated with "a pretty little red-haired girl" who lived in Mt. Olivet. It is not remembered how they met; however, a pretty young redhead who chanced to walk by the site where Donnie was helping to build the church in Mt. Olivet, would surely have attracted his attention in those days! Their chance meeting stimulated a few trips on the road to Mt. Olivet that summer. On one late night return, on approaching Ellisville, Donnie suddenly realized he was about to run out of gas. So, he stopped in front of a country store with one gas pump (long closed for the night), and taking a chance that the owner lived above the store, began blowing his horn. Suddenly, the lights came on, and the aroused storeowner came down, sold a dollar or two of gasoline to Donnie, and sent him on his way (with no hard feelings)!

The "All-Nighter" Flat Tire – There was a time when Jackie Shepherd, driving his late-'40s vintage Chevy, and Donnie Dampier were returning late-night on US-460 from a double date with two young ladies in Georgetown, when Jackie had a flat tire, whereby Jackie was able to pull off the highway into a farm house driveway. Jackie and Donnie then took turns, using an angled lug wrench, in a futile attempt to remove the lugs in order to change the tire. Here were two strong young men, but neither one could get enough leverage to remove those lugs! So, after an hour or two, they decided to wake up the farmer to use his telephone (there were no cell phones in those days) to call an all night service station they knew of in Paris. At the mid-night hour, the dark farmhouse among the trees looked rather ominous, perhaps haunted, but the two brave souls pressed on! The awakened farmer was gracious in the use of his phone, but it took some two hours before someone from the service station arrived to give assistance. Since there was no offer of accommodations with "the farmer's daughter," Jackie and Donnie waited in the Chevy! Since the two did not get home until about 4:00AM, with some explaining to do, the episode had similarities to the lyrics of *Wake Up Little Susie*, made famous by the Everly Brothers of Kentucky, but without the "Little Susies" that had been delivered to their homes in Georgetown hours before!

These two scenarios of the Ellisville storeowner and the Scott County farmer opening their doors in the middle of the night to strangers and giving willing assistance were the norm and not the exception, but rather were the trait of those times! We rarely locked our doors during the day, and frequently not even at night, especially when our parents were sleeplessly listening for us to get home as the clock approached the mid-night hour.

Hitchhiking, which has become a dangerous modern day practice, was a fairly common and acceptable mode of transportation for some, with little fear of the hitchhiker (or, fear of the motorist who stopped to accommodate). So, in the '50s, the "art of the thumb" was frequently seen on the roadways of Central Kentucky and Nicholas County, with members of the Class of 1955 participating, such as Jackie Wells hitching a ride home to Ellisville, or Kenneth Booth to and from Frogtown, or Jock Conley, Jackie Shepherd, and Donnie Dampier to Camp Blackhawk, and Larry

Cameron home to Myers Station. Note that the girls did hitch a ride often with the few who had wheels, but were not often seen hitch-hiking on the road ... but they would have been very successful in the art by utilizing the Claudette Colbert technique of showing a little leg, from the movie *It Happened One Night*, also starring Clark Gable!

As Franklin Delano Roosevelt, president of the United States (1933-45) at the time the Class of 1955 entered first grade, so courageously exhorted to the citizens of America on facing fearful situations, or uncertain times, "The only thing we have to fear is fear itself," so, in like manner, the Class of 1955 and most of the other classes of CHS, had the blessing of growing up and living in a domestic society that was not governed by fear, but in an atmosphere and "Good Samaritan" attitude of trust, helpfulness, and belief in our fellow man. During the '50s the Cold War had proliferated a fear of nuclear destruction across America, prompting numerous communities to encourage their citizens toward the building and stocking of home bomb shelters with instructional plans, like the government pamphlet You Can Survive made widely available. This paranoia was not the case in Carlisle and Nicholas County where few, if any, such structures were built, or even considered. Apparently our parents and other adults of the community had taken to heart the exhortation by FDR to avoid a fearful attitude that he most surely stated or paraphrased numerous times during his famous radio "fireside chats." Some Carlisle comments that memory brings to mind on the issue: "If I build a bomb shelter, whom am I going to let in, and whom am I going to keep out?" "Shall I stand in the doorway with a shotgun and repel, and lose, my friends and neighbors?" "Shucks, I would rather take my chances, and be outside with them, than survive in isolation like that!"

Two Memorials

In the fifty-year period since graduation, the Class of 1955 has lost only two members by death:

Jackie Gene Wells died on August 12, 1992. Jackie G, who joined the class as a freshman, seemed to always be in on everything! He was a fun-loving regular guy, who liked to cut up, and pull harmless pranks. Jackie, possessing that characteristic wink, and with a gleam in his eye for the girls, was named by the class as "the Wolf" (Carole McLean was "the Flirt"), with his lips chosen for the Ideal Male Senior. Jackie had health problems most of his adult life, but on his good days was fun to be around. At our class reunions, his smile was evident and he was still "the class cut-up" with lots of good stories to tell. Jackie Gene Wells was a good friend, and is missed.

Carole Jean Donovan Moreland died on February 8, 1998. Carole Jean became a member of the class in the eighth grade. She was a woman of dignity, pleasantly quiet, with a warm, caring personality, who graduated from CHS with honors. In the senior class play, Carole played the role of proprietress of a nursing home, which was perhaps an omen of her life to come. A few short years after high school Carole was diagnosed with the progressively degenerative disease of MS, but not before Carole was blessed with the joys of motherhood. Carole lived with this deteriorating condition of MS for some thirty years, until she was ultimately confined to the local nursing home. Throughout this ordeal Carole always greeted her visitors with a warm smile, kind words, and an uncomplaining, "not to be defeated" attitude and spirit! Carole was a joy and inspiration to her classmates, friends, and family, and left us all a legacy for living. Carole was dealt many "lemons" in her life, but truly "learned how to make lemonade!"

In Conclusion…

A Kentucky History of The Class of 1955 is a "never-ending story"; therefore, there is no "final chapter!" There are many more unknown or unrecalled events, stories, and memories that could be included in this retelling of the Class of 1955. Each of the two dozen or more individuals who were graduates or significant classmates at one time or another, continue to have an important and ongoing story to tell!

Donnie Joe Dampier
Senior Class President, the Class of 1955
Carlisle High School,
the Musketeers of Carlisle, Kentucky
August 2005

A Budding Buddy Holly?
The Author Donnie Joe Dampier, 1955. Senior Class President, The Class of 1955, Carlisle High School.

Acknowledgements

Some five years ago I first set forth on the venture/adventure of writing this book with its focus on my classmates of the Class of 1955 of the small Carlisle City School, located in the small town of Carlisle, Kentucky. From day one it was quite obvious that I needed help, lots of it, from many individuals and sources. Therefore, in the hope that I do not inadvertently omit anyone, I express sincere appreciation to the following:

First there were my classmates, all interested and supportive. Martha Sue Feeback Taylor got me started by helping me gain access to our class enrollment records, well protected and preserved from long years of archival storage with the Nicholas County Board of Education. These records identified everyone who had ever been a part our class for each grade of our twelve years. Martha Sue was the only classmate who read any of my written work-in-process, and I knew I was well on my way by her comments, "Donnie, this is really good. ... Miss Nancy would have been very proud!" The late Nancy Talbert, herself a 1915 graduate of Carlisle High School, served the school as teacher and principal for many decades, and was our high school English and literature teacher. Many thanks to Larry Cameron for the loan of *Musketeer Memories* year books of 1949-52; to Mary Phyllis Smith Cameron for her scrap books and photo albums (some of which I used); and to Barbara King Warren for her famous scrap book. All of these memorabilia are tattered and yellowed, yet "treasures" which my trusting classmates entrusted to my care! To Pat May Gaunce, with husband, Wayne, through their hospitality in hosting our class reunions at their second home at

Kentucky Lake, which made me aware that a written history, focused on the Class of 1955, should be written of life growing up in a small town in the 1940's and 1950's. To Kenneth Booth and Jock Conley, both always the subject of a good story! And, to Jackie Shepherd for those frequent times when he and I get together and almost always reminisce with good stories!

To the librarians and staff of the Nicholas County and Lexington libraries for helping me muddle through the hours of microfilm research.

The folks of the Nicholas County Historical Society gave me much encouragement, and a feeling of legitimacy, at their annual banquet, first by inviting me as the program speaker, and then with their positive comments at the conclusion of readings from my upcoming book.

Listening to and observing alumni from numerous other small schools, such as Barbourville, Stearns, Eubank, Midway, MMI, Carthage, ILL, etc., continue to be invaluable to me.

The Carnegie Center of Lexington, Kentucky, provided valuable tutorage in their classes on "How To Get Your Book Published", led by noted published authors Crystal E. Wilkerson, author of *Blackberries, Blackberries,* and Neil Chethik, author of *FatherLoss.* They calmed anxieties, as both are quite personable as well as professional.

Much appreciation is directed to the late Joanie Conley, Jock's wife. Although dying in the later stages of cancer she still desired to apply her extensive journalism background to critique my manuscript. Joanie, a longtime, very close friend of Pat and myself, wanted very much for my writing project to be successful, however, she did not "sugar coat" her assessment of my work, first commenting that the writing was interesting, informative, and well written, but badly in need of reorganizing, with the need to focus on my original objective and cut down the content size. I have tried to follow her suggestions, so any success we may gain with this book, Joanie has had a far-reaching hand in.

To my son, David, after listening numerous times to my

descriptions of what I was writing about, was the first to suggest, and encourage me with his comment, "Dad, you need to seriously consider publishing your book!" On numerous occasions throughout the process, David has provided valuable technical assistance and bailed me out of several jams with the cantankerous computer!

My wife Pat, as usual, has always been supportive in my first-ever endeavor of writing a book for publication. It was she who found classes, book signings of other authors, various articles, and other functions to help me learn to navigate through the publishing process. Now that I have chosen the "self-publishing" route and we have selected the fine folks of McClanahan Publishing House in Kuttawa, Kentucky to publish *Finding The Fifties*, she will be by my side, with her special support and encouragement as we set sail on our new venture/adventure over the next months to bring the book, and its message to the reader. Hopefully, we will gain new friendships along the way.

Finally, much appreciation is due to our readers! It is our desire that you find this work informative, interesting, and enjoyable reading.

Donnie Joe Dampier
August 2005

About the Author

Donnie Joe Dampier knows firsthand that of which he writes in Finding The Fifties. Born on December 11, 1936, in the midst of the Great Depression years, Donnie grew up in the small town of Carlisle, nestled in the hills of Nicholas County, on the fringes of the famed Bluegrass Region of Central Kentucky. Growing up during the tumultuous times of World War II in the fear-filled 1940s, he emerged as a teenager in those fabulous '50s to graduate with nineteen classmates from the small independent city school of Carlisle High School, serving as senior year president of the class of 1955.

Donnie continued his education at the University of Kentucky, earning a Bachelor of Science in commerce (business administration) in 1959. It was at the university that he met Pat, his future wife, also a product of the atmosphere of a small town and small school, that of Barbourville High School of southeastern Kentucky's Knox County. They married on August 9, 1959, and have been blessed with two children and two grandchildren, a girl and a boy each.

After spending nearly four years in the city environment of Cincinnati in retail and banking, but always seeking a smaller-town atmosphere, the Dampiers moved to the Kentucky state capital of Frankfort, both compiling long, satisfying careers in state government service. Donnie retired in January of 2003 with exactly forty years of state government service in a variety of positions in finance, computer systems design, education and personnel management, capping off his career as an administrator with the Kentucky Public

Employees Deferred Compensation Authority.

In well over four decades of marriage, Donnie and Pat have traveled in all fifty states, always staying on the earth's surface. Donnie especially loves to leave the highways for the byways to visit "downtown" in the small towns across America, engaging in conversations with the locals. Stimulated from the togetherness of high school, they enjoy ballroom dancing, hiking the trails of natural settings, and the music of big bands, the '50s, brass bands, and classical. Since retirement, Donnie has served as a volunteer guide with the University of Kentucky Basketball Museum, the Kentucky History Center in downtown Frankfort, and currently serves on the Task Force of the Kentucky River Watershed Watch, an environmental protection program through which tests and monitors water quality. From the time that Pat "drafted" him to present a program to her garden club, Donnie has been invited on numerous occasions to speak to other garden clubs on various gardening topics, backyard ecology, the "birds and bees" – and now kids that he is "on the garden club speaking circuit!"

Donnie and Pat, with a Georgetown address, reside on nearly five acres on the banks of South Elkhorn Creek, in a neighborhood of rural setting in Scott County, Kentucky.

Don J. Dampier